# Kingdom

# Kingdom

## The Expression of God's Rule

A Thorough-Going Guide to the Fundamental Nature of Kingdom as the Basis for Christians in Their Governance by God and Toward Each Other

CHRIS WOODALL

WIPF & STOCK · Eugene, Oregon

KINGDOM
The Expression of God's Rule

Copyright © 2012 Chris Woodall. All rights reserved. Except for brief quotations in critical publications or reviews, no part of this book may be reproduced in any manner without prior written permission from the publisher. Write: Permissions, Wipf and Stock Publishers, 199 W. 8th Ave., Suite 3, Eugene, OR 97401.

Wipf & Stock
An Imprint of Wipf and Stock Publishers
199 W. 8th Ave., Suite 3
Eugene, OR 97401
www.wipfandstock.com

ISBN 13: 978-1-62032-118-8
Manufactured in the U.S.A.

All Scripture quotations, unless otherwise indicated, are taken from the Holy Bible, New International Version, NIV, copyright © 1973, 1978, 1984 by Biblica, Inc. Used by permission of Zondervan. All rights reserved worldwide.

Scripture quotations marked ASV are taken from the American Standard Version, copyright expired.

Scripture quotations marked KJV are taken from the King James (Authorized) Version (crown copyright).

Scripture quotations marked (The) Message are taken from Eugene H. Peterson's translation of the same name, copyright © 1993, 1994, 1995, 1996, 2000, 2001, 2002. Used by permission of NavPress Publishing Group.

Scripture quotations marked NASB are taken from the New American Standard Bible, copyright © 1960, 1962, 1963, 1968, 1971, 1972 by the Lockman Foundation, La Habra, California. Used by permission.

# Contents

*Acknowledgments vii*
*Introduction ix*

1  A Biblical Overview  1
2  Kingdom Character Attracts the King's Blessing  51
3  Lessons from Jesus' Parables of the Kingdom  108
4  The Kingdom of God in the Present  150
5  The Coming Kingdom  177

*Conclusion  203*
*Bibliography  207*

# Acknowledgments

I would briefly like to convey my deep sense of gratitude to two groups of people:

- those whose previous endeavors have made the research for this work a pleasure, irrespective of the possibility that my conclusions may not concur with their esteemed findings. If that proves to be the case, I trust they will not be unduly offended; and

- those who will include this work among their future research material to develop their own understanding—and that of others—of the wonderful concept of kingdom as it relates to those who find themselves "in Christ." Again, the conclusions they may reach do not determine the extent of my best wishes directed toward them.

# Introduction

DESPITE SAMUEL JOHNSON'S EVALUATION that it is "the last refuge of a scoundrel,"[1] patriotism can also be a laudable virtue. Indeed, loyalty to one's own country may often be more easily identified than can commitment to one's employer, social subgroup, or even marriage partner. In an age of cross-cultural transmigration, however, there can sometimes be a crisis of identity that ultimately muddies the appropriate subject of our patriotic fervor. Regional issues may also play a part. For example, it might be said that I am first of all a Yorkshireman, secondly an Englishman, and thirdly British. Beyond that, I would readily acknowledge my identity with the whole of the human race before I would concede European status without further qualification.

It is only fairly recently that I have discovered the difference between Great Britain, the British Isles, and the United Kingdom. For many years, I wasn't even aware that they were anything but synonymous terms. The variance between them is not pertinent to the scope of this work. What I can say is that the term "United Kingdom" is something of a misnomer. Whether it ever has been anything else is a subject for another debate. For a few short years, the kingdom of Israel experienced a unity of sorts. In its inaugural years there were minor skirmishes and differences over who should lead the tribes in union, but by and large the Davidic kingdom especially was one of unparalleled success. Once the kingdom divided, however, things were never the same.

When harassed by the Pharisees over the authority by which he cast out demons, Jesus said something as intriguing as it was contentious: "Every kingdom divided against itself will be ruined, and every city or household divided against itself will not stand" (Matt 12:25). It is a principle that has been borne out by the testimony of history.

---

1. In Boswell, *Samuel Johnson*, 182.

*Introduction*

But what precisely do we mean by "kingdom"? In strictly secular use, it refers to a geographical territory or community of people subject to a king. Although these ideas are not entirely absent in relation to God's kingdom, it would perhaps be more accurate to speak of it as the Father's heavenly rule expressed on earth in human lives. In other words, it is the rule of God in action. Moreover, God's kingdom implies his kingship. No room here for strategies devised by men. He is executing a plan according to his own purpose in Christ Jesus. Neither is there any validity in only theorizing or acquiring knowledge about the kingdom of God, save as a means by which to more adequately express God's rule experientially.

Although the exact phrase "kingdom of God"—or any similar alternatives—is completely missing from the Old Testament, the sense of God's kingship permeates its pages. Indeed, his reign is continually lauded by the psalmists[2] and prophets[3] alike. By the time we come to John the Baptist, it would seem that the intertestamental years had so conditioned the minds of those of Jewish background that they were able to understand what was meant by "the kingdom of God/heaven" with little or no need for further explanation. Although the dynamics may have been reasonably clear, however, the details awaited Jesus' elucidation.

It is perhaps a sad indictment of the current standing of the kingdom of God in the minds of so many church leaders that it is a subject that attracts the attention of so few Christians. This is not only true of those of a liberal persuasion, but increasingly so of my fellow evangelicals. This is particularly disturbing, given that the word of God we claim to hold so dear reveals *he basileia tou theou* to be pivotal to both Christ's ministry and to his ethical principles. Everything he said and did was governed by its relation to the kingdom of God. Or to put it another way: the words and ways of the Son were dictated by the will of the Father (see John 6:38; 7:16–17).

The testimony of Scripture is such as to imply that the essence of the kingdom as it relates to God is the expression of his rule. In any kingdom, that privilege is the exclusive right of the king and any other(s) that he might invest with the authority to rule on his behalf. There is a subtle, though distinct, difference between the kingdom of

2. See Psalm 68:16; 97:1; 146:10.
3. See Isaiah 52:7; Ezekiel 20:33; Zechariah 9:10.

*Introduction*

God and the church of Christ Jesus, which must be recognized at the outset lest they be regarded as synonymous terms—they are not. In its truest sense, it may be said that the church is but an agent of the kingdom. The explanation proffered by George Eldon Ladd is perhaps the most lucid I have encountered:

> The Kingdom is primarily the dynamic reign or kingly rule of God and, derivatively, the sphere in which the rule is experienced. In biblical idiom, the Kingdom is not identified with its subjects. They are the people of God's rule who enter it, live under it, and are governed by it. The church is the community of the Kingdom, but never the Kingdom itself. Jesus' disciples belong to the Kingdom as the Kingdom belongs to them; but they are not the Kingdom. The Kingdom is the rule of God; the church is a society of men.[4]

This being the case, then it surely behooves each one of us that claim to be owned by God to discover what he has chosen to reveal through the Bible's pages concerning his rule over the created order generally and, more specifically, in and through the redeemed community.

---

4. Ladd, *A Theology of the New Testament*, 111.

# 1

# A Biblical Overview

## ADAM AS GOD'S VICE-REGENT

THE EXISTENCE OF THE kingdom of God is obviously not an exclusively New Testament concept. Strictly speaking, neither is its domain restricted to the post-creation era. Because God's kingdom necessarily implies his kingship, it may be said to be co-existent with him, for it is inconceivable to imagine a time when God did not reign supreme. However, for the benefit of this work, we are able to speak only on the basis of disclosure, not conjecture. Thus, we begin by looking at the kingdom of God in the history of man: that is, from the point of Adam's creation as recorded for us in the pages of biblical revelation.

### Authority to Govern

Adam's privileged position was both inherent and imparted. He was honored by virtue of being the pinnacle of God's creative act, and he also had God's delegated authority invested in him. It is in this respect that we see the essence of kingdom intertwined with that of covenant for the first time, though it is also implied in pre-creational eternity. The basis of covenant is agreement, with both parties acknowledging the terms, benefits, and potential forfeits of such a contract. In divine covenants, which broadly follow the Suzerain-vassal type, God alone sets the terms. The individual concerned—in this case, Adam—may accept or reject those terms, but is offered no opportunity to negotiate them. Thus, when we speak of Adam's vice-regency, it should not be inferred that there was even the remotest suggestion that God sought Adam's advice; he simply issued the command and expected his appointee to obey.

That said, however, vice-regency does carry with it the authority of the regent. It is both because of this and for this reason that Adam was created in God's image, though we should be careful how far we carry the idea. There are those who suggest that God created Adam in order to meet a need in himself. They argue that the creation was necessitated by God's longing to know himself as other than himself and that this could only be attained in a perfectly created reflection of himself. First of all, God's motive for creation was not need but perfect freedom of the divine will. To have such freedom requires that he be equally free to choose not to do so without penalty. Secondly, the absolute and consistent perfection of God's nature is such that his excellence is neither enhanced nor diminished by anything outside of himself.

Authority is never abstract but must be realized in practical expression. Thus, to give Adam authority without a domain over which to exercise that authority would have been somewhat meaningless. Perhaps this is why he was created toward the end of the sixth day. Prior to that point in time, God had busied himself with the creation of an infrastructure that was ideally suited to Adam's capacity to govern (Gen 1:3–31). On the first three days, the various washes are applied to the canvas:

| day 1 | the separation of light from darkness | (Gen 1:3–5); |
|---|---|---|
| day 2 | the separation of the waters from the sky | (vv. 6–8); |
| day 3 | the appearance of dry land and vegetation | (vv. 9–13). |

The final days of creation saw each of these environments inhabited:

| day 4 | the introduction of light-bearing orbs in the heavens | (vv. 14–19); |
|---|---|---|
| day 5 | the creaturely population of the waters and the sky | (vv. 20–23); |
| day 6 | land creatures are the penultimate act of creation | (vv. 24–31). |

It was a kingdom fit for a king because it had been created specifically for that purpose in accordance with the design of the King of kings. The majesty of heaven had made the earth and all that was in it, but he chose to rule that kingdom via one who could legitimately claim to belong to both realms. Adam was formed from the dust of the ground, but he also had the Almighty's breath inspiring his lungs (Gen 2:7). He had the authority of his Maker to reign on his behalf and a domain in which to exercise that authority. He had almost everything he needed to be a faithful "son," but true faith requires a word from God to obey (see Rom 10:17; Heb 11:6). Adam was given this, too, in arguably the simplest form imaginable:

- fill the earth; and
- rule over its inhabitants.[1]

Adam's first act of demonstrating the authority placed upon him was the naming of the animals (Gen 2:19–20). The last part of verse twenty suggests that there was more to this exercise than simple nomenclature. When a suitable helper was made especially for him, the name Adam gave to his companion was typical of later-known Hebrew practice in that it had meaning that was relevant to that so named. From this fact alone, it does not seem unreasonable to assume that the names Adam had given to the other creatures followed a similar pattern. Indeed, if the Hebrew words used later in the Old Testament for such examples as the cormorant (derived from "casting itself into the sea"), the fox (from the root verb "to burrow"), the hawk ("a flashing speed"), and the lamb ("being pushed out to graze") are anything to go by, then there is a definite sense of them being named in accordance with certain behavioral characteristics.

The authority Adam had is here expressed as a reflection of his Creator. He named the animals by declaring what they were to be called. Right at the very beginning of creation, we are told that there was a kind of cosmic chaos until God began to speak out the creative words (see Gen 1:1). Adam's role as vice-regent was grounded in the declarative will of God; his execution of that role was established by the affirmation of his own will so long as it was expressed within the parameters God had set. We see precisely the same principle in operation, but with significantly different consequences, in relation to Satan's expulsion from heaven. He set his own will against God's and vocalized them thus:

---

1. See Genesis 1:28.

Kingdom

> "I will ascend to heaven;
> I will raise my throne above the stars of God;
> I will sit enthroned on the mount of assembly,
> on the utmost height of the sacred mountain.
> I will ascend above the tops of the clouds;
> I will make myself like the Most High."[2]

## Anointed to Reign

Where divine appointments are concerned, authority and anointing go hand in hand. So much so, in fact, that one might be forgiven for believing them to be synonymous terms. Although closely associated, however, it is possible to distinguish between the two. In simple terms, authority is the right to rule, whereas anointing is the God-given ability to do so. When God breathed life into Adam, he not only became a living being, but one that was distinctly unique from the rest of the entire creation. He was authorized to rule by God's word and he was anointed to reign by his spirit.

Significantly, the Hebrew word translated "breath" is *ruach*, which can also mean "spirit" or "wind" (the Greek equivalent is *pneuma*). When applied to God, it is usually in the sense of creative resourcefulness or dynamic supremacy. The association between God's spirit and anointed leadership is one that runs like a constant thread throughout the Bible. Indeed, this forms the basis for the apostle Paul's instruction to Timothy that: "All Scripture is God-breathed and is useful for teaching, rebuking, correcting and training in righteousness, so that the man of God may be thoroughly equipped for every good work" (2 Tim 3:16–17).

It could be considered both inappropriate and misleading to speak of God as having or possessing a spirit as if it was a mere appendage that he occasionally called upon for a particular duty as and when required. God essentially *is* spirit (John 4:24). There is no article before the word "spirit," definite or otherwise. Thus, it is not that God is a spirit among many or the supreme spirit when compared to others. He simply is spirit, both personal and personable. Because he is a personal God, he is self-conscious and self-determining; because he is a personable God, he is also capable of, and willing to, relate to others. But only spirit can

2. Isaiah 14:13–14.

*A Biblical Overview*

communicate with spirit. In his treatment of the difference between the soul (Greek—*psyche*) and the spirit (*pneuma*) of man, Thomas Chatterton Hammond makes the following interesting observation: "In 1 Corinthians 2:14–15 we have a distinction drawn between 'natural' and 'spiritual' men. The unregenerate man (*psychikos*), or 'soulish,' is unable to appreciate God's revelation, but the regenerate man (*pneumatikos*) is alive towards God."[3]

Anointing for a specific duty—or even for a general responsibility—was usually initiated by a solemn ritual. The fact that it would be difficult to argue for such an event in Adam's case, however, does not necessarily render it inappropriate to speak of him as having been anointed for the task set before him. As in the circumstances of the Adamic covenant, all the other features commonly associated with divine anointing are clearly in evidence. He was uniquely a "son" of God, set apart from the rest of creation in order to fulfill a role only he was able to perform. If Alec Motyer's offering is anything to go by, then Adam certainly fit the bill: "Fundamentally the anointing was an act of God (1 Sam 10:1), and the word 'anointed' was used metaphorically to mean the bestowal of divine favour (Ps 23:5; 92:10) or appointment to a special place or function in the purpose of God (Ps 105:15; Isa 45:1)."[4]

Moreover, the later comparisons between Adam and Jesus as federal heads of the covenants they each represented further fuels the argument for Adam's divine anointing. With reference to Jesus' incarnation, the Old Testament prophets referred to him as a coming Messiah (Greek—*Christos*), the original Hebrew of which (that is, *masha*) does not mean Savior, Redeemer, Deliverer, or Reconciler, but quite simply Anointed One. This is not to suggest, of course, that his anointing was for any purpose other than to save, redeem, deliver, or reconcile, but that he was able to do all of this because he was anointed to do so. If this is true of the last Adam, therefore, it does not seem unreasonable to suppose that it was equally so for the first Adam (1 Cor 15:45).

Although it would be a step too far to suggest that Adam's knowledge was perfect in the truest sense of that word, there can be little doubt that the knowledge he possessed concerning himself, his surroundings, and his Creator was perfectly true. Prior to the fall, he had no first-hand experience of evil or good in relation to it, though it does

---

3. Hammond, *In Understanding*, 71.
4. Motyer, "Anointing, Anointed," in Douglas, *New Bible Dictionary*, 50.

seem reasonable to assume that his perception of good as doing God's will and evil as opposing that will was sufficient to render him responsible for his actions. For him to disobey God would have been contrary to everything he knew to be true; similarly, for him to obey God was the only righteous course of action. Surely this is the hallmark of a godly king in the most comprehensively biblical sense of the term. Adam's appointment to the task before him carried that level of anointing.

However, one area of dominion that is at least as vital as all the others is the capacity to rule oneself. Adam was both authorized and anointed to govern himself within the confines of God-given parameters. Although he was not perfect in knowledge—and it is pure conjecture to suggest whether or not he may have become so had the fall not taken place—he was sufficiently informed to have considered the righteous implications or otherwise of a given choice of action before he took it. And, for a while, he made the right choices. That is, until his gaze was directed elsewhere.

### Distracted From Ruling

Although the subject of Adam's fall will be covered in much more detail in the following section, it is important to consider the initial steps taken toward that breakdown of fellowship between the Almighty and his vice-regent here. One way to view what Adam lost is to reflect upon what has been restored for us in Christ. This is not an entirely adequate premise, however, because if all Christ's atoning work did was to place believers back in the state of pre-fallen Adam, then there would still be the possibility of losing it once more. No, Christ did not give us what Adam lost but what God had originally intended Adam to pursue had he not fallen. Similarly, it is not entirely rewarding to focus exclusively on the actual fall of Adam without considering also the circumstances that were its prelude.

It is often said in some Christian circles that reason has little or no place in the Christian walk, that true spiritual experience is one that pays more attention to the emotions than to the mind. Whether or not this has been a prolonged reaction to the so-called age of the Enlightenment is impossible to prove either way. What there does seem to be more evidence for is that the catalyst for Adam's lapse from trusted vice-regent to sinful rebel was him ceasing to trust his own intelligent thought processes and rely instead almost entirely upon his feelings. The scenario is oft repeated throughout both the Bible's pages and history thereafter. From Israel's erroneous choice of king in Saul because it seemed like a good idea to the Jesus Movement's "if it feels good, do it" mantra of the 1960s and beyond, the initial premise that God's revealed word needs reinterpreting in the light of our emotions is folly at best. The Bible retains the use of the word "sin" in its vocabulary for describing such episodes.

It is noticeable also that Satan knew almost instinctively what strategy to employ to distract Adam: he attacked his authority. The devil unsuccessfully attempted a similar tactic centuries later with the true Son of God, not in a garden, but in the desert. Of course, he was more subtle than to confront Adam directly with a challenge to his right to rule on God's behalf. In fact, it might even be said that Satan's decision not to confront Adam directly was itself the challenge to his authority. In the words of Wayne Grudem:

> Satan . . . in approaching Eve first, was attempting to institute a role reversal by tempting Eve to take the leadership in disobeying God (Gen 3:1). This stands in contrast to the way God approached them, for when God spoke to them, he spoke to Adam first (Gen 2:15–17; 3:9). Paul seems to have this role reversal in mind when he says, "Adam was not deceived, but the woman was deceived and became a transgressor" (1 Tim 2:14). This at least suggests that Satan was trying to undermine the pattern of male leadership that God had established in the marriage by going first to the woman.[5]

Instead of defending the realm of the kingdom over which he had been authorized to rule, Adam's gaze became averted. He became protective over his right to rule, rather than present his case to the rightful ruler. It was he who represented the entire human race, he upon whom was given the responsibility to reign on God's behalf, and ultimately he who would either be rewarded for his obedience or be held accountable for any unfaithfulness (see Rom 5:15; 1 Cor 15:22). When we come to look at his abdication of responsibility in the next section we shall see that, although their respective roles were radically and inextricably different, they maintained the same core features: work for Adam and childbirth for Eve. These were not in themselves products of the fall,

---

5. Grudem, *Systematic Theology*, 463.

but that they should be endured with toil and pain respectively most certainly was (Gen 3:16–19).

When the temptation came, Satan's strategy proved effective, not simply because Eve was deceived, but largely because Adam was paying insufficient regard to his duties. We identified these earlier as quite simply to fill the earth and to rule its inhabitants. As yet, he had not taken the initiative to begin the former, and the fall proved that he was distinctly lacking in addressing the latter. He had failed to offer adequate husbandry to his wife and had allowed the serpent to challenge his God-given role of dominion over the earth's lower creation.

Lest there be any misunderstanding, let us be clear: Adam had not been given authority to make everything that had been placed under his rule subservient to his own will and purpose without qualification. This was only true insofar that his will remained subject to that of the Creator. Again, if I may be allowed to compare him briefly with the second Adam who, when confronted with the threat of the arresting officers, cried out to his God: "My Father, if it is possible, may this cup pass from me. Yet not as I will, but as you will" (Matt 26:39). Were ever paternal authority and filial piety so poignantly displayed?

## Summary

More than any other man in history, Adam could have no excuses for failing to maximize his potential. Created without sin—though obviously with the capacity to sin—he was both authorized to govern on God's behalf and anointed to do so. He was a most privileged individual, indeed. But privilege brings with it not a little responsibility. It is not even as if Adam was not warned of the dangers that might await him (Gen 2:15–17). Integral to the idea of taking care of the garden in the original (Hebrew—*shamar*) is the sense of being continually on guard. Like so many of us since that time, Adam clearly accepted the authority, bathed in the goodness of the anointing, but failed to regard his watchful duties with sufficient seriousness. He allowed himself to become distracted, which ultimately led to him abdicating his responsibilities, as we shall see.

## ABDICATION OF RESPONSIBILITY

Despite being given every opportunity to succeed in his God-given role as vice-regent, Adam failed. He was given authority to govern and was anointed to reign over all creation on behalf of the Creator, but ultimately chose to follow the inclinations of his own will. Even when he was distracted from ruling, it was not at that stage too late to turn back to God; temptation to sin is not the same as commission of sin. But, having allowed his attention to become preoccupied elsewhere, Adam eventually abdicated his responsibility as God's appointed "king" of the kingdom. By so doing, he effectively relinquished his kingly duties in three distinct areas:

- his responsibility toward his Maker;
- his responsibility toward his family; and
- his responsibility toward the created order.

### From the Joy of a Son to the Pain of a Serf

Biblically speaking, the concepts of kingdom and covenant belong together. Thus, it is difficult to engage with the one without also drawing attention to the other. After all, kingdom is founded on covenant. The appointment of Adam as vice-regent of God's kingdom on earth was no accident, but was grounded in the covenant relationship that was established between the supreme being, God, and the pinnacle of his creation, Adam. It is also true to say that the breaking of covenant had a commensurately negative effect on the right to rule. Just as worship without relationship is tantamount to idolatry, so too human kingship in the absence of godly fellowship suspends the right to assume the bestowal of divine favor.

We must first of all observe a subtle, though nonetheless important, distinction between relationship and fellowship. If my wife and I exchange heated words, the level and intensity of our fellowship may become severely hampered for a while (usually until she admits that I was right and she was wrong—I jest). However, our relationship remains essentially unaltered; we are still husband and wife. Probably the most tragic consequence of Adam's rebellion was the forfeiture of his unbroken fellowship with the Creator. It would seem that prior to his act of sin, Adam had enjoyed unparalleled access of communication with God, and yet he was still prepared to make a conscious and deliberate choice to sacrifice that on the altar of unbelief and subversion (see Gen 3:5).

Adam's transgression was fundamentally a denial of dependence. Of course, it would be all too easy to regard Adam as a victim of his circumstance. "It was all the devil's fault" or "If only Eve hadn't succumbed to temptation." The Bible makes it clear, however, that Adam, as God's delegated ruler, was responsible for his actions, for which he would be held ultimately accountable. Oh, Eve and Satan were by no means blame-free and would each have a price to pay but, to paraphrase Shakespeare's *Henry IV*, heavier still lay the head that wore the crown.

The immediate consequence of Adam's rebellion is graphically portrayed in his reticence to meet his God face to face. In the garden, he and his wife "hid from the Lord God" (Gen 3:8), surely implying a tarnished conscience. For the whole of his existence prior to this point, there is no evidence to suggest that Adam had felt anything but comfortable in the presence of his God, as he fellowshipped with him in the cool of the day. Now, however, there was a sense only of unease, remorse, and misgiving at the prospect of being confronted with the one whose image he had so foolishly and permanently sullied.

At the forefront of Adam's abdication—and foremost in the serpent's strategy—was a blurring of the clear distinction of that which exists between the Creator and the creature. When we speak of man in his state of original righteousness as possessing the image of God, this image should not be understood as a perfect and precise replica. Although it was perfectly created, it was not created perfect.

We cannot be entirely sure exactly what this consisted of, but we can rule certain things out on the basis of Scripture's revelation. For example, the image of God in man was clearly capable of becoming tarnished. We know this because it did so. Sin was always a possibility if we are to acknowledge all the reasonable implications of free will. By contrast, God is unable to sin or commit any act that is in any way inconsistent with his intrinsic nature, which is essentially and necessarily pure. Ultimately, the best thing we can say about the image of God in man is that it is a representation or a likeness. Unlike Christ, however, man is not an exact representation or likeness, for there are some godly characteristics he has never shared, nor ever will do so (see any reputable systematic theology on the incommunicable attributes). Self-sufficiency, inherent immortality, omnipotence, omniscience, and infinity are just a few examples.

What we can say with some degree of certainty is that the image of God in man was radically altered by the introduction of sin into his realm. How far he could be held accountable specifically for this effect is unclear, but it would be difficult to argue that God created man in his image with any intention other than that he seek most earnestly to protect it. The moral perfection of that image—that is, original righteousness—was, of course, automatically and irrevocably surrendered. Thus, Adam's kingly responsibility toward his maker was found well and truly wanting.

## Lacking as Both a Husband and a Father

I have recently heard it said by a moderately well-known preacher in the UK that every Christian man is required to be both a pastor and an evangelist in the family home. Thus, he is to extend pastoral care toward his wife and has an evangelistic duty toward his children. I am unsure of the biblical basis for such a premise, but it sounds like reasonable advice nonetheless. In principle, at least, it is a conviction that could surely have been laid at Adam's door; it is also one in which he was ultimately unsuccessful on both counts.

### *Adam's Failed Husbandry*

Although Eve was not entirely guiltless in the episode of eating the forbidden fruit, it was Adam who was held accountable for not having provided adequate watchful protection. The argument that neither of them would have been unduly concerned given that they were relatively innocent, their immediate environment was the paradise of God, and that they may have been oblivious to the potential for contrary behavior, is not really one that bears scrutiny. Adam was commanded quite explicitly to provide wise stewardship over creation (Gen 1:28), which came to include Eve. He was also commanded in no uncertain terms not to eat of the fruit of the tree of the knowledge of good and evil (Gen 2:15–17).

An important feature must be noted here: willful abdication of responsibility does not bring with it the waiving or abandonment of accountability. Adam was still responsible for his actions whether or not he took those duties as seriously as he might have done. The reason for his apparently larger level of liability is not difficult to fathom. Jack Cottrell puts it this way: "the only thing that can explain the clear teaching concerning Adam's greater responsibility is his immediate headship over Eve and his ultimate and representative headship over the entire human race."[6]

In recent times, the concept of a husband's role in the home has become much maligned. The idea that we are far more advanced in the twenty-first century than to contemplate such outmoded ideals is often cited as the definitive end to any potential counterarguments. Equality versus subjection is one that usually finds the latter trailing despondently in the wake of the former. But we need to understand what is meant by those terms and to know that we dilute God's direct commands at our peril. Functional subordination does not necessarily assume that personal equality has been negated. As a pedagogic paradigm, the Godhead itself teaches us as much. The doctrine of the Trinity is undergirded by a presumed co-equality of the three persons: Father, Son, and Holy Spirit. It truly is a tri-unity. Functionally, however, there exists a clear hierarchical structure, which in no way contradicts or undermines the rightful claim of each person to be co-equally God within the one divine being.

### Adam's Federal Responsibility

As covenant head of the entire human race, Adam was federally responsible for all who would follow after him. The mechanics of how—or even why—this is so are ultimately beyond our comprehension. However, the effect of original sin is such that we are all tainted with it and, therefore, in need of a redeemer. Thus, all mankind is born in a state of pollution and corruption because each one of us is symbolically embodied in the sin and guilt of Adam. This is the root cause of man's fundamental inclination toward sin: a federal identification, the fruit of which is manifestly evident in sinful acts. John Murray has this to say of

---

6. Cottrell, *Gender Roles*, 125–6.

it: "The Fall had abiding effect . . . upon all who descended from [Adam and Eve]; there is racial solidarity in sin and evil."[7]

Sin entered the world through the sin of Adam. Equally unequivocal is Scripture's teaching that, with the exception of Jesus, "all have sinned and fall short of the glory of God" (Rom 3:23). There are no other escapees from the principle of sin and there is certainly no biblical evidence to support such a belief. (Indeed, the incarnation event was such that Christ was born in a way that negated the propagation of the sin principle in him.) It does not seem unreasonable to assume, therefore, that in some mysterious way the universality of sin in Adam's seed is entirely due to his personal act of disobedience. As members of the human race through natural generation, we do not enter life pure (as Adam did) with a clean spiritual bill of health until the moment we fail to resist temptation. Rather, we are all somehow tarnished with sin at birth, though from the point of conception (see Pss 51:5; 58:3; Eph 2:3).

Prevalent among the various opinions regarding the transmission of sin is the view that there was such a concentrated form of union between Adam and his race that every one of us actually participated in Adam's specific sin when he did so. Needless to say, the biblical evidence is not sufficiently conclusive to support such a theory. However, in reply to the question: "Did all mankind fall in Adam's first transgression?" the Shorter Westminster Catechism responds by speaking of a covenant having been made with Adam (Hos 6:7), not only for himself but also on behalf of his offspring, whereby all mankind who descended from him by ordinary generation "sinned with him, and fell with him, in his first transgression." While it would be clearly erroneous to speak of the collective will of humanity in Adam, it is by no means unjustifiable to acknowledge the plain teaching of Scripture that Adam sinned as the representative of all mankind, and that the consequences of his action were not restricted to himself only, but thereafter affected all his posterity (see Rom 5:12–21; 1 Cor 15:21–22, 45–49).

## Unwise Stewardship

Climate change, global warming, the greenhouse effect, acid rain, glacier shifts, erratic weather conditions, etc: what do they all have in

---

7. J. Murray, "Sin," in Douglas, *New Bible Dictionary*, 1117.

common? Well, they are all related to environmental issues, they each testify in some way to a planet under pressure, and the blame for them all is almost universally laid at the front door of mankind. There are some who claim that such changes are to be expected as part of a normal cycle of events but that the rapidity on this occasion is largely due to irresponsible human behavior. The testimony of Scripture, however, suggests that, though some of this may be true, the process of earth's decay and that of the rest of the created order was precipitated by Adam's sin.

The whole of creation has been significantly impacted by the fruit of God's wrath against sin on the part of his vice-regent. Although Adam's action was entirely personal, it was by no means private, as we have seen, for its consequences were far-reaching. Not only was mankind alienated from God's perfect purpose, but also creation itself was similarly tainted. Where there had previously been harmony in the cosmos, there now resided discord; where pre-fallen creation knew of abundance, growth, and productivity, there became a seed of death, decay, and repression. No longer would vegetation and the plant world willingly offer up their fruit to the vice-regent over all the earth; instead, Adam would experience only sweat, toil, difficulty, and hardship in providing for himself and his family from his surroundings: "Cursed [was] the ground because of [him]" (Gen 3:17). Dietrich Bonhoeffer confirms that:

> God's Word to Adam proclaims the destruction and division of the primal relation between man and nature. The ground, for the fruits of which Adam . . . previously only had to stretch out a hand, which had brought him what he needed becomes cursed because of Adam's deed. It becomes Adam's concern, his pain, his toil, his enemy . . . This is . . . earth, cursed out of the glory of its creation, cast out of the unequivocal directness of its language and of its praise of the Creator into the ambiguity of the absolutely strange and mysterious. The trees, the animals, which had once represented the Word of God the Creator directly, now indicate in often grotesque ways the inconceivability, the arbitrariness of a despot hidden in darkness. Thus the work of man upon the cursed ground becomes the expression of the disunion of fallen man within nature; it is under the curse.[8]

---

8. Bonhoeffer, *Creation and Temptation*, 85.

*A Biblical Overview*

It is perhaps significant that when the apostle Paul speaks of the "groaning of creation" and its ultimate release from having been "subjected to frustration," he does so in the context of the final revealing of the sons of God in their regal status by virtue of their relationship in and toward the King of the kingdom (Rom 8:19–22). Whether the one who subjected it relates to God as the author of the judgment or to Adam whose sin is responsible for that sentence is not conclusive, though the arguments for the former seem more weighty, especially in view of the fact that God's sovereignty is uppermost in the wider context of this passage.[9]

When God cursed the ground because of Adam's sin, a course of action was set in motion that could only be reversed by global redemption. Just as the perpetrator for sin's effects on humanity and the created order was one man, Adam, so the redeemer for both is the man, Christ Jesus (Rom 8:21). Those who deny that creation's state of decay was anything to do with Adam's sin but that it was inherent from the very beginning seem to put more trust in principles of entropy and thermodynamics than they do in the revelation of Scripture, despite arguments to the contrary. Although they claim to be positing proposals that remain faithful to legitimate biblical exegesis, they are in fact guilty of unbiblical eisegesis by attempting to squeeze their so-called proof texts into a predetermined conclusion.

In order to understand something of the loss suffered by creation because of Adam's sin, it might help us to look at what it will gain when its birth pains are at an end (Rom 8:22). William Hendriksen associates Paul's teaching here to the Roman believers with that of Peter's second epistle (2 Pet 3:7–12), John's revelation (Rev 21:1–5), and Old Testament prophecy (Isa 11:6–9). Here, we learn that the entire universe is to be purged with fire, the results of which will be "a new heaven and a new earth" ushering in true creational harmony and global peace.[10] If this is what is to be restored to creation at the consummation of the present age, then it does not seem unreasonable to suggest that it lost the capacity to become what the new heaven and earth will be, became entirely disharmonious and utterly lacking in the kind of peace God originally intended all because of Adam's transgression.

---

9. See Osborne, *Romans*, 211.
10. See Hendriksen, *Romans*, 266–7.

Kingdom

## Summary

It would be easy to imagine that God's first-appointed king over all that he had created on the earth could not take care of the kingdom entrusted to his care. However, this would imply that he was unable to do so. He had true freedom of will, which must of necessity have included the freedom to have chosen not to succumb to temptation. Thereafter, man's freedom was restricted by the parameters of his sinful nature; not so with unfallen Adam. Thus, it is not that he could not, but that he would not exercise dominion when the first real test of his kingly credentials came along. In this section, we have seen that Adam failed in three specific areas, for which he would ultimately be held accountable:

- his responsibility toward God;
- his responsibility toward his family, both immediate and extended; and
- his responsibility toward the created order.

In so doing, Adam effectively set the pattern for all who would follow him until the coming of the Christ.

## THE KINGDOM OF ISRAEL

A distinction must first of all be noted between the kingdom of God in Israel and God's theocratic rule in and through the kingdom of Israel. For the purposes of this study, the former existed from Israel's inception as a people group, while the latter awaited the establishing of nationhood. Although the primary focus of our attention in this section deals with Israel under monarchical rule, it would be remiss not to set the scene by casting our eyes briefly at the exclusively theocratic government that was evident prior to that time—in admittedly varying degrees—by way of background. Thereafter, I propose to look at some of the key features of the kingdom of Israel under Saul, David, and David's dynastic line up to the point immediately before the division of the kingdom.

*A Biblical Overview*

## Israel Prior to the Monarchy

The book of Judges covers the period between the death of Joshua and the time of Samuel. The time-frame encompassed by it serves as a fitting prelude to Israel's monarchical history. Joshua had been a worthy successor to Moses; his role in leading the tribal groups of Israel into the land of promise is well documented both in Scripture and elsewhere.[11] It is a richly deserved tribute to Joshua's legacy that the Bible records: "Israel served the Lord throughout the lifetime of Joshua and of the elders who outlived him and who had experienced everything the Lord had done for Israel" (Josh 24:31).

Being in the land and conquering it once there, however, proved to be very different propositions. Internal tribal skirmishes, on the one hand, coupled with fearful enemy nations, on the other, meant that there was always going to be more to taking Canaan than merely occupying it.

It is perhaps significant that in Israel's early history, after having arrived in Canaan, their leaders were neither democratically elected or followed any strict hereditary model. Rather, they seem to have been divinely appointed and thereafter acknowledged to be so by the people. While it is admittedly difficult to attribute any definitive time-scale to the book of Judges, it does provide some remarkable insights into the nature of Israelite civilization during the period in question. It would seem that the pattern followed that of Israel's bondage in Egypt, albeit on a much smaller scale and in very different, though not entirely dissimilar, circumstances. Oppression gave rise to pleading, which caused the Lord to raise up a deliverer—usually someone with the least obvious natural leadership credentials—who would defeat the current enemy and usher in a period of relative peace, during which time a state of lukewarmness would prevail until the whole cycle began again.

The book of Judges is many things, but nothing better describes it than being an historical account of Israel's constitutional progression (some might argue "regression") from theocracy toward monarchical structure. Indeed, had it not been for Gideon's good sense, he and not Saul would have become Israel's first appointed king. Thankfully, when offered a throne, Gideon directed the attention of those who sought to honor him so to the true cause of their victory over the Midianites: "I

---

11. See Bright, *History of Israel*; Johnson, *History of the Jews*.

Kingdom

will not rule over you, nor will my son rule over you. The Lord will rule over you" (Judg 8:23). Mighty man of valor he may have been (6:12, KJV), but he was a man with frailties nonetheless, as we quickly discover before half a dozen more verses of that very same chapter have elapsed.

In the restricted sense of their office, the judges were also God's vice-regents insofar that they exercised God's moral government both toward and on behalf of his people. That they were all given to imperfection did not in itself disqualify them from the task they were given nor did it undermine the role each played in the short-lived deliverance to which they contributed. The fact surrounding Gideon's golden ephod, Jephthah's rash vow and self-gratification, and Samson's proclivity to toy with his gift were not swept under the carpet, any more than was that of David's adultery some considerable time later. The testimony of Scripture, however, makes their positive contribution to the unfolding revelation of God's kingdom purpose through Israel the more prominent feature.

Whether the eventual appointment of a human king over Israel ever formed part of God's perfect will has been the subject of much theological debate. No doubt it will continue to be so, though any conclusions drawn can only ever be consigned to the files of conjecture. However, the constant disunity of the tribes throughout the period of the judges provoked a statement that may well suggest otherwise: "In those days Israel had no king; everyone did as he saw fit" (Judg 17:6; 19:1; 21:25).

Perhaps somewhat fittingly, it was the last of the judges (see Acts 3:24; 13:20) who was prevailed upon to usher in the monarchical rule over Israel. Equally poignant is the fact that, whereas "Joshua" means "the Lord saves" or "salvation belongs to the Lord," Samuel's name means "God has listened/heard." Samuel was a child of promise (1 Sam 1:1–20), a man of prayer (7:5–8; 12:17), a circuit judge (7:16), and an inspired prophet (3:19–21; 8:22). He was also not to be found lacking in courage (13:13; 15:16–29).

Samuel's role in helping to inaugurate the monarchy in Israel was a strange one, indeed. He had led Israel with some measure of success, though in later years his leadership credentials were disputed by the tribal elders. No doubt the fact that his sons did not share their father's sense of integrity contributed toward such a challenge (1 Sam 8:1–5). It

*A Biblical Overview*

is not without irony that, despite Israel's rejection of Samuel as leader, it was him they trusted to appoint a more suitable replacement.

## Saul and David

The appointment of Saul as Israel's first king proved to be a radical turning point in their corporate history. Perhaps unsurprisingly, it came at a time of national chaos. Against a backdrop of sustained Philistine threat, the tribal leaders requested of Samuel the prophet that he "appoint a king . . . such as all the other nations" (1 Sam 8:5). Their desire to compete with the surrounding nations on a level playing field almost became their undoing. Where others might point to the valiant exploits of some great Adonis-like figure, whose reputation on the battlefield was almost legendary, Israel's dependence upon a being who had led them in a pillar of cloud during the day and one of fire by night had become an embarrassment to them. They sought something tangible toward whom they could direct the taunts of others and were prepared to sacrifice the blessings of their covenant status with Almighty God in order to be able to do so.

Remarkably, Israel's request for a warrior-leader who was "head and shoulders" above his fellows was granted. Saul certainly fit the description given of him, his every subsequent act being largely dictated by human intellect and brute strength. Looked at in its entirety, Saul's reign was an unmitigated disaster. He failed to unite the people behind his leadership, he was generally lacking in military skills or the capacity to handle the troops, he was unable to discern the parameters of his authority, he was unwilling to be fully obedient to godly directives, and he behaved like a playground bully when it became obvious that another was the object of divine favor.

King Saul would undoubtedly make a classic case study for the modern-day psychologist: his often bizarre mood swings, uncertainties about his purpose in life, the fact that he had to be coerced into a job he never really craved, and the emotional insecurities being possibly linked to an unhappy childhood experience. The testimony of Scripture, however, is not so lily-livered. His disobedience was inexcusable and one for which he ultimately paid with his life (1 Sam 31). It might even be said that God rejected Saul as king because Saul had rejected God's covenant as the basis for his own kingly rule. Perhaps ironically, when his end came it was at the hand of an Amalekite (2 Sam 1:1–10), the very people he had so disobediently failed to eradicate (1 Sam 15).

In stark contrast to Saul, David brought victory, repossession of land, national stability, and the foundation for peace through a dynastic rulership that was to endure for four hundred years. The key factors of his success were God's covenant faithfulness (see Ps 89:28–29) and obedience on David's part to his covenant obligations. Given the hostility that dictated many of Saul's dealings with David, it would perhaps have been understandable for the latter to express relief at the news of the former's death. That he lamented greatly for Saul's loss is testament to the integrity that—bar for a few significant lapses—David maintained throughout most of his forty-year reign.

It is too easy to posit the idea that David succeeded where Saul failed largely in matters of temperament or that David was greatly advantaged by virtue of the favor with which he was looked upon by Samuel. Scripture's epitaph of each man tells its own story:

> Saul . . . an impressive young man without equal among the Israelites—a head taller than any of the others.[12]

> David son of Jesse a man after [God's] own heart.[13]

Initially, David's reign was over his own tribal region only. On Saul's death, his supporters installed Saul's son Ishbosheth as successor to the throne, though it would seem that their motivation had less to do with loyalty and was more stimulated by Abner's desire to manipulate the king in residence. When both were removed from the scene, any real opposition to David's reign dissipated, and he was officially recognized as king of all Israel shortly afterwards.

Arguably David's greatest achievement as king concerned the conquest and establishing of Jerusalem as the nation's capital. For over two hundred years, the Jebusites had withheld the Israelites' advances. Not wishing to give the impression that previous attempts were anything but wholehearted, David did seem unique in his realization of the strategic importance of taking Jerusalem. The politico-religious significance lay in its position, which was ideally suited to uniting the schismatic tendencies that were already emerging. It was also conveniently situated

---

12. 1 Samuel 9:2.
13. Acts 13:22; cf 1 Sam 13:14.

whence to rule, a fact supported by the building there of the royal palace. Jerusalem would thereafter be known as the city of David.

David is rightly revered as Israel's greatest king. Not only does he compare favorably to his predecessor Saul, but he was far superior to any of his own dynastic successors. We have seen that he was a man after God's own heart. This was in part the reason for his accomplishments, though it is not the whole picture. A more legitimate argument might be that, unlike any other ruler in Israel before or since, David realized the limitations of his role and acknowledged that he was only vice-regent to God's absolute supremacy.

David's recognition of the qualities required to lead Israel saw him overlook those assumed by others to be his natural successors. Absalom, Amnon, and Adonijah did not outlive their father and would most probably have proved to be unworthy heirs had they done so. David had been a warrior king of sorts. The period of his reign called for just such a man. In making provision for his death, however, he realized that the current need of the hour was for someone whose strength lay more in the capacity to honor Israel's religious obligations. Thus, Solomon was chosen to sit on David's throne.

## David's Dynastic Line Over the Whole Nation

Although the title of this section sounds rather grand—and in theory should have been more so than it was in reality—the period in question embraces only the reign of Solomon and a few short days of that of Rehoboam (around 1020–931 BC).

As David Hubbard points out: "Solomon was Israel's first dynastic ruler."[14] This, of course, was no mere accident, nor was it an exclusively human choice to revere the memory of David's exploits by way of nationalistic gratitude. It was, in fact, the beginning of the unfolding of God's covenant promise to David (see 2 Sam 7). Though the specifics of the Davidic covenant have been dealt with elsewhere,[15] it is vitally important in this context that we grasp its relationship to the unfolding of God's kingdom on earth. Moreover, such an understanding will help

---

14. D. A. Hubbard, "Solomon," in Douglas, *New Bible Dictionary*, 1127.
15. Woodall, *Covenant*, 33–40.

us to see also the reasons for the erratic nature, repeated failure, and ultimate collapse of the kingdom of Israel in the Old Testament.

In some respects, Solomon's ascendancy to the throne followed a similar pattern to that of his father. Perhaps most notable among these was the fact that a son of the previous king made a last-ditch attempt to seize control. Adonijah did not even wait until the death of his father before having himself pronounced king at En-Rogel. Rallying support from David's once favored general, Joab, and the similarly influential priest, Abiathar, Adonijah's hand seemed to be a strong one. As Israel saw with their choice of Saul, however, human strength and wisdom cannot ultimately prevail against God's will and purpose. Solomon's allies included Benaiah, Zadok, and Nathan, all of whom were to become prominent in the execution of David's earlier promise to Bathsheba's son concerning the passing on of the kingdom (see 1 Kgs 1:11–48).

By the time Solomon actually came to the throne, much of the hard work had been done by his father. So much so, in fact, that it would not be too much of a simplification to say that Solomon's primary objective was merely to maintain what had been handed down to him. In order to make this even easier, he instituted twelve regional administrative centers, each of which was responsible for supporting the newly established central court. In principle at least, this is similar to a local church devolving the responsibilities for providing post-service refreshments to its smaller home/cell groups on a monthly rota basis. Each group carries out those duties for a full month and—if there are twelve such groups—will not be expected to do so again until the same time the following year.

For the most part, Solomon proved to be a worthy successor to his father's throne. He showed admirable trading skills with other nations, taking full advantage of Israel's strategic position both by land and by sea; he initiated peaceful alliances with Egypt, Ethiopia, Tyre, and Phoenicia, each being both beneficiary of and benefactor to Israel's cause at one time or another. Even to the heathen, it seemed that only divine favor could reasonably explain the apparent blessing that accompanied almost every decision taken by this amiable merchant king. And that proved to be his downfall.

Solomon's apparently accommodating demeanor was, indeed, politically expedient, though it often came close to breaching his covenantal obligations. Finally, a step of compromise too far saw him effectively surrender to moral and spiritual bankruptcy. Foreign wives—of which there were many—brought with them their own religions, alliance soon giving way to allegiance. Having completed the building of the temple in accordance with God's revealed design, the words of Solomon's prayer of dedication are some of the most beautiful in Scripture (1 Kgs 8:44–50); they evoked a favorably forgiving response from the Almighty (9:3–9). His waywardness in later years, however, brought only divine disapproval and ushered in the beginning of the end for the united nation of Israel. Hubbard concludes thus: "[The] violent breach of Israel's covenant could not go unpunished. Though judgment was stayed during Solomon's lifetime for David's sake, the seeds of dissatisfaction sown among the people by Solomon's harsh policies of taxation and corvée were to bear bitter fruit during the reign of his son and successor, Rehoboam."[16]

Solomon's wisdom has earned him legendary status. His renown in this regard is not restricted to the parameters of Scripture (1 Kgs 3:16–28; Prov 10–29), but is extensively lauded also in extra-biblical literature. But the wisdom he expressed and extended in judgment upon others was not a natural trait; it was a spiritual gift (see 1 Kgs 3:5–9). Having been granted understanding and wise counsel above his fellows and beyond his natural capacity, his duty thereafter was to exercise them sagely. Is it possible to unwisely employ wisdom? The testimony regarding some of King Solomon's decisions, particularly in later years, suggests that it most certainly is.

Rehoboam's legacy in Scripture is somewhat unique: he was the last king of the united Israel and the first of the southern kingdom of Judah. His father had introduced a heavy tax burden on the people in order to help subsidize royal expenses. When a delegation led by Jeroboam pleaded with Rehoboam that these now be relaxed, the king consulted his advisors. Had he taken that proffered by those more wise and mature, the schism that followed may well have been averted, if only temporarily. Rather, he opted to heed the counsel of his peers, who were just as headstrong and irresponsible as he. The northern tribes rebelled against the even heavier taxation and installed Jeroboam as their own king. We shall follow the intricacies of that division in the coming section.

---

16. D. A. Hubbard, "Solomon," in Douglas, *New Bible Dictionary*, 1131.

Kingdom

## Summary

When God acceded to Israel's request for a king, there could have been little idea of what lay in store or how long such a monarchy would endure. Even the most conservative estimates, based on both the biblical evidence and other known sources, put it at around a hundred years from Saul's inauguration to the division of the kingdom. My maternal grandfather died in 2009 at the grand old age of ninety-seven. Had he lived in Jerusalem around three thousand years ago, he could conceivably have experienced both the beginning and the end of the united monarchy in Israel. Perhaps some did. The period covered by Israel's undivided monarchy did not begin too well. By the time of the separation between the northern and southern kingdoms, the people had begun a downward trend that was to prove irreversible. In between, there had been a time of blessing and favor led by a king who, despite his faults and failings, is still renowned as "a man after God's own heart."

## THE KINGDOM DIVIDED AGAINST ITSELF

Anyone who uses a thesaurus regularly will know that the synonymous value of one word to another is governed largely by context. The list of words offered, therefore, cannot be plucked from liberally without giving some thought to how it is to be employed. On the face of it, "division" and "separation" might appear wholly interchangeable, though there is often a subtle difference. In reality, separation can be a good thing, especially if the bonds of togetherness have been broken somehow. Usually, such separation takes place long after division has reared its ugly head. When a sub-group holds dearly to divinely-appointed principles and yet the larger group to which they belong is prepared to compromise such values, then division is already at hand. Unless one faction is willing to yield ground to the other, then this separation may well be the only mutually acceptable resolution. This was the state in which Israel found itself under King Rehoboam.

### North Versus South

As we saw toward the end of the last section, a united kingdom of Israel did not survive long after Saul's death. In truth, however, the signs of a looming division had begun to appear long before that. It would be easy to proffer the charge that the key to a strong kingdom lay in a firm monarchy. Certainly, the evidence of David's tenure might suggest this to be true, especially in the light of the threats to his position that he was able successfully to counter. However, the danger was foreseen even before the crown of Israel's first king had settled into place. Consider the words of Samuel, the prophet: "If you fear the Lord and serve and obey him and do not rebel against his commands, and if both you and the king who reigns over you follow the Lord—good! But if you do not obey the Lord, and if you rebel against his commands, his hand will be against you, as it was against your fathers" (1 Sam 12:14-15).

Thus, the actual strength lay not in the might of the reigning monarch, nor in the common allegiance of the people to him, but in their mutual commitment to the purpose of the King of the kingdom—God. The history of Israel fully bears this out. Times of blessing coincided with common worship, while periods of turbulence and complacency also went hand-in-hand. The division of the previously united kingdom was essentially the product of Solomon's idolatry; Rehoboam and Jeroboam were really just pawns caught up in the aftermath of God's judgment by withdrawing his hand of favor. The further Israel drifted from clearly defined principles of worship and adherence to their covenantal obligations, the worse the situation in which they found themselves.

When Rehoboam shunned the advances of Jeroboam and his followers, he effectively set in motion a sequence of events that would be more far-reaching than only the division of the kingdom, as we shall see. For the time being, he had enough to manage the breaking of the northern tribes from their own royal house. However, he proved incapable even of that. His show of oppression, it seems, was just that—a show. Perhaps ironically, Rehoboam means "expansion of the people." As if to reflect their similar sounding names, Jeroboam probably means "may the people increase." They were only the first of their respective kingdoms to fail to live up to the meaning of their names.

Thereafter, the kingdom was permanently divided, with hostilities almost constantly raging between the two factions. Attempted allegiances through marriage brought some temporary alleviation to the conflict between north and south, and there were occasions of them being joined together in battle against a common enemy, though the twelve tribes of Israel would never again know the solidarity of oneness.

They could only ever be united as a people if they were so in heart, mind, soul, and strength. Sadly, that was not to be.

For his part, Jeroboam wasted no time at all in establishing his authority over the newly-formed northern kingdom. Whether his initial acts were motivated by a perceived sense of necessity or were simply an attempt to provoke Rehoboam is unclear. The consequences, however, are less shrouded in mystery, as the decision to institute two new religious sanctuaries only served to fuel Israel's idolatrous tendencies and further escalate the rate of their degeneration.

It was not just the erecting of the shrines at Dan and Bethel that serviced such profane infidelity. Jeroboam reneged against the covenants God had initiated with his people in the Old Testament. He set up himself as king, despite the fact that he was not of the line of David (2 Sam 7:16), he established his own priests in contravention of the Phinehatic promise (Num 25:10–13), and he broke the Mosaic covenant commands as represented in the Decalogue (Exod 20:1–17). It has even been suggested that he may have served as high priest himself, thus condensing in his rulership the power to exercise both civil and ecclesiastical governance (see 1 Kgs 12:33). Jeroboam was certainly responsible for the changing of the times when key religious festivals were to be held (vv. 31–32).

The non-dynastic ascension to the throne of Jeroboam became a template for future kings of the northern territories. It effectively became a reign chosen by democratic process rather than a theocratic delegation under God. Kings were chosen by popular whim and removed when that popularity waned. In the words of Hubbard: "[Jeroboam's] royal cult set the pattern for his successors, who are customarily evaluated as perpetuating his sins."[17]

If Jeroboam is emblematic of the pick 'n' mix attitude toward religion, whereby we feel at liberty to choose those elements that sit most comfortably with our sense of aesthetic pleasure, then surely Rehoboam's symbolism consists in that of a bungling authoritarian approach to imposing decisions with no thought except to the plea of tradition. His conduct was far from exemplary of one who looked to such tradition for support. Under Rehoboam's rule, illicit cultic practices began to thrive in Judah, no doubt intensified by the influence

---

17. D. A. Hubbard, "Jeroboam," in Douglas, *New Bible Dictionary*, 566.

of alien women in positions of some persuasion by his side (see 1 Kgs 14:21, 31; 15:13).

Rehoboam's only authentic claims to any semblance of honor are the facts that he was allowed to be buried as a legitimate incumbent of Judah's throne (2 Chr 12:16) and that his name appears in the Messianic line of Matthew's genealogical record (Matt 1:7).

## The Northern Kingdom of Israel

Despite attempts from the very beginning of the northern kingdom to assimilate all authority into the king's hands, God retained a strong prophetic voice, especially through Elijah and Elisha. There was not one king of the northern kingdom, from Jeroboam to Hoshea, who could be spoken of as anything but a failure in spiritual terms. By and large, the demise of each one earned the epitaph that they had done evil in the eyes of the Lord, only Joram, Jehu, and Hoshea having that appraisal diluted slightly (see 2 Kgs 3:2; 10:29–31; 17:2). Indeed, Clarence Benson observes of Jeroboam's successors that: "one was slain in battle, one committed suicide, and six were assassinated, and the history of the nine godless dynasties may be recorded in three words: idolatry, immorality, and bloodshed."[18]

Initially, one could be forgiven for thinking that the northern kingdom carried divine favor with it, especially if one equates this with material prosperity and military prowess. The land it occupied was both potentially more agriculturally beneficial and commercially advantageous, given it proximity to the major trade routes of the period. This was particularly so during the reigns of Omri and Ahab, the former being a notably fearsome battle tactician. Omri (reigned 885–874 BC) seemed to be a syncretist extraordinaire, always willing to replicate schemes that were seen to work for others, whether that be mimicking Solomon's apparently shrewd policy of taking foreign wives to further his cause or imitating the political strategies of flourishing near neighbors. He also made similar provision for the future by espousing his son and heir, Ahab, to Jezebel, daughter of Ethbaal, king of Sidon.

Ahab (874–853 BC) had learned his father's lessons well. He, too, resorted to copying the nations in all matters, thus denying the

---

18. Benson, *Law and History*, 59.

Kingdom

bestowal of unique privilege upon his people as God's covenant nation and with it the opportunity to express God's kingdom rule. Ahab associated power with how he was perceived by others outside the borders of the northern kingdom of Israel. How unlike the great stalwarts of the faith, even those with otherwise less than mimic-worthy traits! "Jacob ... worshipped as he leaned on the top of his staff" (Heb 11:21) and Ahab built a palace inlaid with ivory (1 Kgs 22:39). If ever there was an argument to support the link between idolatry and immorality, Scripture provides it for us in the shape of Ahab, who "not only considered it trivial to commit the sins of Jeroboam son of Nebat, but he also ... began to serve Baal and worship him" (16:31).

The eleven kings of the northern kingdom cited in the second book of Kings differ only in the level of atrocity to which they were each prepared to stoop. Despite being helped in military matters by Elisha (2 Kgs 6:12), Joram (851–841 BC) sought the prophet's death as a scapegoat for the famine in Samaria (vv. 24–31). Having put an end to Ahab's line with arguably more vigor than was necessary (9:7–10), Jehu (841–814 BC) appeared not to be quite so keen to tear down the altars at which the golden calves were worshiped at Dan and Bethel (10:29). Jehoahaz (814–798 BC) generally continued the same godless inclination of his father, his death after seventeen years in power bringing to an end the politically motivated alliance between north and south. Thereafter, there was only disquiet, mistrust, and quarreling on both sides.

From that time on, the downward trend rapidly gathered pace. The single-most positive feature of the reign of Jehoash (798–782 BC) was that he spared Amaziah, king of Judah, when it was within his command to have him killed (2 Kgs 14:13). The reign of Jeroboam II (793–753 BC) was the longest of the northern kingdom if you take into account the eleven-year co-regency with his father. This Jeroboam fared no better than his namesake, however, his lengthy reign being summed up in just a few short verses by the writer of 2 Kings (14:23–29). We learn more of him through the writings of Amos and Hosea, but there is nothing anywhere of credit, except perhaps the overthrow of the Aramean hordes.

After Jeroboam II, there were six kings in Israel spanning some thirty-two years, until Hoshea succumbed to the advancing Assyrian might. Zechariah's reign lasted only six months (753) before he was openly assassinated by his successor, Shallum (2 Kgs 15:8–11), thus fulfilling the prophetic word to Jehu (see 10:30; 15:12). Shallum (752) fared even worse, he too being assassinated after only one month in which to occupy the royal throne (15:13). Apart from taking the kingship by force, Menahem (752–742) was also guilty of other heinous crimes (v. 16). However, he did restore some sense of stability, though at the expense of crippling tribute being paid to Assyria, which he funded by excessive taxation (vv. 19–20). Menahem was the last of Israel's kings of whom Scripture records to have died a natural death (v. 22).

Pekahiah's short reign (742–740), did not trouble the writers of the Hebrew Scriptures unduly (2 Kgs 15:23–26), mention of him serving only to inform us that he, too, "did evil in the eyes of the Lord" (v. 24) and fell victim to an assassin's conspiracy (v. 25). Although Assyria's domination was completed in the reign of Hoshea, much of the groundwork was done during Pekah's tenure (752–732), the last eight years of which were as sole regent. Prior to this time, it is commonly acknowledged that Pekah had set up a rival Transjordanian regime to that of Menahem when Shallum had been killed. The Assyrian king, Tiglath-Pileser, took many of the northern territories and consigned a number of its inhabitants to an exile from which they would never return (v. 29).

Hoshea also acceded to the throne of Israel (732–722 BC) by conspiring to forcibly remove his predecessor (2 Kgs 15:30). Given the political instability of the northern kingdom at the time, it is highly likely that many of his countrymen will have been hoping that Hoshea would live up to his name, which means "salvation." Sadly, their hopes were to be irreversibly dashed. Despite attempts to rid his people of the Assyrian threat, some of which was grounded in the mistaken belief that Egypt would come to his rescue, much of Hoshea's reign was as vassal to Sargon II. When Samaria finally fell, over 27,000 of its inhabitants were deported and integrated throughout the east, and the capital city became an Assyrian province.

## The Southern Kingdom of Judah

The writer of the books of the Kings seems to have had both a general and a more specific criterion for judging the value of each throne's respective incumbent. In general terms, how good or bad they were is governed by their commitment or negligence of worship being directed

Kingdom

to the true God. More specifically, kings of the northern kingdom were compared to Jeroboam, while those of the south had David as their role model. In these regards, all of the kings of the north were bad, following the example set by Jeroboam, whereas few of the south could be said to have emulated King David's pattern of relative goodness.

On this basis, Abijah's three-year reign (913–910 BC) as Rehoboam's successor was not a good one (1 Kgs 15:1–8). His son, Asa, did measure up to the standard set by David and enjoyed a long reign (910–869) in which to prove his commitment to the Lord. Much of this consisted in him removing the symbols of idolatrous practices set up by his immediate predecessors. At the threat of attack from the northern kingdom, Asa formed a successful alliance with Syria. This may be regarded as a lack of trust in divine protection on Asa's part, though Scripture offers no hint that he was rebuked for his actions; quite the contrary, in fact (vv. 9–24).

Jehoshaphat (872–848) shared periods of co-regency with both his predecessor and his successor, though it seems clear that the influence of Asa upon his reign was more beneficial than was his own upon Jehoram. Although Jehoshaphat was rightly praised by the chronicler for his adherence to godly direction (2 Chr 20:32) and sending out itinerant teachers of the Mosaic law (17:7–9), he must also take some share of the blame for Judah's infidelity after his death for aligning them to apostate Israel through the marriage of his son and successor (848–841) with Ahab's daughter Athaliah (18:1). It is a damning epitaph that Scripture speaks of Jehoram's demise in terms of him departing "to no one's regret" (21:20).

Ahaziah's one-year reign (841) continued to demonstrate his mother's influence (2 Kgs 8:26–27), as that of his father had done. The association with the north cost him dearly when Jehu exacted God's judgment on Ahab's house (9:22–28). For the next seven years, Athaliah ruled as queen (841–835), her sole objective seeming to be the complete annihilation of David's line (11:1). Given what we now know of the ultimate fulfillment of the Davidic covenant, it is perhaps not too difficult to imagine the real power behind Athaliah's strategy. Thank God for the legitimate priesthood, one of whom led the well designed and almost bloodless coup to place the young Joash on the throne (vv. 2–21), thus restoring the lawful monarchy to Judah.

*A Biblical Overview*

Joash ruled over Judah for forty years (835-796). It was a lengthy, though unstable, reign. With his uncle's assistance, he restored the temple (2 Kgs 12:1-16). However, there seems to be a clue as to the measure of godly influence Jehoiada exerted upon his nephew while alive (v. 2), for after his death Joash began to tolerate pagan practices once more (2 Chr 24:17-18), even killing Jehoiada's son for daring to challenge his complicity in doing so (vv. 20-22). Joash died an untimely death at the hands of his own officers, who sought to have him replaced as king (2 Kgs 12:20-22).

Of the next four kings of the southern kingdom, only Jotham emerges with any credit. The reign of Amaziah (796-767) continued the trend of instability (2 Kgs 14:1-22), as evidenced by the overlapping of a major proportion of his reign with that of Azariah/Uzziah (792-740). Overall, Uzziah's reign was a mixed one: while he sought the Lord, chiefly through the prophet Zechariah, he knew success (2 Chr 26:1-5); when his accomplishments began to foster arrogance, he knew only divine disapproval (vv. 16-21).

But Uzziah's military achievements did provide the peaceful background for Jotham to be an effective monarch (750-732). It was Jotham who rebuilt the upper gate of the temple, strengthened and enlarged the territory of Judah, and defeated the Ammonites in battle (2 Chr 27:3-6). Despite his successes, however, Jotham was deposed in favor of his son, Ahaz (732-715), by a pro-Assyrian faction amongst his men. Leading Judah from one crisis to another seems to have been Ahaz's only skill. His repetitious appeals to Assyria for help betrayed his spiritual infidelity, just as the sacrificial offering of his own son demonstrated his unashamed apostasy (2 Kgs 16:2-18).

Hezekiah (715-686) was generally a good king, as testified to by the major religious reforms that he undertook during only his first year as sole regent (2 Chr 29:3—31:21). Once again, the chronicler establishes the link between commitment toward God and favor received from God (31:21). Manasseh (697-642), however, undid most of the work of his father (2 Kgs 21:3), despite eleven years of co-regency with him. His enthrallment with Assyrian cults degraded the pure religion of Hezekiah and his lengthy reign was marked only by grotesque idolatry and reactionary governance. Perhaps no other divine rebuke was so well-deserved as that attributed to Manasseh (vv. 10-15).

Kingdom

Amon's two-year reign (642–640) was thankfully terminated before he had much opportunity to replicate his father's atrocities further (2 Kgs 21:20–22). Despite his young age when he ascended to the throne, Josiah (640–649) quickly showed his credentials as a man of reform. Right at the outset we are assured that he was not to be given to compromise (v. 22:2). While following the king's instructions, the Book of the Law was discovered and presented to the still young Josiah. Not only was he grieved by how far from God's requirements the nation had actually stumbled, but he took decisive action to align both his kingship and the kingdom with those requirements (2 Kgs 23). His major error of judgment, however, saw him embark on an ill-conceived military escapade against Egypt (v. 29). When Josiah died, so did the last flicker of light in Jerusalem. His son, Jehoahaz/Shallum, lasted only three months (609) before being deported to Egypt (v. 33), where he became the first king of Judah to die in exile (Jer 22:10–12).

Thereafter, Jehoiakim (609–598), Jehoiachin (598–597), and Zedekiah (597–586) were little more than vassal kings in the hands of Egypt and, later, Babylon. Acting against prophetic instruction, Zedekiah sought to rebel against Nebuchadnezzar, for which he was incarcerated, disgraced, and extradited (see 2 Kgs 25). Thus, the southern kingdom of Judah was brought to an end. When the kingdom divided, the northern tribes had distanced themselves from the Davidic line, insisting that Judah look after its own house (2 Chr 10:16). This it had patently failed to do.

Summary

Although it is often dangerous to equate spiritual faith with natural prosperity, an obvious pattern does emerge when we consider the kings of Israel. Those whose natural kingship adhered to divine kingdom principles were favored, while those who abandoned God were rejected by him. This is true both of the united kingdom and of the two separate kingdoms after the division. That the north never knew anything but divine displeasure is solely due to the fact that none of their kings put their trust exclusively in the God of the kingdom. Following its invasion by Assyria, the peoples of the northern kingdom were not merely exiled or deported, but absorbed into extinction. Even though a remnant from the south returned to Judah after the Babylonian exile, the concepts of kingdom and Israel were mutually exclusive. All the covenant people of God were left with was a prophetic anticipation of a future, though distant, kingdom. Four hundred years of silence enabled the messianic expectation to gather momentum.

## THE KING OF THE KINGDOM IS REVEALED

The time that elapsed between Nehemiah's recorded ministry and the arrival of the Messiah was approximately 427 years. Often referred to as "the silent years," this relates exclusively to the fact that there was no prophetic voice heard amongst God's people until the coming of John the Baptist. The landscape at the beginning of the New Testament, however, was a very different one from that at the end of the Old Testament. This is true politically, culturally, socially, economically, and linguistically. It is no less so spiritually. In the absence of any fresh revelations, the remnant of what had been the southern kingdom of Judah in exile had allowed their circumstances to condition their understanding of the old prophecies. Against a backdrop of centuries of tyrannical oppression, their hope of a messiah became that of a warrior-king who would rise under God's anointing to purge those who subjugated them by rallying the troops. How mistaken they were!

### Matthew—The King Speaks to His Subjects

Matthew's gospel account focuses especially on the relevance of Jesus to the Greek-speaking Jews of his day. By presenting this Galilean carpenter to be the fulfillment of Hebrew prophecy, he systematically sets out to offer Jesus as the promised Christ. While remaining sensitive to their socio-religious temperament, Matthew is not slow to denounce Pharisaical hypocrisy and the lack of responsiveness among the Jews as a people to the fact that this Jesus is, in fact, their long-awaited Messiah.

Although all the gospel accounts speak of and refer to Christ's kingship, none does so more than Matthew, either directly or by suggestion. Moreover, Matthew is especially careful to do so in connection with Jesus' birth as early as the opening verse. By tracing Jesus' genealogy back to David through his dynastic line, the implications would have been all too obvious to Matthew's first-century readership. The claim to office through a family line was peculiarly Hebraistic. Unless evidence could be provided of a claimant's priestly descent, for example, they could not be permitted to exercise the rights and responsibilities associated with such a claim (see Ezra 2:62). At the very beginning of his account, therefore, Matthew was setting the record straight for what was to follow. In purely human terms, Jesus' claim to royal succession was a legitimate one.

Although his ministry is confined to the pages of the New Testament, strictly speaking John the Baptist is the last of the Old Testament prophets. Fitting, then, that it is he who is designated to announce the pending arrival of the kingdom of God (Matt 3:2), a theme to be taken up by Jesus himself immediately following his temptation in the desert by the enemy (4:17). If it can be said of John that he was "more than a prophet" because of him fulfilling what had been written about him (11:7–14), then surely Jesus is more than simply a king. John may have foretold the coming of the kingdom, but Jesus fulfilled the expectation of its arrival; whereas John heralded the kingdom's imminence, Jesus invited us to welcome its appearance.

The recurring theme in Matthew's gospel, then, is of Jesus as the King of the Jews (Matt 27:37). His aesthetic talent for arranging the text around five major discourses displays an obvious pattern, which some have compared to the Pentateuch, suggesting the Gospel to be a new Torah and Jesus a replacement for Moses. Although these comparisons may be of interest to literal typologists, the fact should not be overlooked that Jesus himself said that he had "not come to abolish [the Law and the Prophets], but to fulfill them" (5:17).

Jesus' discipleship manifesto in The Sermon on the Mount (Matt 5–7) forms the content of his first discourse and covers seven principles of the kingdom. These include personal character, influence, fulfilling the Law, private devotions, motivation, relationships, and functional productivity. In his second address (Matt 10), the Master sends out the Twelve with specific instructions about how to implement the authority he has invested in them. There then follows a series of graphic teaching aids by way of parables, designed in order that those who had been prepared to receive might understand more clearly the corporate nature of kingdom objectives (Matt 13). The fourth discourse spotlights the role and attitude of the church as a dynamic agent of the kingdom (Matt

18), while in the final oration Jesus speaks at length on the inevitability of the end-time judgment (Matt 23–25).

So, what are we to do with this Jesus? There is a significant clue in Matthew's genealogical introduction. The order seems important when it is recorded that "Jesus Christ [is] the son of David, the son of Abraham" (Matt 1:1). The Messiah is the rightful object of our allegiance before he is the necessary object of our faith. Indeed, it might even be said that he can only be the latter because he is first of all the former. However, in our approach to him, the order must be reversed. We must acknowledge him as Savior before we can see him as King. In this, too, the one is preparatory to the other. He can only truly be our King if he has first been our Savior. We must assuredly be cleansed of impurity before we can don garments of righteousness.

The message of the kingdom cannot be divorced from that of its King: "Repent!" And yet it is a word that is almost entirely absent in many churches that claim to be built on that message. What kind of church are you? "Oh! We're a God-fearing, Christ-worshiping, Spirit-filled, Bible-believing, kingdom-proclaiming kind of church." Really? And when was the last time this word was declared in your midst? "Well, you don't want to cause offense, do you? I mean, we have to maintain a witness, and we believe the key to that is a healthy relationship with the unsaved amongst us. It wouldn't be right to put them off." A message that fails to bring a person to the point of realizing their absolute need for a Savior because of a condition that is otherwise beyond remedy is not the message of the kingdom, because it was never the message of its King.

## Mark—The Servant King

By way of contrast, the internal evidence of Mark's gospel seems to indicate that it was written with a predominantly Roman readership in mind. The fact that typically Jewish protocols are clarified (Mark 7:3–4), as are both Hebrew and Greek phrases (5:41; 15:16), would appear to validate this view. Indeed, the overriding theme of his account suggests a man intent on declaring the prophetic nature of Christ's work to a people with little or no understanding of Old Testament theology.

It is perhaps for this reason that he is able to so resolutely introduce his work as: "The beginning of the gospel about Jesus Christ, the Son of

God" (Mark 1:1). For Mark's part, the thorough humanness of the Jesus he presents is matched by the absolute divinity of this same Jesus. He is assuredly the Son of Man (2:10, 28), but this does not detract from the fact that he is just as convincingly the Son of God (3:11). Of course, Mark expresses Christ's humanity in ways other than only by virtue of the service he renders, just as the demonstration of his divinity is not restricted only to his kingship. However, it does seem that these are the pinnacle revelations in respect of each milieu. In order to reign, this conquering King had to rule his circumstances in fulfillment of all that the prophets had said of him.

Mark's emphasis, then, is upon the actions of Jesus, particularly in support of his role as the Suffering Servant (Mark 8:31). The key to understanding God's purpose in redemption, argues Mark, is to see Christ not as a political activist, but as the crucified Savior. As Scripture observes, both here and elsewhere, the kingdom of God is an upside-down domain operating on inverted principles where the last shall be first (10:31), weakness is great strength (2 Cor 12:10), chastisement is the true sign of sonship (Heb 12:5–8), and the route to spiritual prosperity is by way of a servant disposition (Matt 20:26). Similarly, the victory of the Anointed One was through suffering and death. The rejection of his closest friends, his family, and even abandonment by his heavenly Father, which appeared to be the final rite of defeat, actually afforded the means of his triumph. Those who seek to be like him would do well to observe the path he chose.

It is almost incomprehensible for us to consider suffering and kingship as anything but mutually exclusive terms. In this, we are not alone. On three separate occasions, Mark records Jesus as specifically predicting his passion to his closest followers in terms that can be hardly described as shrouded in mystery. The immediate response of each, however, suggests that the disciples were utterly baffled by what he was saying to them. Let us take a closer look:

| | | |
|---|---|---|
| 8:27–33 | after Peter's confession of Jesus as the Christ; | Peter betrayed his own fleshly motivation by rebuking Jesus. |
| 9:30–32 | after the Transfiguration, at which God declared Jesus to be his Son; | the disciples were afraid to betray their ignorance by asking Jesus to explain his words. |

| | | |
|---|---|---|
| 10:32–34 | after the rich young man had left Jesus disappointed, having described him as a good teacher; | James and John seemed to see the link between Christ's death and honor, but allowed selfish ambition to dictate their, albeit limited, understanding. |

It is perhaps less than surprising, therefore, that Jesus began to unpack the nature and extent of the sufferings he would endure in the immediate context of Peter's confession of him as the Christ (Mark 8:29–31). Note that Jesus, far from correcting the assignation, seemed rather to take advantage of the opportunity to spell out precisely what his messiahship entailed. Notice also that the imperative "must" (Greek *dei*—"it is necessary") is annexed not only to the suffering of many things, but also to what is parenthetically included in all that follows. In other words, it was necessary for Jesus to suffer many things, it was crucial that he be rejected by the religious leaders of his day, it was essential that he be killed, and it was vital for him to rise again.

Let us be clear about this: the necessity of Christ's suffering(s) was not simply to fulfill the predictive element of prophecy, but because the character of that/those suffering(s) was entirely vicarious. This is the context of Isaiah's imagery (Isa 53), the redemptive nature of which is alluded to repeatedly by Mark (see 9:12, 31; 10:33, 45; 14:21, 24).

## Luke—The King of Compassion

Luke, being the original *Religio Medici*, is meticulously descriptive in his portrayal of Jesus as the friend of the outcast, the healer of the sick, and the dispenser of blessing to the otherwise impoverished. His is the gospel account of grace, divine favor being shown to be extended to those who have and can do nothing to deserve it. The sharp contrast between plenty and poverty, want and wealth, runs consistently through Luke's narrative. Whether richness is to be measured in terms of financial prosperity, natural ability, power, status, or cultural heritage, it is the attitude of self-sufficiency that is the real issue. It is this that hampers the acknowledgment of a need outside of ourselves. The very word "savior" implies the necessity for salvation. Pride must give way to humility; self-righteousness must step aside, exposing sin to the cleansing work of God's Messiah in the heart of the truly repentant (Luke 5:31–32).

Not only is Luke the sole gospel writer to refer to Jesus' identification of himself with Isaiah's prophecy of one upon whom will rest the Spirit of the Lord (see Luke 4:18–19; Isa 61:1–2), but he develops the theme of the Lord's favor in such a way that it becomes the focal point of the whole of his account. The gospel is essentially—and yet remains—for the poor. Precisely what this means has been and continues to be the subject of intense debate. Natural poverty can be relative to the age and culture in which it finds itself. Impoverished emotions can also be conditioned by personal circumstances. Perhaps there is much to be considered worthy of merit in William Hendriksen's association of the original in its broader context,[19] where five chapters later Isaiah speaks thus: "This is the one I esteem: he who is humble and contrite in spirit, and trembles at my word" (Isa 66:2b).

Being of Greek background himself, Luke's writing follows a more orderly pattern than that of his colleagues. His method of presentation is characteristically Greco-Roman, and he takes great pains to argue the original intention in God's heart to redeem fallen humanity. This outlook is nowhere more evident than in the key verse: "The Son of Man came to seek and to save what was lost" (Luke 19:10). And so, Jesus is portrayed as descended from Adam and, therefore, able to identify with the whole of mankind, not only the lost sheep of Israel. If Matthew relates to us the oratory skills of Jesus, and Mark his active obedience to the will of the Father, then it is Luke who discloses Christ's understanding of the human condition.

In a style reminiscent of later Pauline writings, Luke demonstrates both the doctrine and practice of correct behavior. By establishing Jesus as the perfect role model, he shows us not only the good that Jesus did, but also the duty of those who would own him to replicate his conduct as far as it is within their capacity to do so. In the same way, for example, that Jesus went around doing good (Acts 10:38), even to those who often failed to understand the correlation between his message and his mission (Luke 18:34), those who came to him to satisfy anything but their deepest spiritual needs (9:57–62), and those who were determined to oppose him at every opportunity (11:14–54), so we too are encouraged

---

19. Hendriksen, *Luke*, 46–47.

to do likewise in the face of similar self-gratification, self-indulgence, and self-exaltation (18:22).

Amongst other things, Hendriksen cites Luke's gospel account as an ethical guide on how to live aright. He particularly notes what he defines as "the three-fold duty of humility . . . homage, and helpfulness," before elucidating further: "The Christ depicted by Luke entered a world filled with class distinctions and barriers: racial, national, social, sexual. He insisted that by means of the application of self-sacrificing love for everyone these barriers be broken down . . . We must love even our enemies, must proclaim the gospel to all nations, and in our enthusiasm for the mission cause must not forget to strengthen the brothers. All this must be done 'to God's glory.'"[20]

True compassion is not merely about sympathy, though it will involve that. It is not concerned primarily with feelings at all, though they will become engaged in the expression of compassion. The principal motivating factor of compassion in the biblical usage of the word is an innate desire to see justice prevail where currently there is only wrongful discrimination. Thus, the Lukan account presents Jesus' urgency in making it clear that his ministry was not exclusively directed towards those who could lay claim to the historic divine covenants (Luke 7:1–9), highlighting his particular concern for the plight of women (vv. 36–50), to look for the good in those traditionally despised by his own people (10:30–37), to demonstrate a pastoral heart toward all those entrusted to his care (15:1–7), and to reach out to those habitually disenfranchised by society (17:11–19).

The kingdom of God belongs to such as these because the King of the kingdom is anathema to the self-righteous, the self-sufficient, the autonomous spirit, and the egotistical disposition.

## John—The King of Heaven

Finally, John reveals Jesus to be the eternal Son of God (John 1:1–18), endowed with the Father's authority to bring forgiveness to a needy world. John's gospel account is vastly different from the synoptics, both of necessity and of circumstance. His presentation is singularly Christological, his purpose in writing glaringly self-evident: "that you may

---

20. Ibid., 253.

Kingdom

know that Jesus is the Christ. The Son of God, and that by believing you may have life in his name" (20:31). Here we see a familiar strategy, as taken up by Paul in his epistles, where the design is two-fold: doctrine and application. For John, the reasoning behind his account is quite simple: he wants his readers to understand the doctrinal significance of who this Jesus is, but in a way that produces life as God intends it to be lived, which can only be achieved in his name.

Although he never contradicts the other writers, John does provide some supplementary evidence concerning the person and work of Jesus. Much of John's narrative is exclusive to him and, likewise, there is a lot that appears elsewhere that is notable by its absence here. This is quite possibly because he wrote his account many years after the synoptics had been widely circulated and would, therefore, assume that much of their content would be universally well-known. The whole of this work—his letters, too, for that matter—attest to the deity of Christ, concentrating primarily on Jesus' private dealings with his disciples and being written predominantly for the benefit of fellow believers.

Only two books in the Bible open with the words "In the beginning": Genesis and John. Even allowing for the subtleties of linguistic nuance and translation, one is left to wonder whether this was intentional on John's part. Given the theme of his account thereafter, such wonder surely fades as acknowledgment takes its place. In the beginning was only God (Gen 3:1) and yet, in that same beginning, was the Word, who was with God (John 1:1a). There seems little need to clarify any further, but just in case the penny has failed to drop, "the Word was God" (v. 1:1b).

The seven miracles of Jesus, as represented by "the disciple whom [he] loved" (John 13:23), point to the identity of Jesus' subject; they are markers as to who he is. Whereas these signs demonstrate Christ's personality, the seven "I am . . ." sayings demand a practical response. If he is "the light of the world" (8:12), then we must walk in accordance with that light; if he can legitimately claim to be "the Good Shepherd" (10:11), then it behooves us to come in to his sheepfold; if he really is "the way and the truth and the life" (14:6), then can we do any other than simply follow him, believe in him, and live in him?

It is not just the fact of Christ's unique sonship that is important, but the implications of that filial relationship in terms of the kingdom he came to usher in. Because Jesus is God's Son, he is matchlessly equipped to make the Father known both personally and in respect of his expectations of us. Thus, Christ brings illumination as both the light *of* the world (John 8:12; 9:5) and light *for* the world (12:35, 46). Why was it necessary for him to be revealed in this way? Well, we can infer it from the clues that John presents in his gospel account, most notably in relation to Christ's work of atonement, but he is more explicit in his first epistle: "The reason the Son of God appeared was to destroy the devil's work" (1 John 3:8). His whole life bore testimony to this fact, though it was most overtly demonstrated at the cross.

It is from John's account of the crucifixion that we derive the acronym INRI, which are the initial letters of the Latin phrase *Iesus Nazarenus Rex Iudaeorum*, meaning "Jesus of Nazareth, the King of the Jews." The Eastern churches often use INBI based on the Greek version of the inscription, while some change this to INBK to reflect his global kingship (*basileus tou kosmos*—king of the world). Perhaps Pilate's reluctance to have the sign removed was in part due to Jesus' refusal to renounce the title when given the opportunity to do so (John 18:33–37; 19:19–22).

As we have seen, John's literary style is vastly different from that of the other gospel writers. This is to be expected. They not only select episodes from the life of Jesus to correspond with the emphasis they each seek to bring, but they present them in such a way that fully engages with their own traits and characteristics. John's approach is fairly easy to follow. There is not the specific Hebraism of Matthew, the frenetic pace of Mark, or the precision of detail to be found in Luke. And yet, the profundity of John's portrayal is without equal. It is simple yet sublime.

## Summary

The four-fold gospel in the New Testament is just that: one multifaceted gospel. Each writer depicts Jesus in a certain way that does not contradict, but rather complements, the others. The impeccable orator speaks to his subjects in a tone that is both authoritative and loving; the Suffering Servant offers himself as a sacrifice for the needs of fallen humanity; the Shepherd heart reaches out with compassion to the poor, the sick, and the destitute; and this Son of Man is also the Son of God. What unites them all, of course—apart from the subject matter being one and the same person—is that they are all aspects of the King of the

Kingdom

kingdom gloriously revealed. Although neither God's kingdom nor the kingdom's King have their origins in this world, they both find ultimate expression here as the rule of God on earth and the exercise of Christ's kingship in and through his people.

## THE KINGDOM OF GOD AFTER PENTECOST

Strictly speaking, the title of this section should be *The Kingdom of God from Pentecost to Around the Middle of the Sixteenth Century*, as we shall be looking at more recent developments and the effects of the kingdom of God on society and *vice versa* in later chapters. Suffice for now to embark on a fleeting history lesson covering a little more than one and a half millennia. Along the way, we shall discover that, for the most part, the kingdom of God as expressed through the New Testament church has followed a similar pattern to that of its Old Testament counterpart, with a succession of ups punctuating lengthy periods of downs. The "ups" may have been arguably higher, but the "downs" were also significantly lower. Viewed from our perspective, it would be easy to imagine this to have been a spectacular roller-coaster journey; it was anything but, as we shall see.

### Kingdom Explosion

If the new covenant era of the kingdom of God was heralded by John the Baptist and personified by Jesus Christ, then it was unleashed in power on the day of Pentecost by the Holy Spirit. This is not to say, of course, that the Third Person of the triune Godhead replaced the Second, either in terms of emphasis or significance. What it does mean is that, while Christ remains central to the demonstration of the kingdom of God in the book of Acts, it is the Holy Spirit who is busy to promote that centrality.

From the very outset of Luke's account in Acts, he links the beginning of the Christian era with Messiah's personal pledge. On one occasion, prior to him ascending into heaven, Jesus reminded his disciples of that promise, commanding them to wait in Jerusalem until they were "baptized in the Holy Spirit" (see John 14:16–26; 16:8; Acts 1:4–5). Thus, there was an acute sense of expectation in the upper room as they tarried, but it is unlikely that they will have been adequately prepared for the sheer dynamic potency of what was about to happen to them and, subsequently, through them. There had been Spirit-filled people before, isolated individuals scattered throughout Israel's checkered history; never had the world encountered a Spirit-filled body. In the words of Arthur Wallis: "The dynamic of the early church was not in Spirit-filled individualism, but in Spirit-filled corporeity."[21]

Jesus himself had given clues, not only in his teaching, nor even in the things he did, but also in the teaching that emanated from the things he did. Bewildered by his spiritual insight and the stories he had already heard, imagine Nathaniel's utter amazement to be told that he would witness even greater things than these (John 1:47–50). How on earth could he possibly be expected to see events of greater magnitude than that of the sick being healed, lepers made whole again, the blind seeing—both physically and spiritually—and the dead being restored to life? In qualitative terms, it was impossible. But quantitatively it would be greater because Jesus' healing power would no longer be restricted to just himself. In an environment such as this, is it really any wonder that the church was being added to at a rate that has never since been equaled (Acts 2:41, 47)?

The conditions at the time were ideally suited for the kingdom to advance as rapidly and as widespread as it did. Politically, commercially, and linguistically the situation could hardly have been better. Relative stability, developing trade routes, and a common language were just some of the features that facilitated the gospel traveling much further afield in such a short time-frame. What we refer to as the acts of the apostles were only possible because these sent ones were filled with and were open to the prompting of God the Holy Spirit. In many ways, they were also only achievable because God the Father had prepared for those events to unfold as they did.

Arguably the single most influential feature of the kingdom's advance—from a human perspective, of course—was the singleness of purpose to be found amongst those first-century Christians. Can there be any more definitive evidence than this: "All the believers were together and had everything in common. Selling their possessions and goods, they gave to everyone as he had need. Every day, they continued to meet together in the temple courts. They broke bread in their homes

---

21. Wallis, *Radical Christian*, 70.

and ate together with glad and sincere hearts, praising God and enjoying the favor of all the people" (Acts 2:44–47a).

Only a short time before his arrest, Jesus had prayed most urgently that his disciples at that time and those who would come to believe in him through their message would express the same kind of unity that he and the Father enjoyed together (John 17:20–21). Here we have evidence of that prayer being fulfilled. The immediate impact was numerical increase. Many churches in our day spend countless hours of prayer, sitting on committees, debating the legitimacy or otherwise of yet another annual evangelistic push, agonizing over the potential remunerative devaluation of the church coffers if we decline at the present rate, and yet God seems to have given the answer in a very simple cause and effect strategy. The only question we really need to ask is: "Are we prepared to meet the conditions that such growth will inevitably follow: express God's kingdom rule as they did in our commitment to care, fellowship, the sacrament of the covenant meal, and worship?"

The real test of the genuineness of the kingdom's advance came in the form of hostile oppression, the chief protagonists of which were the religious leaders of the day (Acts 4:1–19; 5:17–40; 23:12–21). Whether coincidentally or by design, the church has always seemed to thrive more when it has been under the most threat. Or to put it another way, the kingdom of light shines brightest when it is seen in starkest contrast to the kingdom of darkness. This should hardly come as any surprise. What is perhaps more astonishing—and not without a lavish dose of irony—is the fact that the kingdom's number one detractor became one of its greatest ambassadors for growth and expansion in those early years. What Peter was to the Jewish Christians, Paul became to the Gentiles: God's delegated apostle.

Thus, Luke's supplementary volume might just as readily be known as *The Kingdom Rule of God in Action through the Acts of the Apostles and Other Early Christian Believers*. It recounts a resilient faith and the initial surge of Christianity, the hallmarks of which were simplicity, corporeity, evangelism, and love.

## Muddied Waters

The first few centuries of the Christian church were a strange mixture, indeed. Although there had been a certain order to proceedings, this quickly gave way to organized institutionalism in the years that followed. Functional descriptions associated with leadership soon became titles of honor, sense of community was displaced by authoritative decree, the earlier attitude of being outward looking was replaced by a more introspective approach, and, though love was still expressed, its focus was increasingly idolatrous rather than genuinely godly. The effects of the kingdom of God on society were diminished largely because its King was dethroned in favor of rituals invented and orchestrated by men.

Arguably two of the most influential contributory factors to the relative decline of true spirituality during the immediate aftermath of the apostolic age were pagan practices and philosophical ideals. In the strict sense, Scripture allows for only two designated sacraments: the covenant meal and water baptism. Though they may be correctly described as rites, the evidence of the New Testament is such that there was no ritualistic expression of either in the early days that became so prevalent thereafter. Whereas the setting of the Lord's Supper was informal, yet reverent, it became increasingly more ceremonial. The elements lost their symbolism and were imbued with alleged mystical powers. David Matthew takes up the commentary: "The literalist idea of the 'real presence' of Christ in the bread and wine could actually confer spiritual life: the more you ate, the more of Jesus you took in! By the third century the Lord's Supper was actually being viewed as a re-sacrificing of Christ by a priest upon an altar, the whole thing surrounded by a grim religious mystique. The elements could therefore be 'consecrated' only by a priest, being too sacred for the 'laity' to handle."[22]

The ordinance of baptism, too, became formalized to the point where it was barely recognizable as that practised in the pages of the New Testament. Whereas the biblical evidence suggests its association with repentance as an immediate outward sign of an inner spiritual condition, periods of probation and its ritual application on babies—who could hardly be expected to have made a conscious decision to turn from their sin, let alone articulate such a choice—seemed a far cry from that carried out by the church in its infancy. The veneration of martyrs, mediation through the sanctified dead, the church-promoted scheme of selling relics, ascetic lifestyles, and the supreme earthly authority of

---

22. Matthew, *Church Adrift*, 58–59.

an "over-overseer" were but a short step away, and yet so far removed, from biblical warrant.

Doctrinal matters also provided an unexpected opportunity for church leaders to become disengaged from their God-appointed task of caring for the flock entrusted to them and proclaiming the message of the kingdom to those who currently stood outside its parameters. Of course, those so engaged could have pointed to the apostle Paul as an example of one who also spent a great deal of time addressing issues that were controversial and likely to have had an adverse effect on the gospel message if left unchecked. There were two significant differences, however: Paul managed to bring correction without it having a potentially negative influence on his capacity to fulfill his primary function; he also often wrote his more theologically detailed epistles from a prison cell, where he had little else to occupy his time.

That notwithstanding, however, there were an alarming number of heresies to make their mark at this time. It seemed that hardly had one church council been convened to consider the merits or otherwise of the latest challenge to acknowledged orthodoxy than yet another was required for the same purpose. Gnosticism was the first to rear its ugly head. It had been around for quite some time, the apostle John taking pains to counter its effect, which was based on the pseudo-religious belief in a "knowing" elite. The true humanity of Jesus was denied, as it contravened the Gnostic theory regarding the essential evil of matter.

Arianism, Sabellianism, Nestorianism, Monophysitism, and many others besides were all to rise and fall before successive church councils. There is no question that the countering of heresy has played a major beneficial role in the pursuit of legitimate biblical doctrine. Only a fool would suggest otherwise. But at the same time, one can hardly help but wonder if the shift of focus—necessary though it was—did otherwise irreparable damage to where the emphasis of God's kingdom agents should have been, as more typically exemplified by their first-century forbears.

One enormously beneficial feature to emerge from this early period in the church's history was the acknowledgment as canon of what we now have as the New Testament. This is especially noteworthy in the context of our study, because the books that form it so shape our understanding of the kingdom of God since Christ. Again, the circumstances were brought about by controversy. Amongst the heresies of the day, some were appealing as evidence for their positions to documents that others did not recognize as authentic. Criteria were finally agreed, which basically consisted of:

- asserting the authenticity of the claim to authorship;
- the approval of the original addressee(s); and
- the internal evidence of the work under consideration.

Although I have painted a generally depressing picture of the period, there were also some notable luminaries, through whom there was retained at least some measure of the expression of the kingdom of God on earth. In the context of the promise both experienced and proffered by that first generation of Christian believers, however, the scene was indeed a gloomy one. Things could hardly become worse, could they?

## Reform or Restore?

Well, they could and they did. For some considerable time, the kingdom of God and the might of the Roman Empire seemed to be on a collision course, such was the diametric opposition between them. Imagine the sense of relief, then, when it was announced that Emperor Constantine had come to acknowledge the Christian faith as his own, claiming his victory over Maxentius at the battle of the Milvian Bridge in AD 312 to have been God-ordained. One of Constantine's first acts of benevolence toward other adherents of his new-found faith was to promise restitution for the damage done by his predecessors. Paul McKechnie paints the picture thus: "Full legality and the return of the churches and burial places were probably the most any Christian had hoped for. Compensation for buyers who had bought confiscated church property from the treasury helped to prevent future disputes. But Constantine also made large gifts: in Rome, he gave the Lateran Palace to the church, and it was the residence of the bishops of Rome for the next thousand years."[23]

Church historians are generally divided as to whether the church-state relationship that developed into the Middle Ages was actually beneficial to either party. It seems that Constantine's allegiance to Christianity was genuine enough, even if some of his expressions of it were often misguided. His previous allegiance to sun worship continued to

---

23. McKechnie, *The First Christian Centuries*, 236.

dictate his perceptions, most notably so in his decision to make the first day of the week a holiday and identify it as "the venerable day of the Sun" (i.e., Sunday). This was almost ten years after his conversion experience. While not the last pagan influence to be adopted as ecclesiastical practice, nor even necessarily the most harmful, it did pave the way for all that would follow. Saturnalia became Christmas, candles and incense made the transition from pagan to Christian worship, and many of the paraphernalia associated with Mariolatry can be traced back to the worship of Artemis of the Ephesians.

Thereafter followed centuries of instability where various bishops and emperors struggled for supremacy. Ambrose's dictate that the emperor was within the church but not above it failed to avert imperial interference in ecclesiastical matters. By the end of the fifth century, the idea had developed that the emperor was subject to the bishop of Rome and should govern the empire almost exclusively on that basis. Again, this was not the rule of God in action as an expression of his kingdom agency on earth as it had been witnessed only half a millennium earlier; it was one human agency seeking to lord it over another for the sake of prestige and power.

A thousand years later and the empire had long since disappeared. The bishop of Rome, however, had become arguably the most powerful man on earth. Following Gregory's lead, the self-acclaimed assignation "Vicar of Christ on Earth" for whoever was appointed Rome's patriarch was largely based on the assumed succession of Peter in lieu of a manipulated understanding of Christ's promise (Matt 16:13–19). The rock had, indeed, become a stumbling stone (see Isa 8:13–15; Rom 9:30–33).

The Christian church in the Middle Ages was about as far removed from its inception as it was possible to be. Erroneous practice based on doctrinal error might be overlooked as innocent human frailty, if it wasn't for the infrequent abuse of power, political gamesmanship, and evangelism by conquest. Far from deriving inspiration from a garden near a hill on which there was an empty cross, the expression of the kingdom as it was demonstrated through the church seemed to have more in common with a tree in another garden, wherein a serpent was causing its mischief. All in all, the living Word was not preached because the written Word was not adhered to. David Matthew has this to say: "It is significant that the Bible played a very small part in the life of the church at this time. Unknown and unavailable to the vast majority of supposedly Christian people, it remained the object of study of a few monks and scholars alone . . . Life was borne along purely by the momentum of the ecclesiastical machine, which no longer needed the life of God and the power of the Spirit to fuel its progress."[24]

But the Spirit of God will not hover indefinitely where chaos exists. What is known historically as the Protestant Reformation of the sixteenth century was in many ways inevitable and hardly unannounced. Pockets of radical resistance to the traditional *status quo* had been in evidence for some time. John Wycliffe (1329-1384) in Oxford, England, John Hus (1372-1415) in central Europe, and Thomas à Kempis (1380-1471) in Holland had all voiced concerns over issues such as the meaning and significance of the Lord's Supper, the authority of Scripture, and the calling to a discipleship that seeks to replicate Christ's character. But it was the invention of the printing press that inadvertently became the instrument whereby God's kingdom advance would take center stage once more.

When Desiderius Erasmus (1466-1536), another Dutchman, produced the first printed copy of his Greek New Testament, it heralded the beginning of a movement that was to sweep through not only the established church, but also the then known world. Indeed, not without warrant has it been said that "Erasmus laid the egg of the Reformation and Martin Luther hatched it." Luther's angst had been aroused by the conviction that justification requires faith alone. Thus, he saw the sale of indulgences as necessary only for a profit to be earned from marketeering: a "holy trade," he called it. Excommunicated by the Pope and outlawed by the Emperor, the stand this otherwise obscure monk decided to take signaled that Christian Europe would be forever changed thereafter.

Other spokesmen quickly followed suit, each identifying another chink in the right of Rome's bishop to command doctrine and practice that could not look to Scripture for support. The debt of gratitude today's Christian church worldwide owes to men like Ulrich Zwingli (1484-1531), Thomas Cranmer (1489-1556), Martin Bucer (1491-1551), John Calvin (1509-1564), John Knox (1514-1572), Theodore Beza (1519-1605), and others too numerous to mention, is as unpayable as it is unquantifiable. They were not without their faults, many of which were products of the age in which they found themselves. But

---

24. Matthew, *Church Adrift*, 81-82.

had it not been for their fervent endeavor, then it is conceivable that the current church universal would have been truly Catholic.

It must be noted that it was never Luther's original intention to be the harbinger of a Reformation that was estranged from Rome's auspices but rather to reform from the inside. Others were similarly inclined, but that choice was taken away from them by the orders of expulsion that quickly followed. For the most part, the changes brought about were a mere tinkering with the model, thereby implying that only minor adjustments were necessary. The latter part of the twentieth century saw a renewal movement with similar aims, though in admittedly different circumstances. What was required, however, was a completely radical approach in order to be restored to the initial concept of God's kingdom rule being expressed through his people, as demonstrated in the church's first few years.

## Summary

Although this section has been a necessarily potted history of the expression of the kingdom of God on earth since Pentecost and ends rather abruptly with the Protestant Reformation, we have seen that men appointed for the task more often than not resorted to their natural proclivities rather than seek true spiritual guidance for their doctrine and practice. This trend has continued even to the present day. Church leaders are all too often driven by ungodly motivation and believe that by cloaking it in religious garb they will somehow attract divine favor. The antidote is not to look to a better past, nor even the best it has ever been, but to what God requires as demonstrated in and through his revealed Word. In the next couple of chapters, we shall be looking at the character of the individual and the characteristics of the corporate as unveiled to us by Jesus in the Beatitudes and in his kingdom parables respectively.

# 2

# Kingdom Character Attracts the King's Blessing

"Blessed are the poor in spirit, for theirs is the kingdom of heaven.
Blessed are those who mourn, for they will be comforted.
Blessed are the meek, for they will inherit the earth.
Blessed are those who hunger and thirst for righteousness, for they will be filled.
Blessed are the merciful, for they will be shown mercy.
Blessed are the pure in heart, for they will see God.
Blessed are the peacemakers, for they will be called sons of God.
Blessed are those who are persecuted because of righteousness, for theirs is the kingdom of heaven."[1]

DESCRIBED BY SPURGEON AS "the kingdom manifesto," the Sermon on the Mount (Matt 5–7) is the first and longest of Jesus' didactic discourses as compiled by Matthew. In contrast to Moses' Decalogue, the emphasis is not upon external ritual but a heart attitude toward God and others. As such, the way in which we are exhorted to relate on a peer level is presented as but an expression of our relationship to Father God.

Before we look in detail at each of the kingdom characteristics, it may prove helpful to note some general observations. First of all, the word "beatitude" derives from the Latin *beatus*, meaning "blessed." There are those who translate this to mean nothing more than simply "happy." Although it is true that there is to be anticipated an expression

---

1. Matt 5:3–10.

of joy in the lives of those who qualify for such promises, this kind of bliss is much more than a manifestation determined by external conditions; it is the realization of divine favor, irrespective of what can be seen, producing a real inner joy in the heart. It is not mind over matter, it is faith above feelings—a countenance not governed by circumstance.

Secondly, each beatitude contains both a qualification and a promise. Moreover, in every case, the pledge is suitable to the prerequisite. For this reason, many commentators prefer to speak of "macarisms," from the Greek *makarios*. In this regard, Vine observes: "the Lord indicates not only the characters that are blessed, but the nature of that which is the highest good."[2] In other words, the reward for each condition is one that progresses naturally from the character trait described. For example, those who are merciful are to receive mercy; the promise for maintaining a pure heart is to gaze upon the One who embodies purity; mourners are to be comforted as those in Zion, who receive "a crown of beauty instead of ashes" (Isa 61:2–3).

## "BLESSED ARE THE POOR IN SPIRIT . . ."

". . . for theirs is the kingdom of heaven" (Matt 5:3).

First of all, it is vital to recognize the significance of the sequence to the Beatitudes. There is, if you will, a logical progression to the order that militates against the idea of random selection. That Jesus mentions the need for his disciples to be poor in spirit at the very outset is surely no accident, for it is the key to all that follows. This is true both here in the text and in life. Not only is spiritual poverty fundamental to salvation as a crisis point in time, it is also the foundation upon which we build toward sanctification. It is a pouring out of self-dependency, sinful desires, and satanic influence that there may follow a pouring in of godly grace. It is an emptying that precedes being filled, a tearing down that we might be thereafter built up. Everything else that may come along after it is of no real consequence unless it proceeds from this having first become firmly rooted.

---

2. Vine, *Expository Dictionary*, 125.

## What It Means To Be Poor

Initially, it may prove helpful to consider what is meant by poverty of spirit. It most certainly is not material deficiency, spiritual unawareness, lack of the Holy Spirit, or to be economically destitute. In the Old Testament, God's people are often referred to as "poor" by the use of a Hebrew word that can equally be translated "humble" and "lowly," in stark contrast to "proud" or "presumptuous" (see Prov 16:19; Isa 66:2). To be "poor in spirit," therefore, is to acknowledge our own inability to earn God's commendation, thereby placing all of one's trust in Yahweh's redemptive provision—it is the truest expression of repentance. As such, it should come as no surprise that those who possess this quality own God's rule also in their day-to-day living.

In the United Kingdom, as I envisage is the case in most so-called developed countries, poverty is relative; it is almost as if there is an imaginary scale of affluence by degrees. I may be perceived of as poor because I cannot afford the overtly luxurious lifestyle of my neighbor. The Greek word translated "poor" in the text is *ptochoi*. This is important. Had it been *penes*, then the inference would have been of those so poor that they have to strive to attain their needs (in this case, spiritual), as would a laborer. The root of the Greek *ptochos*, however, is one that is akin to stooping down in a beggarly fashion, suggesting a state of poverty so desperate as to incur urgent pleas for support. It is not a case of "I have a 28 inch flat-screen digital TV, but would really like a 46-inch HD with plasma screen" (see Eccl 4:4); it is more a matter of "Where is my next meal coming from?" In other words, we are speaking here of those who have come to recognize that what they desire more than anything else is beyond their own capacity to accomplish.

The corresponding passage in Luke's gospel account reads: "Blessed are you who are poor" (6:20), which may well be closer to the original. Colin Brown suggests that what we have here is Matthew's attempt at "an interpretative paraphrase which brings out the Hebrew meaning."[3] However, given the intended original readership of the two accounts, I cannot help but think that this would have made more sense had the situation been reversed. If Matthew was so careful to avoid damaging Jewish sensitivities by referring to "kingdom of heaven" instead of "kingdom of God," then surely that same Jewish audience would have been

---

3. Brown, *Dictionary of New Testament Theology*, 824.

all too familiar with their own background regarding what precisely was meant by "poor." Unless, of course, it was the distinction between the Greek adjectives that Matthew believed it necessary to reinforce.

On the basis of Luke's version being taken in isolation, there are those who take great pains to preach a message of natural poverty. Down the ages this has found expression in monastic settings, ascetic lifestyles, Amish values, etc. But Scripture does not present this to be a necessarily—or, at least, exclusively—valid interpretation. Poverty is not a condition of spirituality, any more than salvation is prohibited by wealth *per se*. Remember, we are essentially dealing here with beautiful *attitudes*. Money itself is not "the root of all evil," but the lust thereof (1 Tim 6:10). Dependence upon riches is without question to be shunned, but wise stewardship of what we have is equally to be encouraged. Neither am I advocating what has become known as "the prosperity gospel." This, I believe, is an ungodly indictment against the millions around the world—many of them Christians—who die for lack of food, while the rest of us abuse our bodies through relatively gratuitous extravagance. The key is surely to learn, with Paul, the secret of contentment in all circumstances, whether in need or in plenty, well-fed or hungry (Phil 4:11–12).

Of course, Jesus is not speaking here of economic embarrassment but of spiritual impoverishment. It stands in complete antithesis to the philosophy of the age, for it is representative of an altogether different kingdom. To succeed in society frequently requires that one must be wholly self-assured, fully reliant, absolutely confident, and finding total expression in what the individual is able to achieve. The enemy has promoted this "other" gospel in the business arena, where the power of positive thinking forms the basis of its manifesto. The world of national politics has openly acknowledged a need for so-called "back to basic" family values, a fairer criminal justice system, care in the community social programs, etc., believing that by simply voting a bill through government we can of ourselves attain some kind of Utopian ideal.

To be "poor in spirit" is to be spiritually bankrupt. This is not to say that we necessarily have nothing in our account so much as what we do have is of the wrong currency. Thank God for his *bureau de change*! True happiness stems from a recognition of the spiritual impoverishment of self-achievement and the blessings to be had in complete and absolute dependence upon him. To continue to live in the apparent security of our own ability is to pay scant regard to Jesus' words that "apart from [him we] can do nothing" (John 15:5). To trust him finally is not merely to be elevated to a place where there is a better chance of success, for "nothing is impossible with God" (Luke 1:27). An admission of reliance upon God's glorious grace is the first step toward receiving that grace. Even the recognition of our state is not one we come to of ourselves. That, too, is an act of God's wonderful redeeming grace.

## Treading a Well-Worn Path

Even to speak of spiritual bankruptcy in today's financial climate requires further qualification. So far removed is the stigma that was once attached to being declared bankrupt that it is now often regarded as a preferred option to protect one's outside (or offshore) business interests. Seldom does it actually mean that the one so pronounced is actually destitute.

The Old Testament is littered with episode upon weary episode of man attempting to live up to God's righteous standard, and no one ever did. Not even the best of them. And yet when Jesus came announcing the fulfillment (that is, literally "filling out to the fullest potential") of the Law, and issued an ethical code of love to live out (not up to), perhaps far too many of us have turned it into a new "Law" that will somehow earn us the right to be saved, if only we can measure up to its demands. It is what the apostle Paul identifies as having "fallen away from grace" (Gal 5:4). This is not to lose one's salvation, as some teach, but to become as legalistic in our approach to the gospel as the Pharisees and their ilk were to the Hebrew Scriptures. Only one man has ever lived the Christ-life successfully, because only he could. His name is Jesus. We do not need to try to measure up; rather, we need to die that he might live through us. I apologize if that sounds too simplistic, but it is my understanding of New Testament Christianity. I believe it is also encapsulated here in the opening verse of the Beatitudes.

Of the list in Hebrews 11, in what has become known as "the heroes of the faith" chapter, there is not a man or woman recorded there of whom it could be said: "they were not poor in spirit." They all achieved mighty exploits, but each was swift to acknowledge the source of their power. The same is true of countless others in both Testaments, some unnamed, who knew the reality of this dictum in operation. Even Jesus,

God in the flesh, omnipotent though limited in that power for a while, was forced to concede his total dependence upon God the Father. Oh what a mystery!

The spirit of independence is rooted in pride, self-sufficiency, and egocentricity. This should hardly come as a revelation, for its father is the author of all three—the devil. Even now, he seeks to promote a disposition of arrogance in the hearts of those set free from his grasp. The slightest problem gives vent to distrust, breakdown of communication yields insularity, and shared misgivings often pave the way for a go-it-alone mentality. And yet God's chosen way of establishing his kingdom is through a body, a committed vanguard, each member of which has learned the secret of how to relate, where to release, and in whom to relax. The benefits are manifold, for as we give blessing, encouragement, love, and support, so we find that we receive edification, joy, assurance, and warmth.

Absolute power is most in evidence where there has been confession of abject weakness. There is no secret formula regarding how to become "poor in spirit." The blessing is simply for those who are that. No mere words can achieve it; it has to do with turning away from self and looking to Jesus. For, in fixing our gaze his way, we first of all see our own utter inadequacy to accomplish anything in ourselves of any eternal value and, at the same time, the potential to draw upon an endless resource, as we allow him to live through us in the power of his resurrection life. This is presumably why Paul declares to the believers at Corinth that "flesh and blood cannot inherit the kingdom of God" (1 Cor 15:50).

Notice finally that the state of blessedness for the "poor in spirit" is not presented as a future promise but is cited in the present continuous tense: "theirs *is* the kingdom of heaven." For the majority of those beatitudes that follow, the blessing is seen to be present in principle, though the promise awaits future fulfillment (see vv. 4–9), as we shall see. Not so here.

### Have We Really Understood?

It is thought by some that the Sermon on the Mount was Jesus' first preaching engagement (e.g., John Chrysostom). The internal evidence suggests, however, that this might not be the case (see Matt 4:14, 23).

That notwithstanding, there is surely some significance to be attached to the fact that on this occasion those who are poor in spirit are given prime attention. Why this is so can only ever be the subject of speculation, though Thomas Watson's theory is not without merit:

> Christ does it to show that poverty of spirit is the very basis and foundation of all the other graces that follow. You may as well expect fruit to grow without a root, as the other graces without this. Till a man be poor in spirit, he cannot mourn . . . When a man sees his own defects and deformities and looks upon himself as undone, then he mourns after Christ . . . Till a man be poor in spirit, he cannot "hunger and thirst after righteousness." He must first be sensible of want before he can hunger. Therefore, Christ begins with poverty of spirit because this ushers in all the rest.[4]

Although material want is not implied by the text, the acknowledgment of spiritual poverty that is suggested certainly seems to militate against the idea of marketing Christianity as a business commodity in which the religious entrepreneurial might expect to prosper. Thus, those who aspire to personality cult status and those who are poor in spirit are poles apart.

In some quarters, even the church has succumbed to this school of thought. Pastors are often elected into office on the basis of what amounts to nothing less than an audition sermon and are then unceremoniously disposed of if they dare to try and lead the flock anywhere it chooses not to go. Where such is the case, biblical fellowship is usually reduced to little more than weekly comfort zones. Solutions to difficult problems are typically found within parameters allowed by the premise of diluting everything to its lowest common denominator. Faith is preached with an emphasis almost exclusively on "What's in it for me?" with little or no mention of personal or corporate sacrifice. Even the increasing penchant for naming mission organizations after the individual founder speaks of only one thing: self has usurped the throne reserved solely for Jesus.

But thank God not all is like that within Christendom! Nor, by the way, is it true that everything claiming to be church *is* church. There are still those—and not just a remnant—who know what it is to adopt a scriptural structure of ecclesiastical government, where leaders truly

---

4. Watson, *The Beatitudes*, 23.

lead, build, and equip in accordance with godly principles. In such settings, problems are addressed openly and honestly, and solutions are founded on understanding rather than ignorance. Our coming together should be comfortable, but it is a coziness that owes nothing to pretense or fear, as everything is governed by a sense of mutual edification out of love for one another.

There are no escape clauses to faith "in case it doesn't work out"; no investment plans offered in the event that we get it wrong. "After all, brother, it wouldn't be right to put all your eggs in one basket, now would it? I mean, that's only common sense." No; that is the spirit of the age. It is the philosophy of commerce breaking in upon the church. Moreover, it is the enemy's attempt to prevent you and I from obeying Scripture by laying up for ourselves treasure in heaven and investing in godly kingdom-extension programs. We are not into personal empire plans; what we are committed to is sowing seed into God's kingdom rule, that we might thereby yield an abundant harvest. Much more of that to come later, but it all begins here for those who are "poor in spirit."

## Summary

Scripture is awash with examples of those who were poor in spirit. Although it is a condition that is prerequisite to blessing, it is not one from which we are encouraged to emerge into richness. The Christian walk is one that progressively makes its way towards sanctification, but each step is one that necessarily carries with it the same attitude of utter dependency upon God. Thus, to be poor in spirit and to be vigorous in the faith are not mutually exclusive terms. Abel, Enoch, Noah, Abraham, Joseph, Moses, Rahab, Samson, David, Samuel, and many more besides find themselves honored in the New Testament by the writer of the book of Hebrews. They are all commended for their faith. None of them earned that acclamation by commensurately relinquishing their poorness in spirit, for both are linked to a godly reliance. Unless we can grasp the true meaning of this blessing, none of the others will make any sense. However, the converse is equally true: once we have come to terms with what it really means to be poor in spirit, we can then go on to enjoy the blessings that follow.

## "BLESSED ARE THOSE WHO MOURN . . ."

". . . for they will be comforted" (Matt 5:4).

At first glance, this beatitude seems at best to be a contradiction, at worst downright ridiculous. "How on earth can those who mourn be happy?" asks the cynic. Well, viewed from the earthly perspective, we might easily agree. This is especially so when we consider that the Greek as used here is *pentheo*, meaning to lament or express deep heartfelt sorrow.[5] Just as the poverty of spirit was not related to financial insolvency or economic penury, so this kind of mourning has absolutely nothing to do with mortal bereavement. They are heavenly states, spiritual attitudes, and eternal problems, though they may well find substantial expression in the natural realm also. Therefore, we should hardly be surprised that such teaching is regarded as alien by the irreligious.

### A Special Kind of Sorrow

At the risk of stating the obvious, it is of great consequence that beatitude number two follows hard on the heels of beatitude number one. What I mean is this: poverty of spirit is prerequisite to spiritual mourning. Or to put it another way: acknowledgment of inadequacy paves the way for inner sorrow. "I can do nothing of myself to alter my condition; where, then, shall I turn?" To be confronted by the holy standard of Almighty God and realize our absolute helplessness to attain such a mark will precede the kind of mourning addressed here by Jesus in Matthew 5:4. A Christian is not one who does not know sin, but he/she who realizes the enormity and awfulness of their sin. They are released from its power by believing in the atoning work of Christ and are thence set free from habitual sin. When subsequent un-Christlike behavior and the guilt associated with it might seek to rob one of the joy of salvation, the knowledge that such conduct is both displeasing and dishonoring to God causes such lamentation that only this promise can bring adequate remedy: "he will be comforted."

It should hardly need saying that to mourn is vastly different from being merely disappointed. Anyone who has suffered bereavement, especially of a close family member, knows that the grieving process is a

---

5. See Vine, *Expository Dictionary*, 759.

lengthy one; it can sometimes last a lifetime. Although there is a sense in which the level of grief is exacerbated by the perceived finality of death, the hope of resurrection for the deceased believer may have only a minor softening effect for those left behind. Indeed, many experts are of the opinion that the grief process is an essential tool in coping with the loss and readjusting to an environment in which the departed is absent.[6] As numbness, shock, and initial non-acceptance give way to longing and desolation, there then follows a coming to terms with the reality of loss and a resolution to bring to mind only happy memories concerning the loved one who no longer inhabits this earth.

The kind of mourning to be inferred is that of godly sorrow. Were it any other kind, then it is improbable that it would be rewarded with the promise of comfort, for as the apostle Paul reminds his Corinthian readers: "Godly sorrow brings repentance that leads to salvation and leaves no regret, but worldly sorrow brings death" (2 Cor 7:10). William Hendriksen's comments deserve our attention in this regard: "Godly sorrow turns the soul towards God. God, in turn, grants comfort to those who seek their help from him. It is he who pardons, delivers, strengthens, reassures . . . At times the comfort consists in this, that the affliction itself is removed. Often, however, the affliction remains for a while, but a weight of glory outbalances the grief."[7]

As with any fundamental truth, the principle that brought us *to* Christ will keep us *in* Christ. We do not build any differently toward maturity than the foundation we laid in new birth: stone upon stone, brick upon brick. We are being saved in precisely the same manner that we were saved. Sin brings mourning and mourning gives way to comfort. It is what David cried out to God for, having committed adultery with Bathsheba: "Restore to me the joy of your salvation" (Ps 51:12). And God honored the sincerity of his heart. Sadly, it took the prophet of the Lord to challenge David about his condition, and how downcast must he by then have become!

But it need not be that way for us. If the sorrow is genuine and prompt, then the comfort too will be immediate in its effect. This is why it is so important to keep short accounts with God (and each other), instead of constantly developing a penance mentality: that we might not be robbed of the peace that could and should be ours. Now, someone

---

6. See Parkes, *Bereavement*; Kübler-Ross, *Living with Death and Dying*.
7. Hendriksen, *Matthew*, 271.

will try to convince us that it is not quite as simple as that. Maybe some form of self-imposed torture is required, or we must fast more, pray harder, or not miss a church meeting for the next three months in order to earn God's approval once more. But why? We are no more capable of maintaining our walk without the grace of God than we were of coming to him in the first place. Allow me to tell you whose interests are best served by having you believe otherwise—his name is the devil.

## Comfort that Is Uniquely Spiritual

In any given situation, the comfort required is commensurate to the pain endured. We are not talking here about the small boy who falls over, grazes his knee, and runs to mommy for her to rub the injured area gently and say, "There, there!" The intensity of inner turmoil suggested by the word "mourn" necessitates a level of comfort that far exceeds a mere expression of sympathy. Consolation that does not also include encouragement simply joins us in the mire without offering any hope that things will not always feel this way. In some ways, it might be argued that this is a prophetic ministry. At the beginning of Paul's teaching to the Corinthian church on spiritual gifts, he says this: "everyone who prophesies speaks to men for their strengthening [Greek *oikodomen*], encouragement [*paraklesin*] and comfort [*paramythian*]" (1 Cor 14:3).

Now note the original meaning of the three qualifying nouns in verb form:

| | |
|---|---|
| *oikodomeo* | literally "to build up"; figuratively to do so by means of edification; |
| *parakaleo* | to beseech or exhort by drawing alongside; |
| *paramutheomai* | to speak intimately with a measure of tenderness.[8] |

In the natural realm, of course, the funeral service often provides the catalyst for coping with what lies ahead, most notably for those left behind. The spiritual equivalent in salvific terms would be the sacrament of baptism, where the previous way of life is buried, along with any sensations of guilt that may have been associated with it. The newness

---

8. See Vine, *Expository Dictionary*, 148, 199, 223, 356.

of life that begins when we emerge from the baptismal waters is one that we undertake with the guidance of the Holy Spirit—the Comforter (Greek *parakletos*).

The Heidelberg Catechism reflects upon it thus:

> Question: What is the only comfort in life and death?
>
> Answer: That I with body and soul, both in life and death, am not my own, but belong unto my faithful Saviour Jesus Christ; who, with his precious blood, has fully satisfied for all my sins, and delivered me from all the power of the devil; and so preserves me that without the will of my heavenly Father, not a hair can fall from my head; yea, that all things must be subservient to my salvation, and therefore, by his Holy Spirit, he also assures me of eternal life, and makes me sincerely willing and ready, henceforth, to live unto him.

As I write this, that reminder is particularly poignant. From time to time we all experience prolonged periods where nothing seems to go right for us. It is not that there are necessarily major catastrophes to deal with, such as bereavement or news of a terminal illness. But a sustained sequence of minor nuisances can often have more of a damaging effect in the short term. Within the last couple of days or so, I have had to deal with a faulty toilet syphon; a wash basin faucet that, after a couple of years of promising to give up the ghost, finally has; and the rear offside tire of my car picked up a nail, probably on a visit to the local waste-disposal site. Having located a relatively inexpensive tire replacement firm, I had the new one fitted this morning, only to find that the implement for removing the old tire has substantially damaged the alloy wheel, which will now also need repairing.

Minor difficulties, you might argue, and, of course, you would be right. After all, it hardly bares comparison to a first-century Christian missionary shipwreck, public flogging, imprisonment for the faith, and personal disloyalty, all of which Paul regarded as but "light and momentary troubles" (see 2 Cor 4:16–18; 11:23–33). Neither will it alert any potential compilers of a twenty-first century revised book of martyrs.

It is not so much the cost of putting these things right that I find so objectionable (though they are expenses I could have managed without); it is more the time-consuming inconvenience of having to arrange for their repair. In the midst of feeling disproportionately disgruntled, my wife telephoned home during her lunch break to ask for an earlier pick up from work than usual. Sensing my ill humor, she asked what was wrong, so I told her. A short time later, I received an email from her to say that she had bought me a small gift to cheer me up. It arrived within seconds of me having read the above quotation from the Heidelberg Catechism. Words like "perspective" and "context" spring to mind, swiftly followed by self-counseling advice, such as "get a grip."

## Learning the Lesson

It is yet another lie of the enemy to suggest that the unsaved can be truly happy without Jesus. Brought up in an age where it is considered weakness to admit to being needy, such people choose not to allow themselves to mourn, searching instead for solace in all manner of pleasure-seeking activities. This is why the sports arenas, cinemas, leisure facilities, discos, bingo halls, and other entertainment auditoria are often packed to the rafters. They are filled with people of a questioning demeanor, all apparently pursuing the meaning of life, but with little idea of where to look or whom to consult. Not that I am for one moment suggesting that there is anything intrinsically wrong with such places or that they necessarily should be out of bounds to the Christian. But nothing that is material by nature can ever possibly satisfy a longing that is essentially spiritual.

Part of the reason why certain parts of Christendom have remained ineffective in attracting the unchurched may well be due to a misunderstanding of this very verse (that is, Matt 5:4). It has often been interpreted that to truly mourn is to assume a posture of continuing sorrow, a show of piety, if you will. It seems clear from the text, however, that all of these attitudes are to do with inner disposition, not outward appearance. It simply is not correct that one must be miserable to be a Christian, though oftentimes the unsaved can hardly be blamed for believing so. "Ah, but," you may say, "wasn't Jesus a man of sorrows and familiar with suffering?" Yes he was; he was also anointed with the oil of joy more than any of his contemporaries. The one does not automatically negate the other; they may both be equally valid.

Another reason, of course, why the church has generally failed in its mission thus far has been its tendency to the opposite extreme. As many have tried to counter the above accusation, they have often done so by attempting to put on a semblance of overwhelming glee and happiness, which has hovered between banal superficiality and unmitigated deception. Unbelievers are not so deficient in their capacity to perceive as we might sometimes imagine. They can frequently see through peripheral veneers far more easily than we would necessarily like to give them credit for.

Third—and perhaps more significantly in its effect—is the shallow sense of what we might reasonably expect to be at the very heart of the gospel message. Many a church so presents its regular program as an entertainment schedule that it almost carries with it the hidden suggestion that: "If you were to become a member here, you too could enjoy this 'buzz' every single week." Or maybe they major on the opportunities to share in body ministry, with the subliminal implication that: "Play your cards right with us, and who knows; we might just put you on our preaching rota so that you, too, could be addressing the crowds from behind our diamond-encrusted Perspex pulpit." Others emphasize making new friends, joining the choir, playing a musical instrument as part of the worship band, fun activities to be had as part of a midweek homegroup, etc. Not that any of these things are necessarily to be discouraged in their rightful place, but they can all obscure the truth of what becoming a Christian actually involves: repentance.

Oh, how the devil would love to eliminate that word from our vocabulary! As I understand it, repentance comprises three components: recognition of sin, remorse for wrongdoing, and a subsequent redirection of lifestyle. None of these alone constitutes the whole, though where any feature is lacking there remains arguably a diluted gospel message and commensurately deficient Christian experience. The first step is not "to feel at home in the house"; it is to acknowledge our true condition before God in humble repentance with sincere mourning. We may then be comforted by "the Father of compassion and the God of all comfort, who comforts us in all our troubles, so that we can comfort those in any trouble with the comfort we ourselves have received from God" (2 Cor 1:3–4).

There is a tendency—even in Christian circles—to view comfort from an almost entirely humanistic vantage point. To do so in this context would be to ignore the obviously paradoxical nature of the Beatitudes and to fall headlong into the anthropocentric trap of interpreting Scripture through the filter of postmodernity. Perhaps the fact that Luke

*Kingdom Character Attracts the King's Blessing*

sets them in a background of Old Testament prophecy regarding Jesus as the Messiah, who would proclaim Yahweh's favor to the poor and brokenhearted, should provide its own clues (see Isa 61). If the good news to the poor is that theirs is the kingdom of heaven, then surely the comfort for those who mourn is that they will have bestowed upon them "a crown of beauty instead of ashes, the oil of gladness instead of mourning, and a garment of praise instead of a spirit of despair" (cf. Matt 5:4; Isa 61:2b–3a).

## Summary

The *Concise Oxford Dictionary* defines an oxymoron as: "a figure of speech in which apparently contradictory terms appear in conjunction." Initially, the Beatitudes may seem like nothing more than an elaborate catalogue of oxymoronic couplets. In that context, this one is perhaps the most vivid of them all. For someone to speak so of the delight of distress, the pleasure of pain, and the bliss of brokenheartedness is either certifiably insane or truly one of the most insightful statements ever uttered. But this is not an exclusively New Testament teaching. Indeed, it is wholly consistent with what is revealed in the Old Testament of what God finds pleasing in those who own his name. Arguably Israel's greatest natural leader knew what it was to find himself a stranger in God's presence; he also discovered the secret of what was required to re-establish the relationship so damaged by his iniquity: "a broken and contrite heart" (Ps 51:17).

## "BLESSED ARE THE MEEK . . ."

"... for they will inherit the earth" (Matt 5:5).

Historically, there have been a number of occasions when there have arisen those who, either individually or as leaders of a corporate enterprise, have sought world domination. They have usually attempted to do so through violation of power, expressions of aggression, political expedience, tyrannical conquest, industrial blackmail, policies of de-selection, or strategic extortion in the realm of trade and commerce. And yet here we have such a simple, though profound, statement that

Kingdom

the earth will one day belong to those who have demonstrated that they will not abuse the right to rule—the meek.

## Meek Submission, Not Weak Surrender

The word "meekness" has often been used in a context that suggests it is almost a synonym for weakness. This is simply not true. Neither is it akin to timidity, indecision, or natural affability. Scripture speaks of Moses as having been the meekest man "on the face of the earth" (Num 12:3), and yet none of the above character traits could possibly have been used to describe him. It was in meekness that Moses was prepared to endure physical injury without retaliation or resentment, while at the same time he remained uncompromising in his personal call to leadership. Jesus himself was "meek and humble in heart" (Matt 11:28), even when he turned over the tables of the moneylenders in the temple and pronounced woe upon Pharisee and Sadducee alike. The testimony of Christ is again our best example, prophetically announced of the Messiah (Zech 9:9), and arguably no more fully demonstrated than in his stand before Pilate and the mob.

The Greek word *prautes*, translated "meek" in the New Testament, usually refers to the inner condition as affected by God's Spirit. It is to be distinguished from gentleness, which may be considered part of its outward fruit (see Gal 5:23). According to Vine, it is: "an inwrought grace of the soul, the exercises of [which] are first and chiefly towards God . . . It is that temper of spirit in which we accept his dealings with us as good and, therefore, without disputing or resisting."[9]

In such circumstances, adversity is not engineered, but neither is it ignored. For the meek are fully aware of God's ultimate control in all matters, his instinctive goodness in every situation, and that their reward is to be the whole earth. If repentance is the acknowledging of all wrongs, then meekness involves the waiving of all rights.

William Hendriksen suggests that the third beatitude and the first are so closely alike that one is hard pressed to distinguish between the two. However, he then goes on to state that: "The first designation describes the man more as he is in himself, namely, broken-hearted;

---

9. Ibid., 727.

whereas the second pictures him more definitely in his relation to God and the fellow-man."[10]

To be meek, then, is to trust. Or, as the buzz phrase was when I first came to salvation: "Let go and let God!" The sons of Korah put it this way: "Be still and know that I am God" (Ps 46:10). This is reminiscent of Moses' advice to the Israelites, who panicked at the prospect of being faced with the Red Sea on one side and the advancing Egyptian hordes on the other. Talk about being caught between the devil and the deep Red Sea! "'Do not be afraid,' said Moses. 'Stand firm and you will see the deliverance the Lord will bring you today . . . the Lord will fight for you; you need only be still'" (Exod 14:14).

As we have already seen, the Beatitudes are not reserved for the elite. This was not the apostle addressing the international leadership conference; it was Jesus laying down the elementary requirements for all believers. If we were to initiate a character study of everyone in Scripture who fulfils the criterion of meekness, I am reasonably convinced that we would find it anything but a natural tendency. Abraham's dealing with Lot, David's response to Saul's unprovoked hostility, Jeremiah's reaction to his contemporaries' hatred were all born of a meekness that was supernaturally acquired.

"Yes, but they were mere mortals," you might well argue. "Having been confronted so dynamically with the awesome majesty of Almighty God, how could they possibly be anything but meek?" Well, what about Jesus, then? Did he not, more than anyone else, have the right to retort with righteous indignation toward his enemies? Yet he, too, learned the secret of submission, for that is surely the soil in which the seed of meekness is best nurtured, that it might produce the fruit of obedience to the Father's will. And how is it to be watered if not by the Holy Spirit of God?

## The Call to Humility and Gentleness

Although meekness and gentleness are not synonymous terms, it would nevertheless be appropriate to speak of them as essentially two sides of the same coin. Thus, when the apostle Paul cites "the meekness and gentleness of Christ" as the grounds of his appeal to the unfaithful

---

10. Hendriksen, *Matthew*, 271.

Corinthians, he is not being unnecessarily repetitive for effect (see 2 Cor 10:1). Whereas meekness is an inward condition, gentleness is an outward expression. Moreover, it would be a valid argument to suggest that the latter is made possible only by the existence of the former. When called before the ruling authorities, Jesus (and Paul, too, for that matter) was able to answer his accusers in a gentle manner because of his meek disposition.

In this context, then, meekness is very close in meaning to humility. It is also perhaps best understood in relation to what it is not. It is the exact opposite of arrogance, is diametrically opposed to self-sufficiency, and is antonymous with independence. There are many notable exemplars in Scripture, including Moses (Num 12:3), David (2 Sam 16:11), Jeremiah (Jer 26:14) and, of course, the apostle Paul (2 Tim 4:16). As so often proves to be the case, however, there is surely no more superior model than Christ himself (see Isa 53:7; Matt 11:29; 1 Pet 2:23).

Perhaps there has never been a time in history when meekness as a character trait has been so at odds with the epithet of the age. This should hardly be surprising, given Paul's counsel to us through his second letter to Timothy: "But mark this: There will be terrible times in the last days. People will be lovers of themselves, lovers of money, boastful, proud, abusive, disobedient to their parents, ungrateful, unholy, without love, unforgiving, slanderous, without self-control, brutal, not lovers of the good, treacherous, rash, conceited, lovers of pleasure rather than lovers of God—having a form of godliness but denying its power. Have nothing to do with them" (2 Tim 3:1–5).

Quite a catalogue of characteristics, which I am sure many of us would agree we are experiencing in increasing measure. There are three points I want briefly to draw your attention to. First of all, the list is headed by a trait that can only be described as antithetical to meekness. If the spirit of the age could be defined in but just one word, then surely that word would be "self-assertion." Secondly, it would appear that the church—in its loosest possible sense—is not to be exempt from the influence of those who seek to promote such values. Finally, Paul's advice is wholly unmitigating. Perhaps the King James Version is closer to the original when it correctly translates *apotrepho* thus: "from such turn away" (2 Tim 3:5).

Deriving inspiration from the twenty-fifth Psalm, Arthur Pink[11] seems close to the mark when he affirms that meekness "consists of a pliant heart and will": "The meek will [the Lord] guide in judgment/justice: and the meek will he teach his way" (Ps 25:9, KJV/ASV). Dr. Martyn Lloyd-Jones put it this way: "The world thinks in terms of strength and power, of ability, self-assurance and aggressiveness. That is the world's idea of conquest and possession. The more you assert yourself and express yourself, the more you organize and manifest your powers and ability, the more likely you are to succeed and get on . . . [Jesus] is an enigma to the world."[12]

Again, we must take note of the logical sequence evident in this list of Beatitudes, for just as the implied sense of mourning is contingent upon spiritual poverty, so both dictate that meekness should follow. It is only when we have an appropriate view of sin and ourselves that we can relate to others in a righteous manner. Meekness is kindred to humility, but it is much more than that. Although there is not a hint of pride, not a trace of self-assertion or hypersensitivity, the meek person will always defend rigorously the honor of godly virtue, as did the examples we remarked upon earlier. Meekness finds expression in approachability, consideration, patience, and compassion. It no longer fights for its rights because it realizes that they were all signed away on becoming poor in spirit. In fact, I do not think it too harsh to ask if someone is always embroiled in self-pity, continuously seeking his or her own interests, and locked in to the "my ministry" syndrome, then have they ever known the true value of the cross at all in their lives? I very much doubt it.

## An Inheritance to Savor

The root of the Greek *kleros* (translated "inheritance") and its derivatives originally signified the stone or other determinant object by which lots were cast. The same word is used of the soldiers at Jesus' crucifixion to determine who from amongst them would receive his seamless undergarment (John 19:23–24). It is also used of the disciples' method of choosing a successor to the apostolate to replace Judas (see Acts

---

11. Pink, *An Exposition*, 22.
12. Lloyd-Jones, *Studies in the Sermon on the Mount*, 63.

## Kingdom

1:24–26). Thus, the word "inheritance" may be understood in terms of determining one's allocation in accordance with God's will. Any suggestion that the matter is put to a vote of recognizably suitable candidates is to misappropriate the typically idiomatic use of *edokan* (that is, "to give") instead of the admittedly more common *ebalon* ("to cast"). In the words of Ernst Haenchen: "The human factor is excluded; it is God who is choosing."[13]

In modern parlance, as here, it is more usual to speak of an inheritance in the future tense: what we are due to inherit. There must come a time, however, when what is anticipated passes from the "not yet" to the "now." More often than not, what triggers this is the death of the benefactor. There is, of course, a sense in which the death of Christ made possible much of what he had promised, though it is equally true that his subsequent resurrection guaranteed that (see Rom 1:4; Phil 3:10). It must also not escape our attention that on this occasion the fullness of the promise awaits the natural death not of the benefactor but of the bequeathed. However, such an acknowledgment should not obscure from our view the wonderful truth that the kingdom of God, as the rule of God in action, has burst upon the present, as its citizens both live by and make known to others his revealed will in and for society.

Robin Nixon is correct to say that "The object of Christian inheritance is all that was symbolised by the land of Canaan, and more."[14] Israel took the land it was promised largely through successful military encounters (that is, by force). Given what we know of Israel's failings throughout the whole of the period covered by the Old Testament, it could never hope to make a significant impact outside of strictly defined parameters, as that would have required a gentle approach emanating from a meek temperament. For this, ancient Israel was wholly ill-equipped. Or, as Paul puts it to the Roman believers: "the law was powerless in that it was weakened by the sinful nature [so] God . . . [sent] his Son in the likeness of sinful man to be a sin offering. And so he condemned sin in sinful man, in order that the righteous requirements of the law might be fully met in us, who did not live according to the sinful nature but according to the Spirit" (Rom 8:3–4).

You will see immediately that I have slightly adjusted the sense of Paul's wording by use of ellipses and the introduction of a couple

---

13. Haenchen, *Acts*, 162.
14. R. E. Nixon, "Inheritance," in Douglas, *New Bible Dictionary*, 515.

of extra words (in squared brackets). I offer my apologies if the reader believes that in so doing I have dramatically altered the text, but I believe this interpretation to be fully in keeping with both the original Greek and Jeremiah's prophecy regarding the coming initiation of the new covenant (see Jer 31:31–33).

Again, we see that the reward is perfectly suited to the disposition. We may thus identify the following in relation to the inheritance of the earth by the meek:

- it becomes a "right" only by virtue of the grace of God toward those who are otherwise without such merit;
- its certainty is both guaranteed and irrevocable; and
- man will not—nor is it possible for him to—receive it by way of anything other than a gift from God.

Many of those who heard Jesus' words at the Sermon on the Mount will no doubt have been familiar with the original setting of this blessing. According to the psalmist: "the meek will inherit the land and enjoy great peace" (Ps 37:11). Meekness and peace seem to go hand-in-hand. In natural terms, the few pacifists who are known to me are also extremely meek in their persona. In the course of human history, there have been many attempts to gain world domination by political warrior-like figures. Think of characters like Alexander the Great, the Caesars of Rome, British empiricism, Adolph Hitler, the threat of Soviet communism, or more recently militant Islam. The attempts to achieve their common aim have often failed ultimately because of a distinct lack of meekness and peaceful strategies. The abdication of morality and promotion of ruthlessness is not a recipe for success. "But," says Jesus, "the earth will be gifted to the meek" and, according to David, they "shall delight themselves in the abundance of peace" (Ps 37:11, KJV).

## Summary

Meekness, therefore, recognizes that we have no personal rights to defend, looks to the welfare of others first by esteeming them more highly than ourselves, and yet is not afraid to stand for the truth of the gospel when God's honor is called into question. It is bridled strength. It always involves a faith response to God's revealed Word, a relinquishing of all other "yokes," refusing to be owned by anything else, and a willing submission to the lordship of Christ. In reality, if we could only see the value of our promised inheritance, then meekness would be a much more sought-after character trait. To view all circumstances as opportunities, each setback as a learning process, and every trial as a setting for faith to arise can only be achieved from an eternal perspective and with a meek disposition.

## "BLESSED ARE THOSE WHO HUNGER AND THIRST FOR RIGHTEOUSNESS . . ."

". . . for they will be filled" (Matt 5:6).

In many Christian circles, the pursuit of righteousness is almost unheard of today. The emphasis on personal evangelism, anointed ministry, power through prayer, spiritual maturity, with signs and wonders to accompany the preaching of the Word have all conspired to relegate Christ's command to "seek first his kingdom and his righteousness" (Matt 6:33) to the theological backwater like some spiritual lower division. And yet, the promise of Jesus is that, by so doing, "all [of] these other things will be given to you as well."

### The Pangs of Emptiness

So far, we have looked at man's failed attempts to attract true happiness. Where humanity places itself at the top of its list of priorities, the kind of happiness such practice inevitably brings can only ever be fleeting, temporal, external, and ultimately unsatisfying. The first key is surely to acknowledge a need outside of oneself, even if we initially fail to understand the source of that desire. Indeed, it may well be the frustration of not knowing that will produce the sense of mourning required to finally bring us to the conclusion that "there is absolutely nothing in me that can effect the blessing I so deeply long for." Then we find that this perception of worthlessness helps us in how we relate to others in all meekness.

Now we come to the next step in the process of spiritual insight: true blessing is to be found in seeking with all that we have to cultivate a correct relationship with our Father, God. There are, of course, those pseudo-spirituals who would contend that this instruction should be first, but notice the grace of Jesus that he does not take us immediately to where we should be, instead coming to meet us where we are. Commenting on Matthew 5:6, the late Dr. Martyn Lloyd-Jones wrote: "If this verse is to you one of the most blessed statements in the whole of Scripture, you can be quite sure you are a Christian; if it is not, then you had better examine the foundations again."[15]

To hunger and thirst is far removed from merely being peckish or a little dry. The verb "thirst" is a translation of the Greek *dispotes*, from which we derive our English condition dipsomania, meaning "an intense craving for fluid intake." It is also vastly different from eating and drinking. Where hunger and thirst are precipitated by acute need, eating and drinking facilitate that desire. We usually fail to eat or drink by denial, whether that is through choice (as in fasting), opportunity, or provision. In this case, however, it is a longing to be like Christ, a yearning so desperate, an appetite so insatiable that the only appropriate way to describe it is to say that we hunger and thirst. The psalmist put it this way: "As the deer pants for streams of water, so my soul pants for you, O God" (Ps 42:1). In his own inimitable style, C. S. Lewis had this to say: "If I find in myself a desire which no experience in the world can satisfy, the most probable explanation is that I was made for another world."[16]

Sadly, this too does not seem to be as prevalent in the professing church as one might hope to see. The latest fad, the most recent fashion accessory, the newest gizmo and gadget are all purchased in the vain hope that they will somehow live up to the claims of the marketing people by bringing instant happiness. And for a while they do, that is, until the novelty wears off or something better comes along. Or what about the brother who is perennially seeking the latest spiritual high and will hop from one fellowship to another in pursuit of his aim, chasing blessing at one celebration gathering after another, or even globetrotting to where God's Spirit happens to be at present in power.

I remember some years ago, when what became known as "The Toronto Blessing" and other similar phenomena were in full swing, being invited to spend some time teaching God's word to a number of brothers in Kenya. While in the throes of considering the invitation,

15. Lloyd-Jones, *Studies in the Sermon on the Mount*, 74.
16. Lewis, *Mere Christianity*, 106.

another brother advised: "Oh, you'd be far more blessed if you went to Pensacola instead. My wife and I have just come back from there and man, I tell you, the sense of God's presence was absolutely tremendous. The glow lasted for weeks. Brother, it would do you good."

Now it is neither my place nor desire to pass judgment on the legitimacy or otherwise of such experiences. The reports I heard at the time from some trustworthy sources suggest a mixture of both the authentic and the counterfeit. Giving the benefit of any doubts there may be, however, (and I acknowledge there are some grave ones) my main concern is to point out that the reason God chooses to pour out his favor on such occasions is usually because someone somewhere began to hunger and thirst after righteousness. Conversely, the most reasonable explanation for why he withholds his presence in quite the same way elsewhere is because of a lack of that hunger and thirst. So, all I really achieve by traveling to "where it's at" is first of all to abdicate my responsibility and, secondly, I end up piggybacking on someone else's faith. The question that remains, then, is: "Do we hunger and thirst?"

### The Precept of Righteousness

The implication of Jesus' use of the word "righteousness" in this context is that it is that quality of life which pleases God's holiness in every detail. It is to display the fruit of the Spirit at all times, to walk resolutely in the light of pure actions and motives. Given that true righteousness was only made possible by virtue of Christ's atoning sacrifice, there seems to be more than a hint in Jesus' words of his coming substitutionary death and resurrection. This is certainly true of imputed righteousness as a forensic state before God; it is no less so concerning imparted righteousness as a moral condition. In the words of William Hendriksen: "The two are inseparable. Though it is impossible for good works to justify anybody, it is just as impossible for a justified person to live without doing good works. The term 'righteousness' as used by Christ is, therefore, very comprehensive, embracing both."[17]

Thus, we may say that righteousness as a state and righteousness as expressed in behavior, though not one and the same, belong inextricably together. Those who avail themselves of Christ's sacrifice, that they

---

17. Hendriksen, *Matthew*, 274.

may thereby become reconciled to God, are also those within whom the sanctifying work of the Holy Spirit takes place. The converse is equally true: sanctification is the sole and unique claim of those who have been made "at one" with their God. The promise is attainable because the conditions have been fully met.

Precisely what Jesus has in mind here when he speaks of righteousness—or, at least, the expression of it—will hopefully become more clear as we look at the remainder of the Beatitudes. For the time being, however, suffice to say that this set of eight "blessings" may be divided into two groups of four, the last in each group concerning itself with righteousness:

| | First group | | Second group |
|---|---|---|---|
| v 3 | poor in spirit; | v 7 | merciful; |
| v 4 | mournful; | v 8 | pure in heart; |
| v 5 | meek; | v 9 | peacemakers; |
| v 6 | hunger and thirst for righteousness. | v 10 | persecuted for righteousness. |

In many ways, this section mirrors what the apostle Paul instructed the Philippian believers about the attitude of Christ (Phil 2:5–11). The first group is a step-by-step descent as we progressively become aware of our deep-seated emptiness, until finally we are filled. The second group represents the pedagogic climb, as we learn to apply the principles of the righteousness that has been made available, until finally we are harassed, browbeaten, and generally maltreated because of it. No Christian was ever persecuted for righteousness who did not first of all hunger and thirst for it. Looked at another way, when we ask God that he would fill us in this way, do we really understand what lies further along that path? The inevitable consequence of hungering now is not only that we shall be filled, nor simply that we shall be filled in order that we may bless others, but that we can expect to be reviled for it.

Therefore, it might also be reasonable to argue that if the most fruitful conditions for being filled with righteousness are a poor spirit, a mournful disposition, a meek character, and a deep yearning, then the most recognizable evidence of having been filled with righteousness are acts of mercy, purity of heart, and a capacity to bring peaceful resolutions to hitherto hostile situations. And for this, we will be persecuted.

## Kingdom

A man or woman who is hungry and thirsty for one thing cannot be placated by the abundance of another. This is true even if the analogy is of something far less wholesome than we have in mind here. Someone on the point of physical starvation has no use for gold; those with a pang for power cannot be assuaged by assurances of the finest single malt in Speyside; the volume of "friends" accessible through a Facebook account is of no use to those who crave the solitude of a rural setting. To offer a man wealth who seeks only righteousness is both injurious and insulting.

Maybe this is part of the blessing. Just as those who long for righteousness cannot be satisfied with anything else, so the craving for righteousness renders all other potential hankerings obsolete. Lust, avarice, ambition, material wealth, praise from one's peers, the need to be liked at all costs, to be known as the king of the gadgets or queen of accessorizing are all lay slain on the altar of our hunger and thirst for God's righteousness.

### The Pleasure of Fullness

Citing this verse in relation to the activity of faith, Louis Berkhof reminds us that: "When men really hunger and thirst spiritually, they feel that something is wanting, are conscious of the indispensable character of that which is lacking, and endeavour to obtain it . . . In eating and drinking we not only have the conviction that the necessary food and drink is present, but also the confident expectation that it will satisfy us."[18]

It is also worth mentioning that there is a significant difference between postponing disaster and being fully satisfied. Anyone who has engaged with the discipline of fasting for any substantial period will know that at the end of the allotted time span, you will eat almost anything that is put before you. There is an old saying that has somewhat fallen into disuse in recent years: "Beggars can't be choosers." The hunger and thirst we have in mind here, however, is not born of an "anything will do" mentality. Junk food will not suffice, despite what those who have promoted the McDonaldization of the church may say to the contrary. The tragedy is that many seek to satisfy the soul with those things that appeal to the appetites of the flesh and then wonder why they still feel so empty

---

18. Berkhof, *Systematic Theology*, 495.

inside. The Old Testament prophets foretold this long ago: "Come, all you who are thirsty, come to the waters; and you who have no money, come, buy and eat! Come, buy wine and milk without money and without cost. Why spend money on what is not bread, and your labor on what does not satisfy? Listen, listen to me, and eat what is good, and your soul will delight in the richest of fair" (Isa 55:1–2).

The promise is that they who are as intense as this about their need, those who are so passionately aware of the urgency of their situation, "shall be filled." This is literally the most charismatic experience we can possibly know, for it is—more than anything else recorded in Scripture—a gift of God's grace: that we may be filled with righteousness. It is both a crisis and a process. We shall be filled, once and immediately; and we shall be being filled, constantly and continually. The amazing thing is that, just as the promise is in the present continuous tense, so is the condition. Although we may well be satisfied with God's provision to meet our need, yet we ache for more. Oswald Chambers had this to say of it: "There is only one Being who can satisfy the last aching abyss of the human heart, and that is the Lord Jesus Christ."[19]

Jesus said as much himself. Having miraculously met the material needs of the crowds only the day before, they had largely failed to see the spiritual significance and so tracked him down on the other side of the lake for what they hoped would be another free meal. Jesus went on to clarify the lesson further: "I am the bread of life. He who comes to me will never go hungry, and he who believes in me will never be thirsty . . . For my Father's will is that everyone who looks to the Son and believes in him shall have everlasting life, and I will raise him up at the last day" (John 6:35–40).

Although different words are used in the original Greek, the tense indicated in this promise is the same as that of Ananias when called to lay hands on Saul of Tarsus that he might receive the Holy Spirit (Acts 9:17)—it is the present continuous. The sense is to "be being filled." That is to say, having come to a place of recognition that we are hungry and thirsty for righteousness, the receiving of the promise is not a once-for-all-time blessing, so that it may serve as a reminder of the good old days when we were in the thick of the action. As long as we continue to yearn for God's righteousness, we may avail ourselves of it.

---

19. Chambers, *My Utmost*, 154.

Kingdom

In Luke's account, not only are the hungry encouraged with the hope of being filled, but those who have satiated themselves with second best in the present are told not to anticipate what might otherwise have come their way: "Blessed are you who hunger now, for you will be satisfied . . . Woe to you who are well fed now, for you will go hungry" (Luke 6:21a, 25a).

Arguably the most encouraging feature about this beatitude is, perhaps paradoxically, that which also gives most cause for sober reflection. This is that, having come to Christ, the measure of righteousness we receive is commensurately proportionate to the intensity of our desire. Put in simple terms, we can now be as holy as we choose to be. If we are anything less than that which God intends for us, then the remedy is at our disposal.

Summary

It is not just the condition that merits the promise but due recognition of the fact. It may be said of the vast majority that they perish for lack of righteousness. But it is only they who acknowledge their need who are assured of a positive outcome. It is not even the hungry and thirsty who are given hope of satisfaction without qualification. There are many pews—even pulpits—that are occupied by those who hunger for recognition and thirst for fame. However, it is only when righteousness is the object of our most urgent desire that we may take comfort in Jesus' words of blessing.

## "BLESSED ARE THE MERCIFUL . . ."

". . . for they will be shown mercy" (Matt 5:7).

So far in our study of the Beatitudes we may have noticed a common thread: the emphasis is consistently upon what we are rather than on what we do. Of course, this will find outward expression, but the point here is that the Christian extends mercy because, in Christ, he/she is a merciful person; they do not extend mercy in order to become that. This may seem too obvious to many, but it is a fundamental truth that needs grasping: we do not behave in a certain way so that we may become worthy of salvation; we conduct ourselves in a godly manner because we are partakers of the divine nature, having understood at the outset our poverty-stricken inability to warrant God's approval.

## What Does it Mean to be Merciful?

It is worthy of note that one of the Hebrew words translated "mercy" in the Old Testament can also mean "keenness," "eagerness," "goodness," and "loving-kindness." When used in relation to God, it is almost exclusively the latter, and particularly in connection with his covenant love. It is *hesed*, translated by the Greek *eleos* in the Septuagint version of the Hebrew Scriptures. Another Hebrew word commonly translated "mercy" is *hen*, of which Norman Snaith posits: "It is the gracious favour of the superior to the inferior, when there is no obligation to do so."[20]

In the New Testament, *eleos* is retained as the principal noun (*oiktirmos* and *splanchnon* being the others) Of *eleos*, Vine has this to say: "It is the outward manifestation of pity; it assumes need on the part of him who receives it, and resources adequate to meet that need on the part of him who shows it."[21]

Indeed, mercy is just that—unmerited favor. By way of illustration, there is perhaps no finer example than Jesus' parable of the good Samaritan (see Luke 10:25–37). To be merciful is not simply the disposition of anyone who expresses pity or sympathy, but belongs to those who are actively compassionate toward any who require—though do not necessarily deserve—to be shown mercy. In fact, if we deserved to be looked upon favorably, then it would not be mercy but merit. If there is a difference between grace and mercy, it is that where grace bestows upon us the favor we have not earned, mercy withholds from us the penalties that should be ours. The cross of Christ is where we find both, for each is instigated by Jesus in what is commonly known as "The Great Exchange."

Interestingly, Wayne Grudem cites mercy alongside grace and patience as derivatives of God's goodness, reminding us that they are often mentioned together in Scripture (e.g., Exod 34:6; Ps 103:8):

---

20. N. H. Snaith, "Loving-kindness, Mercy," in Richardson, *Theological Word Book*, 80.
21. Vine, *Expository Dictionary*, 732.

Kingdom

- God's *mercy* means God's goodness toward those in misery and distress.

- God's *grace* means God's goodness toward those who deserve only punishment.

- God's *patience* means God's goodness in withholding of punishment toward those who sin over a period of time.[22]

Although Grudem's argument is well reasoned, I am not fully convinced by it. For instance, though God is slow to anger, neither will he contend with man forever. Therefore, it must be assumed that his patience has limits. This is not something I would acknowledge exists in relation to something that is essential to his being, such as goodness. Moreover, are we therefore to assume that when God is finally angry that he is so outside of his intrinsic goodness? Surely such an argument would be difficult to maintain.

As an attribute of God, mercy shares certain features in common with his other attributes. Some of these are not so much inexplicable as they are incomprehensible. For example, the qualities of God are eternal; that is to say, they are from everlasting to everlasting. They are also, therefore, objective. What this means in relation to God's mercy is that *it* is entirely objective. It does not require subjective expression in order to become real. God was full of mercy before there was anything or anyone toward which or whom to be merciful.

Furthermore, although his mercies toward us as needy recipients are new every morning, as an essential quality his mercy is unchangeable: he is never less than full of mercy, and he can never be any more full than he consistently is. This should give rise to both sober reflection by us and spontaneous rejoicing within us. In these respects, God's mercy is inimitable; we cannot replicate them. However, there is one feature that we would do well to both note and seek to mimic: the mercy of God is not a feeling, nor is it governed by fleeting emotions; it is an act of the will.

All of this notwithstanding, it must also be acknowledged that the expression of God's mercy toward humanity is not restricted to his soteriological dealings with them. The fact that common grace extends to all during their earthly life, irrespective of what they each may do with

22. Grudem, *Systematic Theology*, 200.

the opportunity to avail themselves of the salvation on offer, surely also emanates from God's mercy. If we accept the covenant aspect of mercy, bound as it is between the Hebrew *hesed* and the Greek *eleos*, then it must relate just as much to the so-called covenant of works as it does to the equally misnamed covenant of grace.

## Like Father, Like Sons

A number of years ago, I was a member of what might loosely be described as a Christian rock band (the "rock" part is the loose bit). People who knew of our existence always seemed to want to pigeonhole us into some category or other. "What sort of music do you play, then?" they would ask. "Good music, I hope." "No, I mean, what particular genre would you say best describes what you do?" "Well, some songs are jazz-flavored, others are melodic rock, a couple are fairly heavy, and there's also a progressive edge to our musicianship." "Oh, so you're AOR, then?" Having for the sake of temporal placidity agreed to that one, the interrogation went on. "Do you do Chris Rea?" "No: I happen to like his material, but we write our own music and tend to play that mostly." "Is it Christian music?" And here we come to the point.

Because all six members of Dry Land were Christians, though from very different backgrounds, the music we wrote and performed together was Christian by virtue of the fact that we did so from the perspective of being in a living relationship with Christ. But that is not what the questioner meant either. What was implied was: "Does every song mention Jesus by name or perhaps some great theological truth?" Or: "Do you confront the issue of sin in the church or wax lyrical about the second coming?" Or whatever else might have been their particular pet theme for the month. Well, no we didn't, but are the same criteria used to catalogue the Psalms as being either secular or overtly Yahwistic? Of course not. What we do is Christian—within moral boundaries, of course—for no other reason than the fact that we are Christians who are doing it. The principle is valid whether you are washing the car, feeding the cat, mowing the lawn, loving your wife, bringing godly discipline to your children, singing songs, or "whatever you do [as long as you] do it all for the glory of God" (1 Cor 10:31).

By the same token, we show mercy because we are merciful. When Jesus has touched your heart, there is no need to don Christianity as a garment; it will be self-evident in your character. When the resurrected Christ is living in you, you won't feel obliged to wear a fish badge, just in case people are unable to tell the difference. The difference will be recognizable because of the change in our behavioral patterns.

In Luke's account, Jesus is recorded as having said: "Be merciful, just as your Father is merciful" (Luke 6:36). This is not so much advice to behave in such a way because that is what God would want as it is a command to continue the family trait as honorable sons. Also, its placement suggests that these words are in the form of a summary of what immediately has preceded them. From verse 27 onwards we read of loving our enemies, doing good to those who hate us, blessing those who curse us, praying for those who mistreat us, turning the other cheek to those who strike us, giving more to those who presume to take from us what does not belong to them, and generally conducting ourselves toward others in a way that we would like them to behave toward us. All of this is reviewed at the end of the passage in the context of being merciful.

Thus, a merciful disposition is hugely significant:

- it signifies the absence of a vengeful spirit (see Rom 12:19);
- it signifies a loving attitude toward those who have caused us offence (Rom 12:20–21); and
- it signifies a willingness to release forgiveness to those who seek it (Luke 23:34).

Strangely, it is only possible to exercise mercy where there is legitimate cause to be anything but merciful. The need for mercy presupposes offense and that we would otherwise be well within our rights to exact vengeance. But Scripture teaches quite clearly that part of the unwritten contract of salvation involves signing away such rights. Moreover, we are warned in the lesson of the Lord's prayer (Matt 6:12) and in the parable of the unmerciful servant (18:23–35) that our forgiveness—in some measure, at least—is dependent upon whether we have forgiven those we believe are in our debt. The seeking of mercy is not to be found on the lips of the innocent. Those who are without guilt, and yet have been found as though they were not, will plead for justice; but the man who knows he is blameworthy as charged will beg for mercy.

Neither is the expression of mercy simply a matter of doing the right thing because we know that we should, even though it might be through gritted teeth. What we do must spring from what we are; otherwise, it is just another form of deception. Perhaps the true test of whether or not our motives are pure lies in the honest answer to the following question: "Can we be merciful and keep it to ourselves or do we want to boast about it from the gallery?" be that in the course of conversation, self-congratulatory testimony from the pulpit, or—worse still—in the thinly cloaked guise of public prayer. Mercy does not need to be announced, only extended.

## The Circle of Mercy

William Hendriksen seems to suggest that the fruit cited respectively in the fifth, sixth, and seventh beatitudes are a direct consequence of the like seed being planted by God in the heart of the recipient.[23] This may well be so on the basis of Scripture's overall revelation. However, although I do not often find myself at odds with this particular commentator, it is difficult to arrive at his conclusions on the evidence of these verses in isolation. Surely, the parable of the unmerciful servant would have served Hendriksen's purpose far better in this regard. For example, had verse 7 read: "Having been shown mercy, the blessed shall thence be merciful," I could have more readily followed Hendriksen's argument without question. But the way it reads in the English translation implies that the receipt of divine mercy is, to some extent at least, governed by the precondition of being merciful.

The same principle applies to verse 8 regarding purity of heart and seeing God, and to verse 9 relating to peacemakers being identified as the sons of God. In each case, on the basis of the textual evidence, the blessing is conferred as a direct result of the condition having been met. Even if the conjunction "for" was to be understood in the sense of "on account of" instead of "as a consequence of which," this would require the tense of what follows to be changed from the future to the past: viz., "Blessed are the merciful for they have been shown mercy."

That notwithstanding, the weight of evidence elsewhere cannot be ignored. It is to be expected of Christians that they be merciful if for no other reason than it reflects the restored image of God in them. To look at the same argument negatively, mercilessness is anathema to the spirit

---

23. Hendriksen, *Matthew*, 275.

of Christ in the believer. Thus, we have here in Scripture something of a paradox: the relationship between God's mercy and human mercy is such that the latter is both the fruit of and the prerequisite to receiving the former (see also Matt 6:14–15; Jas 2:13).

Remarkably, John tells us that God forgives us not because he is merciful but because he is faithful and just (1 John 1:9). How can this be? The apostle makes it appear as if it would be an act of injustice to deny us forgiveness. Of course, the context makes it clear that this act must be preceded by confession, but the question remains: on the supposition of our confession of sin, how can divine forgiveness be perceived as a right? Simply because the price has been paid; God's mercy resolved the sin issue by providing a Savior. Thereafter, it is only just that the repentant claimant be forgiven. Thus, we see divine mercy and justice perfectly united in the reconciliation of the creature with his Creator. In the words of Mary Evans: "Mercy is not the opposite of justice—injustice is."[24]

But let us not forget the progression of the Beatitudes. To understand where we are right now in this fifth blessing, we must appreciate how far we have come in the previous four. The supernatural disposition of mercy has systematically been produced by spiritual poverty, an attitude of mourning, meekness, and a hungering and thirsting for righteousness. If it is not a contradiction in terms, for such a person to embrace all of these godly values, then to be merciful is the most supernaturally natural response imaginable. If all that has gone before is truly our experience, then can we help but be transformed in our outlook toward others? I think not. For we, more than anyone else, must know the real source of their condition and, indeed, would still be subject to it ourselves were it not for God's mercy toward us. We, too, can cry with Jesus: "Father, forgive them, for they do not know what they are doing" (Luke 23:34).

The ability to forgive is more powerful than the authority to condemn, the capacity to be merciful more potent than the charter to judge. James puts it this way: "judgment without mercy will be shown to anyone who has not been merciful. Mercy triumphs over judgment!" (Jas 2:13).

---

24. M. J. Evans. "Mercy," in Atkinson and Field, *New Dictionary of Christian Ethics*, 590.

## Summary

Perhaps the most helpful way to summarize this section is by looking at what the psalmist had to say concerning the nature of God's mercy and the conditions in which it is meted out:

> "Remember O Lord, your great mercy and love, for they are from of old" (Ps 25:6).

> "Do not withhold your mercy from me, O Lord; may your love and your truth always protect me" (Ps 40:11).

> "Have mercy on me, O God, have mercy on me, for in you my soul takes refuge. I will take refuge in the shadow of your wings until the disaster has passed" (Ps 57:1).

> "Turn to me and have mercy on me, as you always do to those who love your name" (Ps 119:132).

> "O Lord, hear my prayer, listen to my cry for mercy; in your faithfulness and righteousness come to my relief" (Ps 143:1).

## "BLESSED ARE THE PURE IN HEART..."

> "... for they will see God" (Matt 5:8).

The word "pure" as used here is the Greek *katharos*. Given that it signifies something or someone that has been cleansed rather than merely that which is clean, perhaps "purified" would be a better rendering on this occasion. Whereas *hagios* refers principally to a quality of holiness that is intrinsically resident in the divine being and/or his representatives on earth, *katharos* is indicative of the cultic or ethical rectitude in those who relate to that divine being. Thus, to be pure in this sense is to be void of any outside influence except that which comes via the Holy Spirit of God. As Roderick Finlayson puts it: "the pure heart is the undivided heart, where there is no conflict of loyalties, no cleavage of interests, no mixture of motives, no hypocrisy and no insecurity. It is wholeheartedness Godwards."[25]

---

25. R. A. Finlayson, "Purity," in Douglas, *New Bible Dictionary*, 1002.

## Kingdom

### Climb Every Mountain, But Be Prepared for the Descent

Many commentators agree to being baffled by the position of this verse in the context of the whole of the Beatitudes. That it should be included at all is not called into question, but why here? If the suggestion of a logical sequence in their order is correct, then perhaps we might be forgiven for expecting everything else to lead to this wonderful climax, the zenith of our walk. And therein, I believe, lies the key to our understanding.

As someone who enjoys little more than to be walking the fells and dales of northern England, I am convinced there is nothing under the sun to compare with the sheer beauty of seeing God's creative handiwork from the peaks of Helvellyn or Cat Bells in the Lake District, Longstone Edge or Kinder Scout in the Peak District, or even Pen-y-ghent or Attermire Scar in my own beloved Yorkshire Dales. This is especially so if I know there is to be refreshment provided at the end of the walk courtesy of Messrs. Jennings, Derventio, or Theakston. I realize, of course, that those who have tackled any of the major mountains of the world may well ridicule my sense of excitement over these comparative molehills, but I'm not in the least bit troubled by that. Depending on the weather conditions and my level of fitness on the day, the climb can be quite strenuous. But all that exertion of energy soon pales into nothingness by the splendor of the view and the prospect of a picnic somewhere on the tabletop plateau.

One can only begin to imagine the sense of awe sampled by Peter, James, and John in the company of Jesus, Moses, and Elijah on the Mount of Transfiguration (Matt 17:1–13). So much so, in fact, that they wanted to make a shrine out of it (v. 4). For us, too, the Christian journey can be such a struggle, the walk so difficult, the climb so treacherous, and the sacrifice so demanding that, having come to that place of perfect rest, we want nothing else but to sell up and set up home there permanently. But there is a descent that must be followed. Having been touched by God, we must live that blessing out experientially in the fullness of his Spirit.

When we come down from it all, the circumstances may not have changed one iota, but we will have done so. There will be those who fail to understand us, the abuse will continue to rage on, our superiors at work may maintain their policy of overlooking us for promotion, the

*Kingdom Character Attracts the King's Blessing*

school bully will continue to ill-treat us and cause public humiliation. Maybe even in the local church setting, we will be considered pseudo-spiritual or out of touch with reality. But we will have met with our God.

This is where the previous five blessings have been heading. Remember, we began with a poor spirit, which was essentially a recognition of the *im*purity of our heart. We mourned concerning our desperate plight, undertook a disposition of meekness that caused us to hunger and thirst after righteousness, which in turn produced a merciful demeanor in us toward others. We have learned to walk by God's rule, received comfort from his Holy Spirit, found in ourselves a godly compassion for the whole earth, been filled with that which we so diligently sought, welcomed God's mercy, and now find a purity of heart that allows us to view things from his perspective.

In the episode of Jesus' dialogue with Nicodemus, the following well-known, much used, and—it has to be said—commonly misunderstood phrase emerges: "You must be born again" (John 3:7). What is not immediately apparent from the text is that Jesus was clarifying his teaching earlier in the same passage, in which the following narrative unfolds:

> Now there was a man of the Pharisees named Nicodemus, a member of the Jewish ruling council. He came to Jesus at night and said, "Rabbi, we know you are a teacher who has come from God. For no one could perform the miraculous signs you are doing if God were not with him." In reply Jesus declared, *"I tell you the truth, no one can see the kingdom of God unless he is born again."* "How can a man be born when he is old?" Nicodemus asked, "Surely he cannot enter a second time into his mother's womb to be born!" Jesus answered, *"I tell you the truth, no one can enter the kingdom of God unless he is born of water and the Spirit.* Flesh gives birth to flesh, but the Spirit gives birth to spirit" (John 3:1–6).

If we are to understand the two statements of Jesus, which begin "I tell you the truth . . ." as containing effectively the same information, then we may deduce that, in relation to the kingdom of God, seeing and entering are essentially synonymous terms. Therefore, seeing God may be regarded as an idiomatic form of saying that we have entered into him.

# Kingdom

## The Heart of the Matter

Ask any group of people what their goal in life is and you would be correct to expect a number of different responses. Much will depend upon the age, background, gender, experience, social status, work environment, level of financial stability, and a whole host of other variants. Answers might include things like a secure future for their offspring, a settled retirement, a second home abroad or in a more rural setting, the wherewithal to do what they please and when they choose to do it, freedom from ill health or disease for both themselves and their partner, etc. Ask a group of Christians the same question and maybe the replies would not be so very different. The promise here, however, is that for those who are pure in heart they shall see God. This is the definitive reward, but is it our ultimate objective? As I heard one preacher put it recently: "The heart of the matter is a matter of the heart."

The ancients believed that the human heart was the core of that individual's being, out of which sprang everything else (see Prov 4:23), including the emotions, the motives, the desires, issues of loyalty, our capacity to pursue good or evil, etc. If our heart is pure, everything that emanates from it will be similarly unadulterated. On the basis of their original meaning, therefore, a legitimate paraphrase of Jesus' words might be: "Blessed are those whose core is free from impurity and corruptibility, for they shall be people of divinely-appointed vision."

Christianity is substantially to do with a response of the heart. In stark contrast to the teaching of the religious leaders of his day, Jesus resolutely affirmed a gospel that had absolutely nothing to do with external issues; it had the power to reach right down into the inner man, thus effecting radical change. Only such a deep-rooted transformation could possibly implement love for one's enemies (Matt 5:44); only by such an intensive cleansing of the heart can man conceivably hope to exercise justice, mercy, and faithfulness (Matt 23:23); and only a person who is free from any kind of impurity can weep with compassion as Jesus did (John 11:35).

You see, the Pharisees, the Sadducees, and the scribes kept the law in every detail as an external code of conduct. They tithed rigorously, fasted religiously, prayed fervently, held a mission policy second to none, and sought recognition for their office relentlessly. And yet, Jesus summed up their reward this way: "Woe to you . . . hypocrites!

## Kingdom Character Attracts the King's Blessing

You clean the outside of the cup and dish, but on the inside they are full of greed and self-indulgence . . . You are like whitewashed tombs, which look beautiful on the outside, but inside are full of dead men's bones and everything unclean . . . on the outside you appear to people as righteous, but on the inside you are full of hypocrisy and wickedness" (Matt 23:25–28).

It is interesting that the law of Moses, which the rabbis sought so enthusiastically to promote, was never intended to be interpreted in such a shallow way. Indeed, when asked by one expert for his opinion on the Torah, Jesus gave this insightful précis: "Love the Lord your God with all your heart and with all your soul and with all your strength and with all your mind . . . and love your neighbor as yourself" (Mark 12:28–31).

Israel had largely failed to understand this for centuries. So much so, in fact, that some six hundred years before Christ, the prophet Jeremiah had spoken of God establishing a new covenant that would bring about the inscribing of God's righteous law in the minds and hearts of his people (see Jer 31:31–33). It is a covenant that the apostle Paul is pleased to identify as one "not of the letter, but of the Spirit; for the letter kills, but the Spirit gives life" (2 Cor 3:6). It does so by gaining control of the heart, because God knows that when he has your heart, he also has your will, your mind, your emotions, your expressions, your actions, your relationships, your fears, your anxieties, your everything, your all.

This is why—with the greatest respect to Prime Ministers Cameron, Gillard, and Harper, Presidents Obama, Hollande, Zuma, and others of their ilk—that man's difficulties can never be solved by addressing his surroundings, status in life, social standing, or material wherewithal of any kind. The real problem the world over is man's predicament in Adam, reflected through the condition of his heart. Moreover, our first parent did not fall in the inner-city areas of London, Birmingham, or Glasgow, nor in the ghetto districts of New York, or the many sites of political unrest and instability in the Middle East, or the rice fields of communist China, or the trouble-torn provinces of South Africa, or in a poverty-stricken slum of northern India, but in Eden—the paradise of God. Man's dilemma is essentially one of the heart.

Kingdom

## Purity of Heart Governs Clarity of Vision

There is a clear allusion in this beatitude to the twenty-fourth Psalm, where David answers his own question:

> Who may ascend the hill of the Lord?
> Who may stand in his holy place?
> He who has clean hands and a pure heart,
> who does not lift up his soul to an idol or swear by what is false.
> He will receive blessing from the Lord
> and vindication from God his Savior.
> Such is the generation of those who seek him,
> who seek your face, O God of Jacob (vv. 3–6).

The fact that the psalmist links clean hands with a pure heart suggests both outward and inner holiness; the former alone is not enough. By linking it with other similar passages, William Hendriksen makes the following valid point: "Sincerity or integrity is not sufficient in and by itself. A man may be *sincerely right*, but he may also be *sincerely wrong* . . . the 'pure in heart' of Ps 73:1 are those who in all sincerity are guided by 'God's counsel' (v 24). The *faith unfeigned* of 1 Tim 1:5 adheres to 'sound doctrine' (v 10). And the people to whom Peter refers (1 Pet 1:22) are those who have purified their souls 'in obedience to the truth.'"[26]

Moreover, the fact that David identifies the blessing from God with a "generation of those who seek him" implies an age where such a pursuit, if not commonplace, will certainly belong to more than a handful of isolated individuals. They, like Jacob, will receive the blessing simply by asking for it.

Wayne Grudem defines corporate ecclesiastical purity in the following fashion: "The purity of the church is its degree of freedom from wrong doctrine and conduct, and its degree of conformity to God's revealed will for the church."[27] Although the context suggests that Dr. Grudem is looking primarily at local churches, I would have no qualms about applying the same definition to the church in its global sense. Not only so, but neither would I be disinclined to apply the same classification to individual believers on the basis that the whole comprises essentially the sum of its parts. Grudem then goes on to list twelve factors, which he asserts to be characteristic of a pure church:

26. Hendriksen, *Matthew*, 277.
27. Grudem, *Systematic Theology*, 873.

1. Biblical doctrine;
2. Proper use of the sacraments;
3. Right use of church discipline;
4. Genuine worship;
5. Effective prayer;
6. Effective witness;
7. Effective fellowship;
8. Biblical church government;
9. Spiritual power in ministry;
10. Personal holiness of life among members;
11. Care for the poor;
12. Love for Christ.[28]

Again, though Grudem makes no claims that such a catalogue is exhaustive, I would have no difficulty in anticipating similar qualities to be evident in those individuals who are deemed to be pure in heart. If these are to be perceived as traits by which a particular church's compliance to God's intended purpose might be measured, then surely the same may be said of the individual believer's conformity to his revealed will.

There is an important principle in operation here that goes much deeper than the promise for having met the condition. I would even go so far as to suggest that it is a rule in life that is always applicable. It is quite simply this: the kind of person you are dictates the object and extent of your vision. Or to put it another way: what you see will be governed by who you are. Seeing is not believing, but seeing and being are inextricably related. Thankfully, this is not necessarily a constant. Who we were last year, last month, last week, yesterday, or even an hour ago may not be precisely who we are at this moment in time.

But there is another equation that we may deduce from this beatitude. It is this: true happiness is heavenliness, but it only resides where there also exists holiness. The converse is equally true. Heavenliness is not happiness to the impure. We see a glimpse of this in the here and now. Unbelievers generally feel uncomfortable in the presence of God and those who truly represent him. In this sense, church meetings that focus

---

28. Ibid., 874.

on being "unbeliever-friendly" not only militate against their purpose, but also do a great disservice to the gospel of Christ Jesus. It is a myth to suggest that the duty of the church or its members is to "make" God relevant to the world in which it finds itself; rather, it is to demonstrate his perpetual relevance to every generation. Eschatologically, however, the presence of God will not be a place of blessing to those who have previously failed to engage with his provision of a Savior.

## Summary

To be pure in heart is to be like Jesus in thought and deed, motive, and execution. It is a heart that is free from all ungodly distraction. It is to live with the glory of God as our chief desire, set apart for his use only, that we might thereby see him (Heb 12:14). We do not see him face to face as a man, but the very conscious awareness of God's majesty enables us to perceive his prolific handiwork in the wonder of creation, in the unfolding of history, in our individual experience, and in his dealings with others. I also believe there will come a day when we shall view him personally. Now, I know that Scripture says "*every* eye will see him" (Rev 1:7), but only those who are pure in heart may expect to discover him as he really is, radiant in glory, majestic in beauty, and in the splendor of his holiness.

## "BLESSED ARE THE PEACEMAKERS . . ."

". . . for they will be called sons of God" (Matt 5:9).

If one were to ask a hundred people what a peacemaker is, I would be pleasantly surprised if a significant proportion did not refer to pacifism in their reply. By definition, a pacifist is someone who believes that war and violence of any kind are morally unjustified and that it is possible to resolve all disputes by peaceful means. I am reasonably confident that a similar definition could be attributed to the word "peacemaker." In practice, however, pacifism is more related to a philanthropic mindset that may or may not be annexed to a religious conviction. It often resorts to avoidance rather than confrontation to achieve its aims. By contrast, the kind of peacemaker of which Jesus speaks attains his or her goals by facing up to the challenges that threaten peace.

## The Peace of God in Christ

The world cries out for peace and fights towards that end, which makes about as much sense as embarking on a crusade of promiscuity in the name of chastity. But billions of pounds sterling, US dollars, Russian rubles, Japanese yen, South African rand, and Euros, are spent discussing tactics, devising strategies, and employing safeguards to global peace. And yet, the Bible says of those behind such schemes: "The way of peace they do not know; there is no justice in their paths. They have turned them into crooked roads; no one who walks in them will know peace" (Isa 59:8).

So, what kind of person is a peacemaker in the sense implied here by Jesus? Well, in the logical progression we have followed, he must be a man who is poor in spirit, has mourned his condition before God, is of meek disposition, hungers and thirsts after righteousness, is merciful, and pure in heart. Only one who has a proper view of himself, others, and his Creator can truly bring the peace of God. Part of the function of bringing that peace to a situation may incorporate the execution of godly judgment. This will call for impartiality, wisdom, integrity, spiritual insight, and righteous counsel. If such an individual has any subjective involvement at all in the issues at stake, then he or she must not allow self-interest to dictate the course of action being proposed. This may often necessitate personal sacrifice.

As an adjective, the word "peacemaker(s)" occurs only twice in the whole of the New Testament (Matt 5:9; Jas 3:18). In the original Greek, it appears as a compound of a noun (*eirene*) and a verb (*poieo*). Taken together, they simply mean "to make peace." Although it sounds so obvious that it should require no further explanation, peacemakers should be known by their fruit, that is, that they have effected peace. The point is this: they are not those who merely find dispeace distasteful, or try to bring a peaceful resolution to a particularly hostile situation, nor indeed pray fervently for that to become real, but that they are successful in their quest.

Where the Greek word *hesuchios* denotes peaceable or the capacity to be at and live in peace, there is a more conciliatory tone to *eirenopios*, as used here. Understood in this sense, peace is much more than the negation of conflict; it is the positive bringing about of rapport. As such, it involves both removing the tares of discord and sowing the seeds

# Kingdom

of harmony. Not satisfied with sustaining amicable relationships, nor merely freedom from aggression, peacemakers actually take the initiative to produce an effect that is otherwise absent. They step in where hostility exists and perpetuate a change in the conditions, which occasions an environment of peace. Francis Foulkes makes the interesting point that: "In classical Greek, *eirene* had a primarily negative force; but by the way of the [Septuagint], the word in the N[ew] T[estament] has the full content of the O[ld] T[estament] *salom* and nearly always carries a spiritual connotation. The breadth of its meaning is especially apparent from its linking with such keywords as grace . . . righteousness . . . and from its use in benedictions."[29] Foulkes' use of the phrase "negative force" probably relates to its use almost entirely in the context of a direct contrast with war or the consequential outcome of the termination of war.

What an overwhelming sense of astonishment it must have been to the original Jewish hearers of this verse! As I have noted elsewhere, the prevailing interpretation of the Hebrew Scriptures had conditioned their messianic expectations in such a way as to anticipate a radical militant, who would overthrow the ruling power of Rome by uniting the scattered remnant of Israel in martial conquest against their oppressors. They envisaged Christ as a rival king to Caesar, whose political tract would be littered with tactics of warfare. Cue Jesus promoting a gospel of peace. How could this be? Simply because man's logic, his rationale, his powers of reason and understanding, even at their very best, are ill-equipped to fathom the most elementary truths concerning God (see Isa 55:8). Spiritual comprehension calls for spiritual discernment and it is available only to those who have "the mind of Christ" (1 Cor 2:10–11).

## Peace Is Not Wrought Independently

In the previous section, we noted that the pure in heart shall see God. Here, it must be observed, that the primary cause of difference of opinion, dispeace, conflict, enmity, and war is essentially a selfish disposition exacerbated by an impure heart. However, the peace we have in mind here should not be understood in terms of inactivity (see Acts 9:31), though that may well be the image most of us conjure up when we crave peace and quiet. But Jesus did not say: "Blessed are the peace lovers," from which we might have inferred those who are content to sit

---

29. F. Foulkes, "Peace," in Douglas, *New Bible Dictionary*, 902.

around and wait for peaceful resolutions somehow to appear. No, the blessing is promised to those who enthusiastically engage in bringing that resolution to pass.

By embracing the biblical presentation of what is meant by peace, it is not quite so unreasonable to propose that sometimes it can only be achieved by confrontation. Surely this is what Jesus had in mind when he counseled the disciples about the best possible way to deal with those who would seek to sow seeds of discord (Matt 18:15–19). Peace is not the product of compromise, for truth should not be sacrificed in its attainment. Nor should it be confused with a truce, which is basically an agreement to disagree. True peace without justice and righteousness is also an impossible objective.

Moreover, the kind of peace that ignores or fails to address the underlying issues of unrest is not what Scripture calls peace at all; it only maintains the *status quo* at best, which is clearly unacceptable. All such a strategy can ever hope to achieve is appeasement, papering over the cracks, while under the surface lies a volcano just waiting to erupt. This is because—exactly as in the case of the other Beatitudes—we are dealing here with the transformation of the inner man, not simply the control of one's temper while on the inside you quietly rage. Neither is it the avoidance of unresolved concerns that still cause inner turmoil whenever you recollect the hurtful way that a brother treated you or a refusal to discuss long-standing difficulties in the vain hope that your silence will eventually erase the memory of your sister's insensitivity.

Arguably the most important principle to observe when seeking to bring counsel is to tame the tongue. From my experience, this is true of Christians in general, but it would appear to be especially so of those who study diligently. They often seem to feel that it is their mission in life to share the knowledge they have acquired to every unsuspecting soul who has the good fortune to cross their path. Give them a platform to do so in the guise of offering wholesome advice and there is no stopping them, irrespective of whether or not what they have to say has the remotest bearing on the problem being raised. The very first time you pause for breath and they are in, like a dog with a bone.

By the time they have finished, you are probably left wondering whether they have really understood the nature of the difficulty you face at all. What began as a minor irritation has now become so enlarged that "It has something to do with how you were treated as a child," or "It's the product of a dodgy relationship you had in your teenage years," or "A demon has got hold of you, brother." By now, you feel totally drained, utterly useless, completely unworthy, and are probably thinking to yourself: "Was I ever really a Christian, anyway?" "Everyone should be quick to listen [and] slow to speak," says James (1:19), as a prelude to his more detailed discourse in chapter 3 on the potency of this unruly member, the tongue. These sentiments are, of course, echoed in the book of Proverbs, where we are reminded that: "The tongue has the power of life and death" (18:21), with apparently no measure or degrees in between (see also 10:19; 20:19).

If Paul's counsel to the believers at Corinth is anything to go by, the peace of God, at least, seems to be antonymous with confusion (see 1 Cor 14:33). Thus, it may be regarded, at least partly, as the bringing of order where previously there was only chaos and disturbance. It is surely not without reason that, in his personification of wisdom, the writer of the Proverbs can say: "Her ways are pleasant ways, and all her paths are peace" (3:17).

Bringing peace and maintaining peace are very different propositions. It might even be argued that the only basis for lasting peace in any meaningful way is for the situation to be subject to the God of peace. Because conditions of conflict do not exist outside of an environment of unhealthy desires (see Jas 4:1–2), the capacity to bring peace, embrace peace, and enjoy a sustained period of peace lies essentially with our willingness to commit our passions to Jesus, the Prince of peace.

## Genetically Inherent

It should also be noted that the blessing is not so much in the identification as it is in the implied recognition. What do I mean by that? Well, it is quite simply this: I may walk along the street outside my home, see a stray cat, and call it a dog, but it does not for that reason make it so. What registers with me that enables me to identify it as a cat is that I recognize in it traits that are not only common in cats, but in some cases they are exclusively so. Being called "sons of God" is a blessing because it carries with it the implication that there are certain characteristics—in this case, the ability to bring peace—that are instantly recognizable as belonging to those who are sons of God.

Although the idea of linking peace and divine sonship is not unique to the New Testament, it is here—because it is in Christ—where it finds fulfillment. The so-called "priestly blessing," commanded to be given to the Israelites by Aaron and his sons, is especially worthy of our attention in this regard: "'The Lord bless you and keep you; the Lord make his face shine upon you and be gracious to you; the Lord turn his face toward you and give you peace.' So they will put my name on the Israelites, and I will bless them" (Num 6:24–27).

The word "sons," as used in this beatitude by Jesus, is the Greek *huios*. According to Vine: "It primarily signifies the relation of offspring to parent [and is] often used of prominent moral characteristics and without reference to gender."[30] In the New Testament, the word *huios* is usually employed in one of five distinct ways:

- it is used uniquely of Christ's relationship to the Father (see Matt 16:16; Rom 8:32; 1 John 5:5);
- it is used in the natural sense of a male progeny (e.g., Matt 13:55; Acts 1:13; Heb 11:17);
- it appears in relation to Paul and Timothy/Titus to denote the sense of spiritually paternal responsibility and affection (1 Cor 4:17; Phil 2:22; 1 Tim 1:2; Titus 1:4);
- it can signify a change in relationship (Gal 4:7); and
- it is used in a figurative way to demonstrate apparently shared character traits (see Mark 3:17; John 12:36; Acts 4:36).

When contrasting the acts of the sinful nature with the fruit of the Spirit, the apostle Paul reminds his Galatian readership that the kind of peace that God intends is only accessible by those "who belong to Christ [and] have crucified the sinful nature with its passions and desires" (see Gal 5:19–24). Whether intentionally or otherwise, the imagery used here by Paul is reminiscent of Isaiah's prophetic message of a spirit being poured out on high so that the wilderness becomes a fruitful field, wherein reside justice, righteousness, and peace (Isa 32:15–17). Walter Hansen is probably correct to insist that: "Peace is . . . the result of relationships built by loving service."[31] By identifying peace as a spiritual fruit, Paul demonstrates that it runs counter to fallen human nature, but fits perfectly with the restored pre-lapsarian Adamic nature, Adam being the first "son" of God amongst men. Only those who have known

---

30. Vine, *Expository Dictionary*, 1060.
31. Hansen, *Galatians*, 179.

# Kingdom

God's peace can thence resolve to bring solutions to real or potentially hostile situations. Thus, "peace-possessors" become peacemakers.[32]

Therefore, we shall be called children of God insofar as we display the fruit of our sonship. People of God behave in a certain way because of their spiritual parentage. We are peacemakers because our heavenly Father is the "God of peace" (1 Thess 5:23; Heb 13:20). And here, once again, we see the principle of sowing and reaping in operation: it is as much a spiritual law in the realm of bringing peace as it is in being merciful, giving to the needy, showing love and displaying kindness, gentleness, and godly restraint. For "peacemakers who sow in peace" are promised "a harvest of righteousness" (Jas 3:18). Conversely—and if I might be allowed to posit a lateral idea for a moment—if those who are peacemakers are encouraged to anticipate the privilege of being acknowledged as sons of God, what might the reward be of those who are habitual "peacebreakers"?

## Summary

Our understanding of the word "peacemaker" has become somewhat muddied by its constant misuse in the political arena. Government spokespersons and international ambassadors are often referred to as peacemakers when, in actual fact, they often bring little more than resolutions of mutual tolerance through compromise. The peace that God intends is far weightier than the *status quo* achieved by the negotiation of anti-combat agreements. Indeed, this sort of peace can only be obtained in and through Christ. As we embrace this for ourselves in the home, in our schools, places of employment, and across cultural, social, religious, and ethnic divides, it will become clear to others that we are not seeking to reduce individual manifestos to their lowest common denominator, any more than Jesus did in Palestine. But by following his pattern, we bear the hallmarks of our sonship, the spiritual characteristics of our heavenly Father.

---

32. See Hendriksen, *Galatians*, 224.

## "BLESSED ARE THOSE WHO ARE PERSECUTED BECAUSE OF RIGHTEOUSNESS . . ."

". . . for theirs is the kingdom of heaven" (Matt 5:10).

It is worthy of note, as we come to the last of these beatitudes, that whereas the previous seven deal with the blessing of God upon those who conduct themselves in a certain way, this one places the emphasis upon how such people are likely to be treated by others. Although it is true that their persecution is for taking a stand in favor of righteousness, the progression we have observed throughout implies that this follows immediately from the fact that they are peacemakers. How interesting! The world relentlessly pleads for peace, heads of government debate it endlessly, vast sums of money are spent researching its viability, but as soon as the Christian man or woman uncovers the real cost of true peace, they thereby expose themselves to oppression and victimization.

### Persecution Is a Reality

The meaning of the Greek *dioko*, translated "persecuted," is to pursue with the purpose of causing to take flight. The precise word used here, however, is *dediogmenoi*, which is the perfect passive participle, indicative of prolonged endurance under persecution. Luke's account seems to amplify the meaning somewhat: "Blessed are you when men hate you, when they exclude you and insult you and reject your name as evil, because of the Son of Man. Rejoice in that day and leap for joy, because great is your reward in heaven. For that is how their fathers treated the prophets" (Luke 6:22–23).

In typically Hebrew idiomatic fashion, Jesus' discourse of the Beatitudes ends where it began: with the promise of the kingdom. However, the correct application of contextual hermeneutics demands that we extend our scope a little further, as verses 11 and 12 expand on the idea conveyed by verse 10. There are, of course, many lessons that could be gleaned from these few verses alone, but I would like to draw your attention to just three:

- both here and in Luke's account it is made clear that the harsh treatment is based upon an unwarranted premise; the accusations are falsely posited (cf. Luke 6:22; 1 Pet 3:16);

Kingdom

- although not a direct translation here, the usual Greek word for "speak evil against" is a compound from which we derive our English verb "blaspheme." Thus, the object of such calumny is not necessarily God himself;
- Jesus alludes here to a charge he will later lay at the door of the religious leaders of his day: such persecution is characteristic of a prophetic lifestyle (see also Luke 23:37).

As a very young Christian, my mental embracing of the concept of persecution was governed by my limited experience at the time. I was almost seventeen years old, had been birthed into a very traditional Pentecostal church family, had been brought up by grandparents who held conventional values of morality, and was apprenticed to a local colliery. The kind of persecution I knew consisted of little more than being called "holy Joe," being told that my "obsession" was just a passing adolescent phase, and being laughed at for carrying a Bible through a small West Yorkshire mining town on a Sunday. Persecution? "Bring it on," I thought naively. I must confess that I have not encountered much more in terms of intensity in the almost forty years since those days. But Luke's use of defining verbs makes it all the more real somehow. Let us see what Vine has to say of them:

| "hate" | – | *miseo* | – | malicious and unjustifiable feelings toward others; |
| "exclude" | – | *aphorizo* | – | the separation of believers by unbelievers; |
| "insult" | – | *oneidizo* | – | to reproach, to defame, or to upbraid; |
| "reject" | – | *ekballo* | – | to cast out/from/forth.[33] |

It is estimated that during the course of the last two millennia, something in the region of seventy million believers have been put to death for their faith in Christ. That works out at around one hundred for every single day, or 35,000 per year. What is perhaps even more startling is that approximately two-thirds of these have occurred in the last century. These figures are taken from the statistical findings of Italian journalist Antonio Socci, who presented them to a conference in May

---

33. See Vine, *Expository Dictionary*, 164, 528, 954, 1017.

## Kingdom Character Attracts the King's Blessing

2002 at the Regina Apostolorum Pontifical Athenaeum in Rome, under the heading "*I Nuovi Perseguitati*" (that is, "The New Persecuted"). In his report, Socci identified a number of countries where the persecution of Christians is currently at its fiercest. They include the Molucca islands of Indonesia, Bangladesh, India, Nigeria, East Timor, Cuba, the former Soviet Republics, Saudi Arabia and surrounding lands, Vietnam, and China, with Sudan heading the list. He concluded that the attack is spearheaded chiefly by Communist forces and militant Islam.

But the persecution of Christians is not instigated by unbelievers exclusively. Scripture, the testimony of church history, and personal experience all demonstrate that the most severe persecutors of the people of God have been the advocates of organized religion. Consider Moses, constantly at odds with the children of Israel; or Gideon, much maligned by his own townspeople; or Samuel, rejected in favor of a king who would lead by natural strength and earthly understanding; or David, who suffered rebellion from within his own ranks, even from among his own sons; or Elijah, whose refusal to adopt the gods of other nations earned him royal rebuke; or Jeremiah, hated because he declined to go with the flow of Israel's complacency.

Now think of Jesus. His whole life was perhaps best summed up in one brief statement by the thief on the cross: "This man has done nothing wrong" (Luke 23:41). And yet, the religious leaders would not rest until he was done away with. Why was that? Because light will always expose the deeds of darkness and, therefore, evoke feelings of animosity and hatred. Righteousness cannot help but reveal wickedness. We all like to believe we are making a pretty good go of it when everyone else seems to be failing at a similar level. As soon as we see the righteous standard of God, however, and realize how far short of that we fall, then it will either cause us to repent or—as is more often the case—cry out: "Away with this man! Crucify him!" (vv. 18–20).

### Triumph in the Midst of Adversity

Regarding the progression from the previous verse, Donald Carson has this to say: "It is no accident that Jesus should pass from peacemaking to persecution, for the world enjoys its cherished hates so much that the peacemaker is not always welcome. Opposition is a normal mark of being a disciple of Jesus, as normal as hungering for righteousness or being merciful."[34]

However, there are those within what may be described under the general umbrella of Christendom who believe that any form of suffering is the product of a divinely-appointed decree of punitive judgment. Sadly, my late mother fell victim to this kind of mindset almost thirty years ago. She finally succumbed to the ravages of cancer in 1984, and there were still those who claimed that her plight was partly self-inflicted. Only weeks before her death, one self-acclaimed "prophet" accused her of unconfessed sin, his only evidence being the condition of her health. His motive—he claimed—was to rid her of the shackles that were causing offense to the Almighty. I wonder what he and those of his ilk would make of verses like this. Perhaps the irony of Job's "friends" is lost on them. Of course, my mother's prolonged suffering could hardly be described as persecution because of righteousness but neither was it punishment because of unrighteousness.

A similar mentality was equally prevalent during first-century Palestine. William Hendriksen makes the point well: "The impression upon those whom Jesus was addressing must have been tremendous, for it was rather a common idea among Jews that all suffering, including persecution, was an indication of God's displeasure and of the special wickedness of the one thus afflicted. Christ here reverses this view, but only with respect to those who endured persecution for the sake of righteousness (verse 10), himself (verse 11), the kingdom of heaven (19:12)."[35]

Imagine the apostle Paul eavesdropping on a present-day preacher extolling the virtues of "positive Jesus-hood." Here you have a man who worked hard, had been in prison frequently, had been flogged severely, was exposed to death many times, was beaten, lashed, and stoned on several occasions, shipwrecked three times, in constant danger, and inwardly burned with temptation (2 Cor 11:23–29). What is more, he considered all of that to be just "light and momentary troubles" (2 Cor 4:17). Now try giving that as a list of expectations at the end of your Sunday evening appeal, and I can almost guarantee that the hands will go down far more quickly than they went up.

---

34. Carson, *Matthew*, 135.
35. Hendriksen, *Matthew*, 280.

## Kingdom Character Attracts the King's Blessing

The gospel of non-commitment and little involvement may attract more members numerically, but only integrity will produce disciples. Surely, that is the ultimate objective of the kingdom of God. To be quite frank, the kind of triumphalism that prevails in some quarters under the assumed banner of Christianity deserves all the bad publicity it inevitably attracts. The victory of which my Bible speaks is one to be enjoyed in the midst of adversity; we overcome not because there is no wickedness in attendance, but we do so right at the very core of evil's domain.

The co-existence of more than one sphere of rule makes their clashing not only possible but unavoidable. The most helpful way I have found to understand it better is to think of a diagram containing two pairs of circles. One pairing is concentric, that is, they share the same center. As long as this fact remains constant, it is impossible for them to collide. If they do so, it is because one—or both—of them has moved off center. Now think of the other pairing. Their centers are not identical. Although there is no risk while they are kept well apart, the closer they become the higher the potential for their clashing. If the two eccentric circles represent the kingdom of God and that of Satan respectively, then the hazard is increased incalculably.

Any apostle, prophet, evangelist, pastor, teacher, vicar, priest, bishop, brother, or any other such dignitary who ever spoke of the Christian experience without making room for the likelihood of suffering/hardship/persecution needs to expand their vocabulary by at least those three words.

### The Prize Is Worth the Price

Persecution, whether endured individually or corporately, can take many forms. It may involve physical aggression (Acts 16:22), slanderous accusations (Dan 6:23), mocking and insults (2 Kgs 2:23), threatening intimidation (Neh 6:1–9), personal ostracism (Jer 11:19–21; 12:6), and, for some, maybe even imprisonment (Acts 5:17–18), exile (Rev 1:9), or death (Acts 7:54–60). Although it may sound too trite to speak thus, the type and intensity is of little real relevance. What surely matters is how we deal with it. We are not called to be fearful (1 John 4:18), vengeful (Rom 12:14), retaliatory (Luke 6:27–31), easily dissuaded (Mark 4:3–6, 16, 17), dispassionate (Rev 3:14–16), or unfaithful (Matt

Kingdom

26:56), but simply to endure (Eph 6:13). How is this possible? Well, Paul gives what I believe to be a vital clue in his letter to the brothers at Rome: "I consider that our present sufferings are not worth comparing with the glory that will be revealed in us" (Rom 8:18). Notice that the apostle is not saying that he has weighed up the pros and cons of each side and discovered that the coming glory just wins out, or even that it overwhelmingly does so. No, he dismisses the argument altogether as one not even worthy of his effort.

Although it would be difficult to prove by anything other than circumstantial evidence, it does seem that there is some commensurate link between piety and persecution. Anything more than a cursory glance at the historical records reveals that those Christians who have faced the greatest danger have usually also been its most exemplary ambassadors. Within a generation of Paul's counsel to the believers at Rome, the city had witnessed Christian persecution on a scale previously unimagined. Nero used Christians as human torches to illuminate his private gardens, some were forced to watch their own body parts being roasted in front of them, while others were sown into the carcasses of wild animals before being set upon by dogs. Today the level of barbarism may not be quite so intense, but it has been claimed that many of the estimated millions of Chinese Christians have been subjected to hard labor in recent years.[36] Their crime? To love Jesus above all else. Their reward? The kingdom of heaven.

As we saw earlier, the ethos of a righteous character as recorded here by the Lord is to be like him, that is, to attain Christlikeness. It is not something that I must strive to become so much as simply to allow him to dictate every course of action in me and through me. That being acknowledged, we should not only be unsurprised if persecution comes our way, nor even expect it from time to time, but the clear indication of the New Testament is such that if we are conducting ourselves in accordance with its principles, then persecution is inescapable.

If in any doubt regarding the veracity of such a statement, then consider the following words of Jesus to his disciples, and note particularly the setting. He had just spent some time emphasizing the importance of abiding in him as branches to the vine, with his Father as the gardener, and is about to give more detail on the role of the coming Holy Spirit in their lives, when he says this: "If the world hates you, keep in mind that

---

36. Shea, *Lion's Den*, 58.

it hated me first. If you belonged to the world, it would love you as its own. As it is, you do not belong to the world, but I have chosen you out of the world. That is why it hates you. Remember the words I spoke to you: 'No servant is greater than his Master.' If they persecuted me, they will persecute you also" (John 15:18–20). To which Martyn Lloyd-Jones adds his scholarly voice: "If you try to imitate Christ, the world will praise you; if you become Christlike, it will hate you."[37]

A little time later, as if to reinforce the idea in their thinking, he told them quite bluntly: "In this world you will have trouble. But," significantly more than a crumb of comfort, "take heart! I have overcome the world" (16:33). The other New Testament writers were no less transparent on the matter (see 2 Cor 12:10; Heb 12:7; Jas 5:13; 1 Pet 4:12). It might even be argued that the Scripture writers' insistence upon citing this hallmark of a person's genuineness of faith was in part instigated by the potential for distorting the message in order to circumvent persecution.

Much of the time when Christians speak of a desire to become more Christlike, they do so in the hope of imitating his serenity, his fruitfulness, his prayerfulness, his miraculous capabilities, his understanding of the human psyche, his oratory prowess, or any other feature that would appeal to our feeble sense of power and comfortability. When Jesus spoke of us becoming like him, however, it meant something radically different. It included things like taking up our cross to follow him (Luke 9:23), ridding ourselves of all that might seek to take the Father's place in our affections (Matt 19:23), looking to minister to the needs of others, even when it militates against our natural desires (Matt 8:18–22), refusing to draw from our God-given resources if to do so would be against his will or to promote selfish ambition (Luke 4:1–13), being denied by our family and friends in our hour of need (John 7:5; 18:15–18, 25–27), and in some way, however mystical or real, to share in his sufferings (Phil 3:10).

## Summary

No one could possibly accuse Jesus of not being upfront about the Christian life and what to expect from it. Many who present the "gospel" in our own day do so by portraying it as an almost Utopian idealism,

37. Lloyd-Jones, *Studies in the Sermon on the Mount*, 137.

where every demon is rendered totally ineffective, where all problems miraculously and dramatically dissipate, where believers suddenly become immune to health problems, marriages are immediately guaranteed to work with little effort on our part, children cannot conceivably fail at school, and life in general becomes just one ethereal experience after another. In stark contrast, Jesus told it as it really is.

## SUMMARY

The overarching theme of the Beatitudes/macarisms is one of inner happiness as a direct consequence of godly benevolence. This is why its message is so ageless. Men still yearn to be blessed, and there is nothing inherently wrong with that desire, even for a Christian (see 1 Chr 4:10). In fact, children of God should be the happiest people on the face of the earth. And yet, many seem so bereft of life, so woeful in appearance, so perennially tragic in their experience that one might be forgiven for believing in the doctrine of baptism by immersion in lemon juice or caustic soda.

Society appears to be constantly inventing ways to be happy, almost at the same rate that it finds them to be unsatisfying. Today's fad and fashion accessory is fast becoming tomorrow's antique, fit only to be relegated to the attic of disappointment. Computer graphics, high-profile business enterprise, the music industry, career orientation, sexual promiscuity, and many other avenues of similar ilk promise today's generation of pleasure-seekers yet another adrenaline fix and, with it, a momentary happiness buzz. "But," says Jesus, "true happiness that will last beyond today can never be attained outside of God, and this is the way." The root of being happy is not conduct; that is its fruit. Its root is character. The writer of the Proverbs says: "A man's gift makes room for him and brings him before great men" (Prov 18:16, NASB). This is quite true, but only a man of godly character will make the best use of such an introduction. What we do and say essentially springs from who we are, not *vice versa*.

The Beatitudes of Matthew chapter 5 are an inversion of society's values. Where the non–Christian mocks the poor in spirit, God says: "You are blessed"; where the unconverted would seek to trample the meek under foot, God says: "You are blessed"; even though the ungodly dismiss those who pursue personal righteousness as uncool, outdated, and sad, God says: "You are blessed."

There is nothing in the list that would appeal to carnality. Status, pride, arrogance, public approval, and self-expression are all thankfully conspicuous by their absence. In their place, we read about humility, meekness, mercy, purity of heart, and righteousness. Why? Because they belong to different realms. One is of the princedom of this world, the other is of the kingdom of heaven; upon the throne of the first is self as the regent of the devil, while the rightful ruler of the second is God himself. The government of Christ is the realm over which he reigns. If we belong to this kingdom, then its King is our Master.

If you were to ask someone who has no personal relationship with Christ to evaluate the Christian ethic, you would probably find "kindness" to be their response, or "charitable works," or maybe "to avoid moral evil," or perhaps simply "those who go to church regularly." Enquire of Jesus how best we might express our allegiance to him and he would doubtless say: "By this shall all men know that you are my disciples, if you love one another" (John 13:35). "And what kind of character will most amply produce this, Lord?" "Just read Matthew chapter 5, verses 3–10."

# 3

# Lessons from Jesus' Parables of the Kingdom

THE MEANING OF THE Greek word *parabole* is literally to place "one thing beside another with a view to comparison."[1] Although the idea is expressed in the Old Testament (*parabole* being employed consistently in the Septuagint to translate the Hebrew *masal*), it is to the pages of the New Testament that we must turn to find its fuller use.

Although it must be readily admitted that there are some features that are commonly shared by a parable and an allegory, it should also be conceded that these are far outweighed by their differences. Whereas a parable essentially demonstrates but one truth or theme, an allegory typically contains more elaborate detail. Usually, an allegory is not confined to reality but is the product of its author's imagination in order to convey a number of concepts simultaneously. Given that its details are subject to the writer's fancy, each facet can be constructed to suit a particular role in relation to the whole. By contrast, however, a parable is normally taken from an everyday occurrence and so its finer points are more often than not merely incidental. It seems clear, therefore, that to allegorize the parables of the New Testament is to invest them with meaning that is alien to their original purpose.

It must also be noted that no single parable presents the whole message that they corporately seek to convey. Though there is immense gospel value in the parable of the lost son (Luke 15:11–32), and much can be learned from the tale of the good Samaritan about proper Christian virtue (Luke 10:30–37), we must be careful not to afford more

---

1. Vine, *Expository Dictionary*, 830.

*Lessons from Jesus' Parables of the Kingdom*

significance to the parables than God intended. Parables are like arrows: they have but a single point, the details being simply feathers that add balance, weight, and direction. The parable of the laborers in the vineyard, for example, is principally a comparison between the beneficence of the paymaster and the goodness of God; it was never meant to advise on business management techniques or pay structures (see Matt 20:1–16).

The purpose behind Jesus' use of parables seems to be commonly misunderstood. It is often regarded that he spoke to the crowds in order that they might more readily comprehend the matters of which he spoke. Such an argument is often presented in terms of him simplifying spiritual issues for the easy digestion of the natural mind. The fact that on a number of occasions he was required to explain their meaning to his closest disciples, however, appears to negate this particular theory. There is something undeniably enigmatic about many of Jesus' parabolic stories, almost as if the truth of them was intentionally cloaked in riddle form to test the resolve of those who claimed genuine interest in discovering their secrets.[2]

## SOWING AND REAPING

During the course of the past thirty-odd years as a Christian, I have probably heard more sermons or illustrative allusions to the parables of the sower and that of the wheat and tares than any other. I would imagine that to be the experience of many others in a similar position. Despite this fact, it is difficult to remember more than a handful of such occasions when the teaching became elevated to any status much higher than one might expect to be addressed to a Sunday school audience. It is not easy to explain why this might be. Perhaps I have just been incredibly unfortunate. My recollection, however, seems to suggest that preachers of my acquaintance have largely—though not exclusively—failed to identify the kingdom nature of these parables. There are a number of possible reasons for this, the two that immediately spring to mind being ignorance and fear. I trust that what follows will be subject to neither.

---

2. See Grant and Freedman, *Secret Sayings*, 120–2.

Kingdom

## The Parable of the Sower

We begin our consideration of the kingdom parables with that of the sower and the seed. We do so not only because it is presented first in the Matthean account, but also because Jesus hinted at its key significance (see Mark 4:13). Not only is an understanding of this parable elementary to our appreciation of other parables, the message it contains is basic to the Christian walk. The essence of that message is this: though there are a number of possible ways to respond to the message of the kingdom, only one can be expected to be truly productive in the long term.

By employing a scenario that would have been all too familiar to many of his agriculturally-conscious listeners, Jesus was effectively saying that it is the condition of the soil that determines the fruitfulness—or otherwise—of the crop being planted. Translating this to the explanation of the parable, the condition of the individual human heart governs the fertility of what is sown there. William Hendriksen identifies the four soil types thus:

| i) | the path | (Mark 4:14–15) | unresponsive hearts; |
|---|---|---|---|
| ii) | rocky places | (vv. 5–6, 16–17) | impulsive hearts; |
| iii) | thorny ground | (vv. 7, 18–19) | preoccupied hearts; and |
| iv) | good soil | (vv. 8, 20) | responsive hearts.[3] |

The apparent ease in understanding the parable of the sower and the soils is arguably the enemy of our fuller appreciation of its message. After all, Jesus' interpretation is recorded for us, so what else could there possibly be for us to know? The clue, I believe, lies in that short intermediary passage between the telling of the parable and its elucidation (Matt 13:10–17). Here, Jesus explains why he chooses to speak in parabolic form, while at the same time suggesting that there is a distinction to be made between those who remain satisfied with what can be gleaned from a casual enquiry and others who are so hungry for the truth that they are prepared to search more diligently. Sadly, too many preachers of my acquaintance belong to the former category.

When Jesus uttered these words he was addressing his closest followers, those who had spent time with him not just as part of the

---

3. Hendriksen, *Mark*, 156–60.

## Lessons from Jesus' Parables of the Kingdom

crowds but sufficiently close to establish an intimate relationship with him. It was these he identified as those who had been given the secrets of the kingdom of heaven. Surely, he was referring to the kingdom of God personified, that is, encapsulated within his own person. Those who had been impressed merely with his oratory skills, amazed at his capacity to feed multitudes from a small boy's lunchbox, or mesmerized by his ability to bring health, healing, and sanity to the diseased, disfigured, and distressed could not hope to understand. Their own satisfaction was the stumbling block to such insight. This kind of understanding cannot come through verbal instruction, theological study, or the captivating drama of biographical works; it is to be found only in and through Christ.

Exegetical expertise that makes little or no room for practical application is of little or no kingdom use. It is often claimed that if theologians (in the sense of those familiar with biblical doctrine) spent less time with their noses in books and more with their feet on the ground and/or their hands in their wallets, then they might achieve far more for the kingdom. This may well be true of some, perhaps even the majority. But I also thank God for the many of my acquaintance who realize that understanding and application are not mutually exclusive concepts.

As for the parable of the sower, it seems to provide some explanation as to why there are relatively so few who attain a reasonable level of understanding the Scriptures, and, similarly, those who have found the capacity to demonstrate its power to the benefit of both themselves and others appear to be in the minority. Immediate disdain for the truth of the gospel is obviously not the way forward. But shallow ideals that will not stand up under pressure and verbal confessions that are biblically unsound will not suffice either. The genuineness of the receiving is not necessarily in question, nor is the quality of the seed in doubt. No, the difference made to its fruitfulness is dependent entirely upon the fertility of the soil.

I have often heard it taught that the four different soil types are indicative of four different kinds of people. The interpretation given by Jesus certainly lends some credence to such an exposition. However, they might also—and possibly more forcibly—represent four different responses to God's revealed will. "What is the difference?" you may well ask. Well, it is quite simply this: I, as an individual, might experience any or all of the responses at different times, depending upon the status of my walk at that particular time. If my current experience is one of lukewarmness, then I might not be as receptive to God's word as I was eighteen months ago. Equally, if I pay due attention to my present condition, I might be more responsive to the same word six months hence. Emil Brunner puts it this way: "Soil is what it is, but man, in the eyes of God is called to decide for himself. The four-fold field denotes not four different human dispositions, but four different human decisions, all of which are latent in us."[4]

Of course, this is not to imply that the obvious must concede all ground to what might be described as the obscure or that I am proposing we view the matter in a way that denigrates the sovereignty of God. I am merely suggesting that we make room for the possibility of interpretations beyond the superficial. Hardness of heart is not the exclusive domain of the unsaved; it can equally become the experience of those who were once sufficiently pliable to allow the gospel to penetrate their outer reaches but have now become impervious to the pleas of their needy neighbor, indifferent to the plight of the unreached, and generally quite detached from the advance of the kingdom in society.

Instantaneous enthusiasm is so linked to self-gratification as to be almost synonymous. The true test is in what it produces in the longer term. To be captivated by oratory eloquence or swept along by the euphoria of the megachurch congregation with arms aloft singing praises to God can be experiences that last long in the memory. Their true value, however, can only be gauged in terms of whether they provide the catalyst for subsequent growth and productivity. Otherwise, they were but moments of joy that we occasionally have cause to remember with some degree of fondness.

Even seed falling among thorns can be a daily experience for some. We must be walking faithfully, mustn't we? After all, we rise early every morning to engage with God's word and wrestle in prayer before breakfast. We feel that our "quiet times" alone with God before the bustle begins will so set us up for the day that we must simply breeze through its trials. The reality, however, is often that all is forgotten before lunchtime, as the pressures of driving through congested traffic, trying to contact the gas supplier by phone for the umpteenth time, queuing (im)patiently at the post office while dear old Mrs. Hargreaves counts out every loose copper from her purse for that special edition book of

4. Brunner, *Sowing and Reaping*, 14.

*Lessons from Jesus' Parables of the Kingdom*

twelve stamps sporting images of yesteryear's literary giants, and then getting sprayed by last night's rainfall as every passing motorist appears to take great delight at aiming for that part of you that is singularly unprotected. Sometimes, before you have even had the opportunity to put the kettle on for morning coffee, the cares of this life have choked out of you what seemed immovable only a few short hours earlier.

But then there are those who are not hearers of the word only, but doers also. Not content with nodding their agreement or acknowledging mental assent, those who receive instruction as good soil submit themselves fully to the leading of the Lord and to the prompting of his Spirit. To be known as faithfully obedient is reward enough, but a further promise is made to them: that their assiduousness shall yield manifold fruit. Just as the product of the sown grain is yet more grain, so the fruit of sowing God's kingdom is the enlargement of that kingdom.

### The Parable of the Wheat and Tares

There are a number of features about the parable of the wheat and tares, the relevance of which to this study will be immediately obvious (see Matt 13:24–30, 36–43). Again, to those who are agriculturally aware, wheat and tares can look remarkably alike in the early stages of their development, even at close quarters. Characteristically, however, they are very dissimilar. If the tares (Greek *zizanion*) are to be identified with the bearded darnel, as Vine suggests,[5] then it saps nutrients from other plants in its environment and is particularly susceptible to parasites, which can prove toxic if eaten by humans or animals.

This notwithstanding, the reluctance of the landowner to yield to the suggestion of his servants and remove them is based on the possibility that good crop might also mistakenly be uprooted with the bad (Matt 13:29). It is also in the sure knowledge that such a separation will take place at the appointed harvest time, when not only would they become more distinguishable, but the work would also be assigned to those especially trained for the task—that is, the reapers (v. 30).

At the end of the discourse, Jesus dismissed the crowds. At this point—possibly due to a combination of courtesy and embarrassment—the disciples asked him to explain the parable to them. In true

---

5. Vine, *Expository Dictionary*, 1122.

metaphorical fashion, Jesus identifies each key component in turn, arresting their attention immediately by introducing the Son of Man as the one who had sowed the good seed (Matt 11:37). He then goes on to tell them that:

- the field is the world (v. 38a);
- the good seed represents the sons of the kingdom (v. 38b);
- the tares are the sons of the evil one (v. 38c);
- the enemy who sows them is the devil (v. 39a);
- the harvest is the end of the age (v. 39b); and
- the reapers are the angels of God (v. 39c).

Once gathered, the fate of the tares is to be thrown into the fiery furnace (Matt 13:40–42), while that of the righteous (that is, the wheat) is one of beauty, glory, and fulfilled potential (v. 43).

This parable is often cited by those who argue against the idea that the church comprises the redeemed community of believers and them alone. They invariably point to the Lord's apparent acceptance of mixture in the here and now, as symbolized by the coexistence of the wheat and the tares. They even own his argument as their own, that the situation will be satisfactorily resolved at the end of the age, any attempt on our part to intervene before the appointed time bearing the potential for disastrous consequences. However, Jesus identifies the field not as the church but as the world. The influence of the kingdom permeates society as it grows from strength to strength alongside structures and individuals who are subjects of an altogether different kingdom. But not so in the church, either in its local or its universal sense. This is not to imply the impossibility of their being a mixture of truly redeemed and those not so in any given church gathering. But the church in the strictly biblical sense of the word is not about gatherings, buildings, or meetings; it is essentially and necessarily about people. It is the redeemed community.

Notice also that the existence of evil in the world is not random or just the product of Adam's fall. That is most certainly the channel by which it came to be in our world. This parable demonstrates, however, that it is principally the strategy of the enemy of God's kingdom, the design of which is surely in keeping with his own character: theft, murder, and destruction (see John 10:10).

*Lessons from Jesus' Parables of the Kingdom*

The characteristics of the kingdom of darkness are such that it inevitably arouses strong passions on the part of those who belong to the kingdom of God. Animosity, frustration, and hostility could easily give way to aggressive methods, forceful means, and retaliatory tactics, but this is not the way of the children of light, much less the Prince of peace. This is in complete accord with Paul's advice to the brothers at Ephesus that, having donned all that has been placed at their disposal, they simply now stand (Eph 6:13). This is not to imply passive inactivity, but neither are we encouraged to fight fire with fire. The biblical way to defeat a negative force is to adopt an antithetical approach. Thus, we are to love our enemies, pray for those who ill-treat us, feed the hungry adversary, quench the thirst of those who despise us, and generally overcome evil with good (see Prov 25:21–22; Rom 12:17–20).

Jesus' counsel is to: "Let both grow until the harvest" (Matt 13:30). It might have been more palatable had he said that the wheat would grow and the tares would simply coexist, but the development of both is assured in the parable. Why this is so is uncertain. Jesus himself offers no further explanation, from which we reasonably may assume one of two things: either he considered it to be self-explanatory and, therefore, in need of no further elucidation, or it is not required of us to know any more detail than that given. If it is the latter, we do well to avoid unhelpful speculation; if it is the former, we are left to concede the obvious probable explanation that—from our perspective, at least—even that which is evil must come to maturity before it is fully ripe for judgment.

What is beyond the realm of conjecture is the fact that a separation is guaranteed by the most trustworthy and unimpeachable source: the word of Christ. The destiny of each is known in advance: one will be assembled to the landowner's barn, the other will be gathered together to burn. This is a serious affair indeed. So much so that it warrants sober reflection. The issue of judgment should initially evoke somber examination, for faith really is a matter of life and death in their most extreme forms. However, the knowledge that we truly are in Christ and he in us must cause us to rejoice that, whatever they may signify, our destination is not the furnace but the barn.

There are a couple of side issues that I would like to draw the reader's attention to. They are especially significant for anyone who has a proclivity toward Calvinistic theology, though I am sure that those

Kingdom

with an Arminian tendency might also be interested. Consider them and do with them what you will. They are these:

- the seed has no choice in what it will become or what its destiny might be; and
- once sown, there is no cross pollination or transference of allegiance (none of the wheat can decide to become tares or *vice versa*).

This is not to say, of course, that there are not good wheat plants that once served as tares under a kingdom dictatorship set in opposition to the rule of God. But the fact remains that, even when we behaved as tares, conducted ourselves after the fashion of tares, and might justifiably have expected the same fate as that of the tares, we were in fact wheat in the waiting. The mission of evangelism is not to convince tares to decide to switch camps; it is to present the message of the gospel in order that those who are destined for glory but have not yet believed might be given the opportunity to do so. Fine sounding arguments, appeals to anthropocentrically-conditioned sensitivities, and spurious claims to be more just or loving than God cannot eradicate the fact that: "the God and Father of our Lord Jesus Christ . . . chose us in him before the creation of the world to be holy and blameless in his sight. In love he predestined us to be adopted as his sons through Jesus Christ, in accordance with his pleasure and will—to the praise of his glorious grace, which he has freely given us in the One he loves" (Eph 1:3–6).

## Summary

In many respects, these two parables are both the gateway and the key to the rest of Jesus' parables of the kingdom. Understand these and your comprehension of the others will be significantly enriched. Conversely, if you fail to appreciate the key principles inherent in these two parables, then your command of the others will be severely hampered. It might even be argued that the heading I have chosen under which to discuss the parable of the sower and the parable of the wheat and tares could easily have been the general title for all of the kingdom parables, for in some measure they each relate to the overarching theme of "Sowing and Reaping." Let us now consider the next pairing, the parables of the mustard seed and the yeast, which I have decided to discuss under the banner: "Growing and Changing."

## GROWING AND CHANGING

I have long regarded maturity as being unrelated to age, little to do with experience, and all about the acceptance of responsibility. This certainly seems to be true of individuals. I am convinced that it is equally so of corporate bodies, for they are in some measure governed by the nature of the individuals that comprise their make-up. Both the kingdom of God and the church as an agent of that kingdom fall into this category. The parables of the mustard seed and the yeast demonstrate the nature and characteristics of the growth and development of God's kingdom, both of itself and throughout society in general terms. They are coupled together here because they make essentially the same point, though differ ever so slightly in emphasis. They are reasonably familiar to us and so we accept their teaching almost without question. To the original audience, however, a people conditioned to hope for—if not expect—dramatic results, they would probably have seemed alien at best.

### The Parable of the Mustard Seed

According to the assistant keeper of the herbarium at Kew's Royal Botanical Gardens, there is much uncertainty surrounding the precise identification of the New Testament mustard seed (Greek *sinapi*), though the consensus of opinion suggests that it is most probably *brassica nigra* (that is, black mustard). At the period in question, the seeds of this plant were "cultivated for their oil as well as for culinary purposes."[6] The fact that it must be capable of growing to a height that can attract passing birds to its most robust branches (Matt 13:31–32) is perfectly in keeping with this proposition.[7]

Elsewhere in Matthew, the mustard seed is used to define the potency of faith, irrespective of its measure (see Matt 17:20). Here, too, Jesus relates its potential despite the smallness of its size. By comparing his kingdom to a grain of mustard seed the significance is obvious.

---

6. F. N. Hepper, "Plants," in Douglas, *New Bible Dictionary*, 946.
7. See also Vine, *Expository Dictionary*, 766.

## Kingdom

From small beginnings and apparent ordinariness, the kingdom would grow beyond all reasonable expectations, a point not lost on George Eldon Ladd.[8] By the time Jesus uttered these words, they had already proven true in many respects:

- the birth of the King of the kingdom was to humble parents in modest surroundings in Bethlehem, long regarded as of little importance in Israel compared to Jerusalem, just a short distance away to the north;
- his ministry began in relative obscurity in Nazareth;
- his closest followers were generally of an unassuming background; and
- even after his death, the disciples met almost apologetically in an upper room.

Following Christ's death, resurrection, and ascension both the increase of his kingdom and the rapidity of that growth were nothing short of phenomenal. So much so, in fact, that within forty years Christianity had spread throughout the known world, affecting Jew and Gentile, rich and poor alike. Any obstacles that threatened to halt its progress were swiftly cast aside, including religious prejudice and political self-interest. Hostile environments were regarded not as a menace, but as an opportunity for strategic advancement. If the kingdom rule of God in Christ could deal effectively with man's sinful fallen nature, despite opposition from spiritual forces, could anything stand in its way? The mustard seed had not yet become fully grown, nor has it yet, but it had certainly begun to realize its potential.

Where this parable seems to fail is in its capacity to do justice to the extent of growth of the kingdom of God. This is presumably why no single parable can suffice in aiding our understanding. All of the kingdom parables taken together cannot fully explore its treasures. And so here, even allowing for the most generous comparison, there are limitations to the capabilities of agricultural sowing. The kingdom rule of God knows no such restrictions. Seven hundred years before Messiah's birth, the prophet Isaiah spoke these words: "For to us a child is born, to us a son is given, and the government will be on his shoulders. And he will be called Wonderful Counselor, Mighty God, Everlasting Father,

---

8. See Ladd, *Theology of the New Testament*, 98.

*Lessons from Jesus' Parables of the Kingdom*

Prince of Peace. Of the increase of his government there will be no end. He will reign on David's throne and over his kingdom, establishing and upholding it with justice and righteousness from that time on and forever. The zeal of the Lord Almighty will accomplish this" (Isa 9:6–7).

The passage is familiar to many of us and rich in meaning. But I would like to draw your attention to just one of its features concerning the kingdom of God. Remember, we identified the kingdom as essentially the rule of God in action; his government, if you will. Now notice what the prophet says of the government of the one called Wonderful Counselor, Mighty God, Everlasting Father, and Prince of Peace. Had he said of it that there would be no end, that would have been both true and incredibly incomprehensible to finite minds. What he actually said, however, was that there would be no end to its increase. It will never cease to grow. How amazing!

There is another incidental that I would like to mention in passing. Again, there is insufficient evidence to make too much of it; you must decide to do with it what you will. It is this: even when fully grown to its maximum possible stature, the mustard tree is not particularly striking to look at when compared to other similar plants. Its markedness, as we have indicated, is in how it came to such a size from such inauspicious beginnings. In stark contrast to known earthly kingdoms throughout history, the coming of the kingdom of God on the earth was relatively unannounced, without pomp or ceremony, quietly going about its business, and attracting those for whom it was designed before the creation of the world. Its beauty is not in outward displays of grandeur but in inner and inherent glory. It simply is.

As for the birds who take refuge in the adult plant's branches, there is probably an intentional allusion here to similar imagery used by the Old Testament prophets, Ezekiel (17:23) and Daniel (4:12). Some have taken this to be indicative of the Gentile nations,[9] which would certainly strengthen the link to ancient prophecy. However, the argument that it could also relate to the blessings of common grace experienced by the unsaved in the Gospel era should not be summarily dismissed, though the idea that it is representative of doctrinally corrupt infiltration into the church seems highly speculative. Moreover, this demands that the church and the kingdom be understood as synonymous entities, which is clearly not the case. Thus, it seems much more credible to think of the

---

9. R. E. Nixon, "Matthew," in Guthrie and Motyer, *New Bible Commentary*, 834.

birds merely as unbelievers who are also beneficiaries of the kingdom's influence throughout the earth.

Whether this might be in the form of social welfare or simply the secondary effects of divine favor is difficult to argue with any degree of certainty. It is even likely that both are equally true, given that there is much evidence to support such a proposition, both now and historically. For example, such worthy objectives as the abolition of slavery, the introduction of stringent sanitation codes, health service facilities, national welfare projects, the basic legal system, and law enforcement can all trace their origins in the United Kingdom to the endeavor of those captivated by an ethical awareness of kingdom principles, to the mutual benefit of all who reside there. I'm sure this example can be replicated many times over in other countries of the world.

## The Parable of the Yeast

The issue of comparative size is once again misunderstood in the parable of the yeast (Matt 13:33), though this time its growing influence from such insubstantial beginnings is the prominent feature. As yeast that is added to bread mixture pervades the whole batch of dough, so too will the rule of God be. However, Dick France is correct to draw our attention to the minor distinction between this and the preceding parable when he says that: "The leaven is unlike the mustard seed in that it is not in its growth which is remarkable, but in the expansion which it causes in the new dough. So the kingdom of heaven (and those who represent and proclaim it) has a dramatic effect on human society."[10]

The Greek word translated "yeast" (or "leaven" in the older versions) is *zume*, from which we derive our English word "enzyme." The verb form *zymoo* means "to ferment." Of its New Testament usage, I find myself indebted to the Revd. Angel of Abergorlech in South Wales, when he informs us that: "Each instance is in a literary figure: parable, metaphor, proverb and type. The point of the various uses varies from context to context, despite the frequent claims among scholars that in the N[ew] T[estament] leaven is used . . . to symbolize an evil influence which spreads like an infection."[11]

---

10. France, *Matthew*, 528.
11. G. T. D. Angel, "Leaven," in Brown, *New International Dictionary*, 462.

*Lessons from Jesus' Parables of the Kingdom*

Thus, although it is true that elsewhere in Scripture yeast (or leaven) does seem consistently to symbolize a negative attitude (see Mark 8:15–21; Luke 12:1; 1 Cor 5:6–8), to accept that here would place this parable in more than a little contextual disharmony, given the emphasis of the parable of the mustard seed. This being so, a more reasonable and wholly consistent filter might be to say that it always symbolizes an influence of sorts, the immediate context determining whether that be good or bad.

You do not need to be a master baker to understand what a difference adding yeast makes to dough. Anyone who has ever tasted unleavened bread will know instantly. When the bread is freshly baked, so much the better. I am fortunate enough to be married to someone with whom I share a similar dislike for mass produced food stuffs. We boil the chicken carcasses and add diced fresh vegetables to make soup, we create our own savory flatbreads called "the pizza slow train," and—all too rarely in my opinion—my wife will bake. Biscuits, scones, fruit cakes, chocolate gateaux, mince pies, pork pies, steak and kidney pies, quiches, tarts, and *bread*. The very word makes me shiver with glee.

But why do home-made bread and shop-bought bread taste so radically different? Barbara would probably say "It's the love that goes into it." This may well be true—partly. Mostly, however, it is the quality of the yeast. A small jar of saccharomyces (that is, natural leaven) has occupied an appropriately-sized corner of our fridge for something in excess of four years now. It is a live fungal agent, which remains alive despite pieces being occasionally and sometimes ceremoniously spooned from it. Quite prepared to sit undisturbed at the back of our now dated A. E. G. Öko-Santo, its sole purpose in life is to metabolize sugars in dough so that small pockets of carbon form, which, when subject to heat, will cause the bread to rise and rise and . . . well, you know the rest. What a delight!

Such a difference, however, does not come by virtue of the ingredients being dissociately present in the same kitchen; they must be mixed together. Similarly, the coexistence of those whose lives are governed by godly precepts with those whose lives are not is insufficient to bring about the kingdom rule of God outside of strictly defined parameters. Ascetic lifestyles may well prevent those who adopt such a position from becoming tainted by ungodliness, but it also withholds righteous communion from those who arguably need it the most—unbelievers.

# Kingdom

Yeast and flour are not at all similar; they belong to completely different food types and share no natural qualities. It is noteworthy also that when combined, the introduction of yeast to the flour has a dramatic effect on the latter but not so much on the former. In other words, yeast exerts a beneficial influence upon flour, but flour does not have a detrimental effect upon yeast. Moreover, the process of change that does take place begins almost immediately. Such is the effect of the kingdom of God upon society as darkness is invaded by light, chaos gives way to order, insensitivity stands aside for compassion, and lethargy surrenders to yearning.

Thus, the union of yeast and dough is discernible only by the impact of the former upon the latter. It does not announce its intentions in advance, proclaim its strategy as it proceeds, or celebrate its victory at the end. Yeast is quite simply content to do what it does best: get on with the job in hand. Thus, the yeast works strongly but silently, intensively yet invisible, without fuss and without fail, devoid of both hostility and hindrance, until nothing with which it comes into contact is left untouched by its influence. Although many Christians today seem to be more dictated to by the spirit of the age than guided by the Holy Spirit, this parable—perhaps more than any other teaching in the whole of the New Testament—suggests that we are not called to strive for demonstrable success, only to be faithful.

Throughout the centuries of its existence, the kingdom has wrought many benefits for society in general. When we looked at the fulfillment of the parable of the mustard tree, we noted a few of these. In the context of the parable of the yeast, indicative of the permeating influence for good, we can identify still more: the education of those not considered worthy for such a privilege by others, the promotion of godly standards in the business and commercial marketplace, the introduction of divine blessing to those who might otherwise not engage with such an opportunity, the Christlike treatment of war-torn victims, the workforce, women and children, and the underprivileged and disenfranchised. Thus, the influence of the kingdom of God is both rigorous and widespread, concentrated and all-embracing.

The range of God's effective will is both beyond our capacity to measure and outside of the limits of our comprehension. What we can say with some degree of certainty is that, despite what obstructions or barriers men may put in place to prohibit the range of the gospel of

Christ, there is not a square millimeter on the face of this earth—his earth—that lies outside of the domain of God's kingdom rule. The yeast has been added to the dough.

## Summary

Of course, both of these parables are essentially proclaiming the same message regarding the kingdom of God: from the smallest of beginnings will come something so disproportionately large that the end product will barely be recognizable from its inauguration. What is true of the entire realm of God's rule throughout the world is no less so when considered in the context of its agents, whether that be the church universal, its local expression, or redeemed individuals that comprise the whole. There will, no doubt, be readers of this who may well have been committed to living their lives in accordance with God's kingdom rule for many years. For almost as long as they can remember they have harbored aspirations to accomplish something beyond the mundane and the banal in God's service. They reflect upon their achievements with more of a sense of frustration and regret than satisfaction. To them, these parables speak comfort and hope. They say: "Do not despise the apparent smallness of your contribution, for who can tell what harvest a seed sown in faith can truly achieve?"

## BUYING AND SELLING

Again, the parable of the hidden treasure and that of the pearl of great value are two kingdom parables that I have heard preached on or taught from on many occasions. At first glance, you would imagine it difficult to do so in a way that brings dishonor to the text. My experience, however, suggests that this is not necessarily the case. To present them as evidence of the extent of Jesus' sacrifice on behalf of fallen humanity is not only an inconsistent emphasis when compared with the other parables, but it is wholly unwarranted by the context of each, irrespective of how valid the premise might be. The parables before us do convey a singular truth: the immeasurable worth of God's kingdom, for which no sacrifice is too great, each depicting a different aspect of it.

# Kingdom

Their shared focus is encapsulated by the title of this section: "Buying and Selling."

## The Parable of the Hidden Treasure

The kingdom of God is of inestimable worth. George Eldon Ladd puts it this way: "the kingdom of heaven is like a treasure whose value transcends every other possession."[12]

If we assume that the identity of the field in this parable (Matt 13:44) is the same as in that of the wheat and tares (v. 38), then this lends further significance to the fact that the man purchased the field in which he knew the treasure (Greek *thesauros*) to be buried: the kingdom of God "is not of this world" (John 18:36), but it is most assuredly in it. We are not informed of the exact price paid for the field or whether the landowner knew of its true value; these are unnecessary incidentals. We do know, however, that the man who found the treasure joyfully sold everything he had to possess not only it, but also that in which it was buried.

Bizarrely or beautifully—depending on one's perspective—the content of this particular parable is also the nature of parables in general. Solomon wisely spoke of it thus: "It is the glory of God to conceal a matter; to search out a matter is the glory of kings" (Prov 25:2). In other words, the mysteries of the kingdom are hidden by God. This is not so that they should remain beyond discovery, but that they may be found by those who are diligent in their quest. One of the major principles of sound hermeneutics is that Scripture is its own interpreter. Just a few chapters earlier, toward the latter part of his Sermon on the Mount, Jesus said this:

> "Ask and it will be given to you; seek and you will find; knock and the door will be opened to you. For everyone who asks receives; he who seeks finds; and to him who knocks, the door will be opened. Which of you, if his son asks for bread, will give him a stone? Or if he asks for a fish, will give him a snake? If you then, though you are evil, know how to give good gifts to your children, how much more will your Father in heaven give good gifts to those who ask him!" (Matt 7:7–11).

---

12. Ladd, *Gospel of the Kingdom*, 62.

## Lessons from Jesus' Parables of the Kingdom

I count it a privilege rather than a misfortune that I was effectively brought up by my maternal grandparents from an early age. I was taught traditional values of morality, respect, and integrity, for which I shall remain forever grateful. One aspect that I recall with increasing fondness is to hear tales of a bygone age, most notably the struggles of the war years. Apparently, in places where devastation was especially bad, there was always someone willing to take advantage of an opportunity for ill-gotten gain. In the major towns and cities, looting was particularly rife.

Even in small villages, however, house-theft was a problem, especially when the air-raid siren sounded to bring the community together in a reasonably more secure shelter. To combat the threat of the accomplished burglar, homeowners would often resort to burying their most treasured items in their gardens. Years after the war ended, many such items were rediscovered, presumably because the original owners either had died or had simply forgotten about them. Although this parable was invented to present a biblical truth, there is no doubt that its particulars would have been taken from the course of natural events, which may well mirror those described to me by my late grandfather of life in Britain during the 1940s.

In the time of Jesus, the turbulent political landscape might possibly have led to similar precautions being taken, especially in view of the fact that the owners of singularly precious items would have been subject to heavy taxation. Add to this the possibility of invasion from marauding combatants and the situation presented by Jesus would not have been as unfamiliar to his hearers as perhaps we might imagine. Forgetfulness, death, imprisonment, or exile are just a handful of viable explanations for unretrieved hidden wealth.

To the enquiring mind, this parable gives easy cause for speculation. Why was the man digging in someone else's field? If he was planning to claim the find as his own after purchasing the field, knowing it to be there in advance, then why did he not simply take it without buying the field? We are not told and we are not encouraged to indulge in conjecture. We simply know what we need to in order to grasp the point of the parable.

It has been the very real experience of millions since it was first told, none more so than that of the apostle Paul, who had also "stumbled accidentally" across the treasure of the kingdom (Acts 9:1–2). This is his

Kingdom

testimony: "Whatever was to my profit I now consider loss for the sake of Christ. What is more, I consider everything a loss compared to the surpassing greatness of knowing Christ Jesus my Lord, for whose sake I have lost all things. I consider them rubbish, that I may gain Christ and be found in him" (Phil 3:8–9a). Indeed, Paul's reference to "treasure in jars of clay" ("earthen vessels," KJV), though primarily denoting the contrast between the gospel message and its bearers, might also equally apply to a distinction to be observed between the kingdom rule of God on earth and those entrusted as worthy ministers of the message of that kingdom (2 Cor 4:7).

Although not included in the parable, such a scenario usually produces one of three common responses:

- as in the parable, the one who discovers the hidden truth of the kingdom recognizes its value and is only too keen to do whatever is necessary to acquire its benefits;
- others see at once the worth of God's kingdom but, after considering the price, are unwilling to make the necessary sacrifices that they might obtain it; and
- still others stumble across the kingdom and fail even to recognize its beauty.

Of course, there will be those in pseudo-religious garb who would stand aghast at the above suggestions. How could anyone, when confronted with the opportunity to respond favorably to the kingdom of God, fail to do so, let alone allow it to pass by without notice? Well, that is precisely what did happen just a little over two thousand years ago when not only was the kingdom on show, but in the person of its king—Jesus. Many religious leaders acknowledged his messiahship privately, but so clung to their position among the Pharisees that they were unwilling to do so publicly (John 12:42). When it came right down to it, their ambitious desires far outweighed what they knew God would require of them. Their hearts were aligned to their own treasure (Matt 6:21), which was not the kingdom of God.

The kingdom rule of God is upheld by the kingly wisdom of God, of which Job said:

> Man's hand assaults the flinty rock
> and lays bare the roots of the mountains.
> He tunnels through the rock;

> his eyes see all its treasures.
> He searches the sources of the rivers
> and brings hidden things to light.
> But where can wisdom be found?
> Where does understanding dwell? . . .
> God understands the way to it
> and he alone knows where it dwells,
> for he views the ends of the earth
> and sees everything under the heavens . . .
> And he said to the man, "The fear of the Lord—that is wisdom,
> and to shun evil is understanding."[13]

## The Parable of the Pearl of Great Value

It is my conviction that, unless otherwise stated, there is but one central theme to each parable. Those for which Jesus himself provides an explanation are exceptions to this, though that in itself does not give us the right to analogize all the parables where to do so might correctly be regarded as speculative. Thus, there is no sound biblical basis for the assumption that the merchant's fervor in the parable of the pearl of great price correlates to our personal decision to pursue God's favor in salvation. The central theme is the inestimable and incomparable value of the kingdom of God (Matt 13:45–46).

That aside, however, there are some partially hidden secrets implied by the text that we would do well to note. The first is this: the man who found the pearl was not looking for that one pearl; it was not the object of his search. When he set off on his journey, his motivation was to find fine pearls (plural). Although it is not clear from the text (either in our English translations or the original Greek), the idea cannot altogether be dismissed that he might already have been successful in his quest prior to finding this pearl. In other words, he may well have found other pearls before coming across the one of such exquisiteness that the splendor of the others paled by comparison.

This possible scenario might reasonably beg the question: if there were other pearls, would these represent other kingdoms? I would say not so much other kingdoms, for we are only made aware of one other kingdom that stands in opposition to God's kingdom, though its rule is

---

13. See Job 28:1–28.

capable of many wiles. Thus, I would argue that if we do allow for the possibility of the merchant finding other pearls, that they for him—not unlike those faced by Bunyan's Pilgrim—are indicative of other kingdom choices.

This being so—or at least potentially so—could the merchant have come to any decision other than the one he did, in fact, make? This is where Calvinist and Arminianist opinion will divide without even a moment's hesitation. But let us not be so rash as to dismiss the evidence. There were many in Israel who not only saw and heard the One in whom resided the fullness of God's kingdom but also tasted bountifully of its benefits, and yet in the main "his own did not receive him" (John 1:11). In another of the parables that Jesus taught with kingdom allusions, a rich man makes plans for a great banquet, to which many of his friends and local dignitaries are invited. But a significant number made their excuses to be absent (see Luke 14:12–24). How could this be possible? Is the magnificence of the kingdom an illusion? Does it promise more than it can conceivably deliver? Well, no, but it does bear an outrageous price tag.

Such is the superiority of he most valued pearl that the merchant (Greek *emporos*, from which we derive our English "emporium") shows not a hint of hesitancy. And remember, he was not being asked to make room for God's kingdom by getting rid of clutter, nor even sacrificing some of the best stuff he had in his possession; the price was all that he owned. The following translation of the opening verse of an old Swedish hymn, inspired by this parable, may help us to more readily appreciate its message:

> O, that pearl of great price, have you found it?
> Is the Savior supreme in your love?
> O, consider it well ere you answer,
> As you hope for a welcome above.
> Have you given up all for this treasure?
> Have you counted past gains as but loss?
> Has your trust in yourself and your merits
> Come to naught before Christ and his cross?[14]

For some time, I have made it my habit to watch a midday television program as I enjoy a spot of lunch. It provides an ideal break, without encouraging feelings of guilt for having wasted three quarters

---

14. Johan Erik Nystrom, 1842–1907.

of an hour unnecessarily. I would have been eating anyway. For me, *Bargain Hunt* has become something of an obsession, and I don't feel in the least bit troubled by admitting it. For the uninitiated, the idea of the show is that there are two teams of two people, each given three hundred pounds to spend in an hour at an antiques fair (their quest is edited to fit with the broadcaster's schedule). They must purchase three items, with the help of an expert, which will later be sold at auction in the hope of making an overall profit. If they do not spend the whole of their allocation, any surplus is given to that team's expert to buy a bonus item, which they may then opt to use as a sort of "joker" either to get them out of trouble or to add to their profits. Often the teams' choices will bring a loss; seldom is this the case for the experts' bonus buys, as you might expect.

In both cases—the parable of the kingdom and the television program—the one item of singular value is there for all to see and who are willing to pay the price. But not all who have access to it do see, and of those who are able, not all are willing to make the required sacrifice. Many of us have become conditioned by social proverbs that make any decision subject to a process of risk assessment. From a young age we are advised not to put all our eggs in one basket. Why? Presumably in case there is an accident or some other as yet unidentifiable misdemeanor that would render our purchase a waste of time, money, and effort. There is no such risk with the kingdom of God, but that does not make it any the less costly.

The "bird-in-the-hand" philosophy is fine for those who are unwilling or incapable of exercising faith. Such was the case of the young man who went away disappointed, having been told to sell everything he had in order to give to the destitute that he might have treasure in heaven (Luke 18:22). But for people like the merchant in this parable, or Peter and Andrew who, having met Jesus, knew that the life of a fisherman thereafter could never satisfy (Matt 4:20), or those countless others throughout the course of history, such as Stephen (Acts 6:8—7:60), John Wycliffe, William Tyndale, John Huss, Jerome of Prague, Bishops Ridley and Latimer, Thomas Cranmer, Dietrich Bonhoeffer, Jim Elliott, and nameless others who have willingly embraced torture and/or death rather than relinquish their most prized possession, the pearl of great value—the kingdom of God.

Kingdom

I thank God for the many useful methods that different churches employ to make known the message of the kingdom. In recent years, the Alpha initiative has been particularly successful—both in the UK and further afield—at explaining the basics of the gospel to interested parties in a familiar and unthreatening setting. In almost forty years as a believer, I have yet to experience a dearth of interest in the Christian message, even if at times that may have been cloaked in mockery and wummery. For those chosen before the foundation of the world, however, the kingdom of God is not a matter of window shopping but of purchasing, even if it costs all you possess and are.

Summary

The two parables we have considered in this section highlight the complexity of human life. When we make plans for evangelistic endeavor, it is good to be reminded of that fact. There are no hard and fast rules about how best to engage an individual's heart in terms of creating the best possible environment for them to acknowledge Christ as Savior. Ultimately, of course, this is the role of God the Holy Spirit in accordance with the Father's elective decree. From our perspective, however, it does seem that some almost stumble upon salvation as if by accident, while others find it after a long and difficult pursuit. The parables of the hidden treasure and the pearl of great value relate to each scenario perfectly. It is also evident that the worth of the end product is neither enhanced nor diminished by the route by which the candidate arrives.

## SEPARATING AND JOINING

We now come to two parables that I must confess to never having heard preached on as subject texts. This, coupled with the fact that I have heard both referred to many times in passing, suggests that perhaps they have not been afforded the place they rightfully deserve in Christian teaching. I have maintained the couplet idea in this section by looking at the two parables under the heading of "Separating and Joining." On the surface they might appear to be different, even contradictory, concepts. Under the right circumstances, however, they can be complementary. The parable of the net warns against the urge to separate the true from the counterfeit this side of the end of the age, while the section about the wise teacher implies that we are to seek to become joined with those who have learned the value to be had in treasures new and old.

## The Parable of the Net

The parable of the net (Matt 13:47–50) is similar to that of the wheat and the tares in that it, too, warns against the hope of an entirely pure expression of God's kingdom this side of eschatological judgment.[15] It might even be said that this is an aquacultural version of the aforementioned agricultural parable. Taken together, they would be understood by farmer and fisherman alike. Moreover, it seems clear from the explanation that such separation is solely attached to the divine prerogative and those to whom God assigns the task (that is, the angels at the end of the age). The efficacy of this parable—despite its length—is in its simplicity, especially in its original context. As Donald Hagner observes: "It would have been very common in Capernaum, for example, to see the fishermen sitting on the beach, going through the day's catch, keeping the good fish and throwing away the bad ones."[16]

It must also be noted that the "bad" fish would not have simply been returned to the sea, but placed into a refuse heap for later disposal. I must take exception at this point, however, to some comments attributed to Arland Hultgren, wherein he claims that the emphasis of the parable is on the separation of the wicked. He thus—quite emphatically—considers the "righteous [to be] the residue of the process of judgment and punishment."[17] Such a conclusion seems to pay scant regard to both the immediate and the wider context, where it is clear that God's estimation of his kingdom subjects is far loftier than that of Hultgren.

The full stop at the end of verse 47 could lead us to believe that everything that follows over the next three verses serves merely to embellish the central truth that the kingdom of heaven is like a net. It is, in fact, the whole of that section that is likened to the kingdom of heaven. As we have seen in some of the other parables, the rule of God

---

15. See Ladd, *Theology of the New Testament*, 101.
16. Hagner, *Matthew 1–13*, 399.
17. Hultgren, *Parables of Jesus*, 306.

# Kingdom

affects the lives of all with whom it comes into contact, but that does not necessarily mean that it will have a positive effect on determining their eternal destiny.

The language employed, both here and elsewhere, to depict the final destination of the unsaved has evoked much debate throughout the centuries. The fact that it appears in parabolic form has led to the suggestion that Jesus is employing figures of speech to convey the horror of actual and final separation from God. Others have conceded that it behooves us more to be afraid of it than to satisfactorily interpret it. There is perhaps more than an ounce of wisdom in such a position. What we can say with some assuredness, however, is that those who find themselves separated as bad fish do so not because of any curtailment of love on the Savior's part, but because of their own failure to take advantage of the opportunity afforded to them in life. Could the apostle be any more clear: "They perish because they refused to love the truth and so be saved" (2 Thess 2:10b).

The word "love" here (Greek *agapos*) should not be devalued or allowed to become diluted by our twenty-first century misuse of it. It is more intense than perhaps we are accustomed to. Although it can only really be discerned by others by virtue of the actions it produces, its existence is not governed or dictated by them. Thus, Paul did not write to the Thessalonian believers that unbelievers would ultimately perish because they had not been attracted to the kingdom of God, or been fascinated by the mystery of Christ, or found comfort in the unthreatening manner of the Sunday service, or been impressed with the godly character of their Christian neighbors at number forty-two. Nor was it that they had never been given an opportunity to do anything with the truth and so be saved. No; they had actively and willfully refused to love the truth.

Because of the obvious similarity between this parable and that of the wheat and tares, we might wonder at its purpose. After all, it does not seem to add anything of significance that would otherwise be absent. William Hendriksen suggests the apparent repetition may have been to re-emphasize the idea of "the irreversible decisiveness of the coming judgment," thereby reinforcing both "the exceeding preciousness of the kingdom of heaven and the necessity for everyone to take possession of it here and now."[18] His conclusion is not without plausibility.

---

18. Hendriksen, *Matthew*, 579.

*Lessons from Jesus' Parables of the Kingdom*

In the New Testament, there are three Greek words translated "net." In this passage, it is *sagene*, which, as some early English versions correctly translate, is a dragnet. This was a large net designed for commercial use. It would have been weighted along its lowermost edge so that the net could literally be dragged along the bottom of the river or lake, possibly also with wooden floats positioned the length of its uppermost edge. According to Vine, it would be: "let down into the water and drawn together in a narrowing circle, and then into the boat, or as a semi-circle drawn to the shore."[19]

Fishing nets are non-discriminatory. This applies whether they are the handheld nets used by children in crab pools or the dragnets of large fishing vessels, as here. The only way to make them more selective is to increase the size of the knitted mesh so that smaller fish can swim safely through, though the strength of material used can also determine whether much larger fish are able to tear the nets and thereby escape. Generally speaking, however, they catch all with which they come into contact. So, too, the kingdom rule of God does not discriminate between those who may or may not benefit from its existence on the earth. But there will come a time when it will determine favor for those who may rightly be described as its subjects. Those who cannot be thus identified will find their fate will be the same as that of the bad fish in the parable. Their judgment—and that of the good fish—will be a just one, because it will be initiated by the righteous Judge.

It is also important that we understand the basis of separation as indicated in this parable and elsewhere. The use of character traits like "righteousness" and "wickedness" is only really helpful if we qualify precisely what we mean by them. In other words, what really constitutes a good fish or a bad fish? Clearly, it is not determined by acts that we do in life, though it is equally true that we should expect evidence of fruit to demonstrate the genuineness of our repentance. But there will be many who are considered bad fish who may not necessarily have gone out of their way to do anyone a bad turn, just as there will be those who are regarded as good fish whose only decent action was to accept Christ's atoning work for them moments before they left this life.

And that is the key. Good fish are regarded as such for no other reason than they are clothed in the righteousness of Christ, while bad fish remain so by virtue of the fact that they have not claimed his

---

19. Vine, *Expository Dictionary*, 780.

righteousness for themselves. In the final analysis, the one thing that determines the eternal destiny of us all is what we have done with God's Christ. On October 21, 1997, I had the privilege of leading my eighty-six year old grandmother to Jesus about ten minutes or so before she died. Her name is written in the Lamb's book of life (Rev 21:27). She is a good fish. Of course, in God's eternal purpose she always was, but I didn't know that.

Therefore, we may say in general terms that good fish are true disciples of Jesus and bad fish are simply those who are not. Those who fall into this latter category include those who never knew Christ, those who chose never to want to know, those who convinced themselves that they knew but never truly committed themselves to following him, and those who pretended to know in order to keep up appearances. What really matters—as we shall discover in the next section—is whether he says to us "Welcome!" or "I never knew you" (Matt 7:15–23).

### The Parable of the Teacher

The parable of the teacher (Matt 13:52) is not so much about the kingdom of God *per se* but concerns itself rather with those who are entrusted to instruct others about it. Wisdom is attributed to those who bring out of their storeroom—presumably for the benefit of others—treasures both new and old. Whether this can be legitimately equated to teachings from both the Old and New Testaments, the Law and the Gospel, a kingdom that accommodates both Jews and Gentiles, or any other apparently disparate pairing is entirely speculative. What seems beyond reasonable doubt, however, is that those who are obsessively inquisitive about the past at the expense of being sufficiently acquainted with the present are not here represented. Similarly, those who are forever chasing the latest fashionable expression of Christianity where it dismisses tradition as wholly irrelevant will also fail to communicate anything of true kingdom value.[20] In the words of Arthur Wallis: "If we would understand the present and find the right path for the future, we must study the past."[21]

---

20. See Hendriksen, *Matthew*, 580.
21. In Matthew, *Church Adrift*, 7.

*Lessons from Jesus' Parables of the Kingdom*

The Old Testament prophet Joel conveyed a similar thought in the context of the promised outpouring of the Holy Spirit, when God said through him: "And afterwards, I will pour out my Spirit on all people. Your sons and daughters will prophesy, your old men will dream dreams, your young men will see visions. Even on my servants, both men and women, I will pour out my Spirit in those days" (Joel 2:28–29).

Amazing words and at the same time potentially sobering for those of us of a certain age. Now in my fifty-third year, I must confess to becoming increasingly aware of how more frequently I seem to be disturbed by dreams. Almost commensurately—but just as worryingly—I am not so conscious of being envisioned as I was at an earlier age. Am I on the slippery slope to dreamdom only? No doubt time will tell. The fact of the matter seems to be that unless a young man's vision is tempered by an older man's dream, his strategic pool of resources is likely to be limited by inexperience and immaturity. Conversely, if an old man's dream is not being constantly refreshed by a younger person's vision, it will in all probability be consigned to little more than allowing its owner ever more frequent trips down memory lane.

Teaching that is not inspired can hardly be expected to be anything other than uninspiring. What do I mean by that? Well, it is quite simply this: if those who have been entrusted with the role of bringing teaching to the flock fail to embrace their responsibility to seek his guidance, then it should come as no surprise at all if the fruit of their endeavors matches the effort they put in.

A few years ago, my wife and I were part of a relatively new charismatic church in a large university city in the north of England. As a pseudo-pioneer work, it attracted a good number of young working couples from other parts of the country, together with a significant student body to make up the bulk of the young people's contingent. The criteria for leadership seemed to focus perhaps more on youthful exuberance than sober reflection. This was particularly evident at the midweek gatherings, where homegroup leaders would often either delegate the teaching responsibility when required or prepare their notes over the meal table a couple of hours before the occasion. At six o'clock on a Wednesday evening, the pressures of the day would be expected to dissipate, as Wayne Grudem, McCain's pizza, the BBC News bulletin, two-year-old Matilda, and Thomas the Tank Engine all fought for center stage. Four hours later, Everard and wife were bemused at why no one in their group seemed to respond to this week's journey into the Psalms. It is not really difficult to see why, is it? It is not so much that such leaders are careless as that they do not appear to care enough.

As hinted at earlier, there are those who suggest that the treasures old and new refer to the respective covenants associated with the Law and the Gospel. To my mind, such commentators are more guilty of eisegesis than they would care to admit. They are certainly reading more into the text than is reasonably warranted. Perhaps just as misleading—though by no means surprisingly so—is Eugene Peterson's *Message* translation: "He said, 'Then you see how every student well-trained in God's kingdom is like the owner of a general store who can put his hands on anything you need, old or new, exactly when you need it.'" I sometimes feel on the edge of despair at the disservice done to the word of God by those who think they are making it easier to understand.

Of course, to speak of new things in relation to the Bible is not to advocate—much less anticipate—further additions; the canon of Scripture is complete as it stands. In that sense, therefore, the newness does not relate to novelty revelation, though we may rightly expect increased revelation in our understanding of that established word of God. The lessons of church history are such that whenever the kingdom of God has been embraced by a generation of Christian believers, that generation has ushered in a fresh disclosure or rediscovery of a previously hidden or long-neglected truth.[22] It does so not by abandoning what had thitherto been made known, but by building upon it as a sure foundation. Thus, for each generation of believers, even old treasures will be as new to them.

When I was studying for my second degree (on the atonement), I had arranged to spend ten days at a dedicated residential library in Flintshire. I had already done some preliminary background work prior to my arrival. There were a couple of key elements that I was particularly excited about, largely because I had convinced myself that I was the first person in the history of the Christian era to discern them. My subsequent discovery probably said as much about my naivety, the company I kept, and issues of arrogant pride in approximately equal measure. Within just a couple of short hours of research at St. Deniol's, I found other writings that contained the same or similar findings being written almost one hundred and fifty years earlier. In one or two

---

22. Houghton, *Sketches*, ix.

*Lessons from Jesus' Parables of the Kingdom*

cases, they cited others having related them centuries before that. I was crestfallen, I was humbled, and I realized the truth that there really is nothing new under the sun (Eccl 1:9).

I was recently spending some time with a dear friend I have known for almost twenty years. Because of the geographical distance now between us and other commitments, we tend to meet up just once a year when I embark on my Christmas card delivery spree. Last year she was out when I called, so our most recent get-togethers have been two years apart. We were filling each other in on what we had been up to since last we met, and she commented on how she thought I had changed during the course of our knowing one another (my wife would probably say not necessarily for the better). I remarked that I hoped my developing understanding did not come across as arrogance or give vent to egocentricity. In fact—and this is common among many students of the word of my acquaintance—the more you come to know of the riches of God's storehouse, the more you also come to realize how little you know. In this sense, the treasures of the kingdom of God are truly inexhaustible.

Perhaps there are some clues to be gleaned from Jesus' later denunciation of the scribes for being so pernickety over practising the rituals of the law, but failing in their responsibility to administer "justice, mercy and righteousness" (Matt 23:23–24). Presumably, he referred to them as "blind guides" because they were ever seeing but never truly perceiving (Mark 4:12).

## Summary

What I have discussed in this section as two different parables under the heading "Separating and Joining" many commentators treat as all one parable, instruction about the teacher being understood as but a continuation of what has gone before. The fact that this portion of Scripture is not introduced in the same way as the rest may lend some credibility to their argument. Either way, the important thing is that, whether we regard it as a parable *per se*, a parabolic illustration, concluding remarks to the preceding parable, or that the whole of the parables lead up to it, have we properly understood its message? Right at the very beginning of his giving instruction by parables, Jesus told his disciples that understanding the parable of the sower was key to recognizing the significance of all parabolic teaching. Now, in the context of teaching on

Kingdom

the end of the age he checks that they have correctly understood and, at the same time, reminds them not to let go of mysteries previously revealed in favor of those most recently unveiled, but to value them all.

## THE END OF THE AGE

Although many of the parables already discussed in this chapter looked tentatively toward the end of the age, the eschatological focus that Jesus brought just a couple of days before his final Passover is worthy of separate attention. The uncertainty faced by that early group of close-knit disciples concerning the immediate future is in some ways replicated by Christians today the world over. Much of the confusion we encounter regarding the end times is in no small measure due to a lack of proper understanding, often fuelled by inappropriate or erroneous teaching. However, one of those present for most of Jesus' ministry years continues to provide more than a crumb of comfort in the face of increasing hostility toward the message of the kingdom of God: "the one who is in you is greater than the one who is in the world" (1 John 4:4).

### The Parable of the Ten Virgins

From the day of Jesus' ascension, the church has anticipated his promised return (see Acts 1:11). In the parable of the ten virgins a call is issued to meet the bridegroom (Matt 25:1). Of those who had been awaiting his arrival, some did so without wavering (i.e., the wise virgins), while others allowed natural distractions to avert their state of alertness (the foolish virgins). It was—perhaps poignantly—at the time when he was least expected that the announcement of his arrival was made (v. 6).

On hearing the proclamation, the wise had only to trim off the heavily carbonized part of the oil lamp's wick so that the flame would burn with maximum brightness; the foolish, however, had not even supplied themselves with oil in readiness for the event they knew would take place and that was now upon them. Herein lies an almost secondary lesson but one that is worthy of note. Spiritual preparedness is a personal responsibility, as is faith. The pragmatic wisdom of others cannot be distributed to those who find themselves in a crisis of their own making (Matt 25:9) if to do so might jeopardize the benefits of such wisdom by those who invested it appropriately.[23] From a purely human perspective, the period between Jesus' departure and his return is an indeterminate one; it calls for steadfastness and godliness, not complacency and capriciousness.

Regarding the composite features of this parable, Hendriksen is correct to avoid unnecessary conjecture. He rightfully dismisses the many theories about the possible identity of the ten virgins, or the one who made the announcement, by reminding us that: "The fact that Scripture does not answer these questions would seem to indicate that they are not of supreme importance."[24] He demonstrates a similar uncertainty over whether the oil could possibly enjoy symbolic significance, admitting only that: "If it does, it would point to the Holy Spirit, through whose transforming and enabling power men are prepared to welcome the Bridegroom."[25]

My wife and jokes do not get on. In fact, it would not be putting it too strongly to suggest that they are best kept apart. It is not so much that she doesn't get the punchlines; it is not even that she necessarily finds them unfunny, though that is often the case. It is more that she has a tendency to think too much beyond the bare minimum. "Well why would he say that?" or "Who in their right mind would think such a thing?" or "Only an imbecile would behave in such a way!" Barbara thinks I have stopped hearing new jokes; I haven't. It is just so much less stressful to keep them to myself.

The same may be said of those who always seem to want to allegorize parables. Who the ten girls are in the context of the story, why they were staying with friends the night before they were due to meet the groom, or what they might have eaten for breakfast is immaterial. If it were not so, we would have been given more detail. All that is required for us to grasp the gist of the parable is given to us, which is: being prepared for the final phase of the kingdom of God when it arrives is vital; when it comes it will be without delay and there will be no opportunity for getting ready at the last minute.

---

23. See R. E. Nixon, "Matthew," in Guthrie and Motyer, *New Bible Commentary*, 846.

24. Hendriksen, *Matthew*, 874–6.

25. Ibid., 879.

It is a particularly striking feature of the parable that the ten virgins are alike in so many respects:

- they are all waiting with the same objective: to meet the bridegroom;
- they all have with them an instrument by which their path might be illuminated;
- although none of them know the precise hour of the bridegroom's arrival, they are all aware of its imminence;
- they are all similarly excited about the coming event;
- they all fall asleep; and
- they are all abruptly awoken when the announcement is made of the bridegroom's arrival.

However, it is where they differ that is all the more arresting. It may only be in one aspect, but it proves to be crucial: five are faithful; the other five foolish. The folly of the latter group in not having oil for burning is compounded by the fact that they had their lamps with them.

I have a mobile phone (or cell phone for American readers). Nothing remarkable in that, you might think. And, of course, you would be correct. It is not the latest fashion accessory type; I'm not even sure it was when I bought it. It may well have a facility to play games, talk to computers, or order me a pizza on set days of the month without my knowing it. If it can, I don't know it. I only possess it so that I can contact home in an emergency. Or, at least, that is the theory.

You see, I keep forgetting that it needs recharging from time to time. I will go out for the day, perhaps visiting old friends, and have every intention of phoning home if I am delayed by heavy traffic, an engaging conversation, or a last-minute decision to call somewhere else *en route*. The only thing is that nine times out of ten my intentions are scuppered by a flashing battery icon, which informs me in no uncertain terms that, once again, I'll have to make my apologies when I return home. A mobile phone in my pocket with no charge—what is the point of that? It is about as much use as an oil lamp without any fuel. What folly!

There is a sense in which it might be said that the foolish virgins were merely going through the motions, hedging their bets, but not really fully committed to the cause. When the alarm cry went up, they were found well and truly wanting. There is a vital principle here that must be allowed to apprehend our attention: complacency and compromise will never sustain us in a crisis; only commitment can ever do that.

Perhaps startlingly to our minds, the judgment upon those ill-prepared is not a mild rebuke and being allowed in regardless, even if only by a side entrance. Nor is it confined to a suitable punishment, after which we can all get along as before, but "let that be a lesson to you." No, the bridegroom's response is both brief and final: "I don't know you" (v. 12). The loss was not minimal; it was everything. Being ready means just that. It does not mean: "I'll be with you in ten minutes" or "I've just my coat to put on" or "Go start the engine; I won't be long." It means that, if called to do so, we are ready to go right now without a moment's hesitation.

## The Parable of the Talents

The similarities between the parable of the talents in Matthew's gospel account and that of the minas in Luke's are obvious (cf. Matt 25:14–30; Luke 19:11–28). So much so, in fact, that some commentators have suggested they may refer to the same incident. Well, they may, but it is not necessary to believe that they do. Indeed, their differences—of which there are quite a few—make it more likely that they were told on separate occasions:

| Parable of the Talents | Parable of the Minas |
| --- | --- |
| Jesus in Jerusalem; | Jesus outside Jerusalem; |
| three servants; | ten servants; |
| each servant given a different amount according to their capabilities; | each servant given the same amount; |
| the parable focuses almost exclusively on the master's servants; | another group is introduced to the narrative, who sought to rebel against the king's appointment; |
| the reason for the parable is left for us to discern. | we are clearly told at the outset that the reason for this parable is because there were those who imagined that the kingdom would appear in all its fulness immediately (Luke 19:11). |

Kingdom

It is important to note that the word "talent" in this context translates the Greek *talanton*, which was a measure of weight, usually of a precious metal used in coinage.[26] The correspondent value was dependent upon the material being used. For example, a talent of silver would obviously have more worth than a talent of copper, neither of which would amount to as much as the same weight in gold. Similarly, values fluctuated between locations and under different administrations, making trade and commerce often subject to heated negotiations.

Too much should not be made of the differing levels of bargaining ability given to each of the three recipients in the parable of the talents; it is simply an acknowledgment by the businessman that each member of his workforce was capable of different levels of trust. Neither is it necessary to make anything of the overtly ungracious appraisal of the master concerning the one found wanting (Matt 25:24). These are but incidentals. The main point of this parable is the need for the responsible use of such capabilities as gifts from God. The first two servants were commended for their faithful appropriation (vv. 21, 23); the third was condemned as "wicked" (v. 26). I am again indebted to Vine for pointing out that the Greek word employed in the original is *poneros*, which suggests a level of maliciousness that is elsewhere associated with the devil.[27]

The master's evaluation of the first two servants' endeavors is easily lost in our attention being directed to that of the third servant. Five talents of money was a considerable sum in those days, irrespective of the metal used or the governing administration's value set on such a weight. To compliment the trustee on his faithfulness in such a "small amount" (Matt 25:21, KJV) might not seem to convey the gratitude one might legitimately expect. However, the fact that his "Well done" may also be translated "Excellent!" or "Wonderful!" militates against such a notion. We are left, then, with the only plausible explanation for his "small amount," the sense of which is brought out by the NIV. Compared to the next level of responsibility that each is to be entrusted with as a reward for showing themselves worthy, these will be regarded as relatively minor.

Whatever may or may not be inferred from the trust shown in the respective recipients, any hint at favoritism is quickly dispelled by

26. See Vine, *Expository Dictionary*, 1120.
27. Ibid, 1226.

*Lessons from Jesus' Parables of the Kingdom*

the master's praise for those who merit it. The commendation given to the first two is identical *ad verbatum*. They had both doubled the master's investment and were, therefore, worthy of equal praise (see Matt 25:21, 23). Neither is there any mention of potential rivalry between the two servants. The first shows no signs of lording it over the second or grumpiness for earning the same favor, nor does the second betray any feelings of envy towards the first. A first-century pilot run for *The Apprentice* this is not.

Compared to the other two, there appears to be some reticence in the approach of the third servant. Whether we are to imagine that he had been in attendance at their awarding ceremony is not clear from the text. There is a sense with the other two of restrained excitement; they almost cannot wait to tell the master of their good news. Here, however, there is only a sense of foreboding and reluctance. It may well be cloaked in a guise of self-justification, but it is poorly masked.

The lazy servant's punishment is well-earned. Any suggestion that Jesus is here celebrating the wealth of the rich increasing at the expense of the poor must immediately be dismissed. If any principle is to be gleaned from the issuing of the third servant's talent to the already healthy stock of the first servant (Matt 25:28), it is that the faithful will receive the kingdom rights that might otherwise have come the way of the pernicious. Thus, fidelity and slothfulness are both rewarded in accordance with the merits of each.

A subsidiary point for our consideration is that such gifts are not ours to do with as we choose; they are given to us for a purpose and should not be allowed to fail in their objective. Furthermore, being the custodians of talents of divine origin—and making the best possible use of them—requires that personal character be developed accordingly. As Edwin Louis Cole points out: "A man's talent can take him where his character cannot sustain him. If your talent takes you to the level of life where you don't have the character to underguard it, you'll lose where your talent brings you to."[28]

In other words, character is the moral foundation upon which talent can flourish; without such a foundation, however, any gifts we may have at our disposal will crumble and fall when shaken (see Ps 105:19; Prov 22:1). Or to put it another way: depth of character will determine height of achievement. The final words of the master in the parable

---

28. Cole, *Maximized Manhood*, 41.

provide a fitting summary: "For everyone who has will be given more, and he will have an abundance. Whoever does not have, even what he has will be taken from him" (Matt 25:29).

From the very outset, I have maintained that the kingdom of God and the church are not synonymous terms, the latter being but an agent of the former. I have also pointed out that the kingdom of God is essentially the rule of God in action, its influence being extended throughout the earth to the benefit of all. This being so, it does not seem unreasonable to infer from the parable of the talents that the lazy servant corresponds not with unfaithful believers (if that is not a contradiction in terms), but with non-Christians. Their eternal destiny seems to confirm this. In other words, it does appear that, within the sphere of God's kingdom rule, unbelievers also are assigned responsibilities for which they must ultimately give an account. This obviously begs the question: "What would the outcome have been had the third servant fulfilled his duty?" Surely we are not to imagine that this alone would have been sufficient to change his eternal fate. Unless, of course, part of that which was placed at his disposal was the capacity to acknowledge his need for a means of salvation.

## The Parable of the Sheep and the Goats

The eschatological theme is continued in the parable of the sheep and the goats (Matt 25:31–36). It speaks, of course, of final judgment. Those who take a dispensationalist view of Scripture, however, regard this passage as only one of a number of judgments, this being a judgment of the nations' treatment of the Jewish people during the period of the tribulation. It is my conviction that, although different Bible passages seem to identify various component features associated with judgment at the end of the age, they each relate to part of the same final judgment (see also 2 Cor 5:10; Rev 20:11–15). Wayne Grudem also dismisses the dispensationalist interpretation of this parable on the grounds that it speaks not of citizenship—or otherwise—of the millennial kingdom of God on earth, but of eternal destinies.[29]

There are at least hints in this parable at the mystical union that exists between Christ as the head and his body of believers, the church.

---

29. See Grudem, *Systematic Theology*, 1141–2.

*Lessons from Jesus' Parables of the Kingdom*

Men and women are not, it would appear, to be judged on the basis of gender, nationality, skin tone, intellect, ideology, natural disposition, theological persuasion, or denominational allegiance; their final and eternal destiny will be based exclusively on what they have done—or omitted to do—with Christ and those who belong to him. In relation to Jesus' predicted appraisal of the sheep, Hendriksen comments thus: "it is the faithful discharge of humble duties pertaining to day to day living that is given as the reason for the words of congratulation and approbation, and for the cheering invitation to come in and take possession of the blessings of the kingdom in its final stages. What Jesus is saying is, 'In your daily life and conduct, in what are often called "the little things of life," you have furnished proof that you are my true disciples. Therefore, I call you blessed.'"[30]

Of course, the converse is equally true concerning the goats. Whatever was not done for Christ's disciples will be reckoned as if it was withheld from Christ himself. Perhaps significantly, although the sentencings for each group are separate features, the actual judgment is singular. By the one act of calling out the sheep, to whom it would have been second nature to respond to the shepherd's voice (see John 10:14–16), the goats are thus separated as those left behind. However, Jesus had earlier intimated that those who considered themselves sheep but were really otherwise would face the same fate as he now reserves for the goats (see Matt 7:22–23). We can only conclude, therefore, that they are not so much wolves as goats in sheep's clothing.

It is worthy of note that, according to this parable, the fullness of God's kingdom was prepared as an inheritance for the faithful at the foundation of the world (presumably at or immediately prior to its creation). However, the eternal fire was not designed as the final destiny of the unfaithful, but it becomes theirs by virtue of their alignment with those for whom it was prepared: the devil and his angels (Matt 25:41). Whether the word "eternal" in this context refers to everlastingness or simply speaks of its irreversible finality is difficult to argue either way. This may seem to offer some concession to those of an annihilationist disposition, though it seems unlikely that there would be any internal inconsistency. Therefore, one would presume that what "eternal" means for one group it means the same for the other also. Its use elsewhere in

---

30. Hendriksen, *Matthew*, 888.

similar contexts also suggests that it is so employed with the implication of being never ending.

Again, although there are many similarities between sheep and goats, these are far outnumbered by their differences:

| Sheep | Goats |
| --- | --- |
| have a wool coat; | have a hair coat; |
| graze on grass; | browse on branches; |
| prefer open spaces; | huddle together for warmth; |
| meek; | independent; |
| gregarious; | capricious; |
| obedient; | willful; |
| submissive; | rebellious; |
| trusting and trustworthy; | divisive and unpredictable; |
| capable of being shepherded easily; | difficult to control, even by an experienced goatherd; |
| symbolic in Scripture of the Savior (the Lamb that was slain). | symbolic in Scripture of sin (the scapegoat). |

One similarity that is particularly evident from the telling of this parable betrays the true character of what each is used to represent. When judgment is pronounced, neither the sheep nor the goats were aware of having committed the acts for which they were lauded and doomed respectively: "When did we see these needs and help/not help?" The citation for each is similarly parallel: "As much as you did/did not do these things for the least of my brethren, you did/did not do them for me." This is surely the essence of what is the true test of discipleship: that they have love for one another and express that love so naturally that they hardly realize they are doing it (John 13:35).

At first glance, it appears that the qualifying criterion for eternal security is good deeds. On closer examination, however, it soon becomes apparent that those who had lived in such a way as to earn the Lord's favor could only have done so by cultivating a relationship with him, as sheep responding to the Shepherd's voice. In other words, it was not their good works that saved them, but these were seen as the evidence of an inner faith, which did. Goats will not do this. In countries where both are prevalent, they may often be seen happily grazing together during the day. When the time comes for the sheep to be gathered together at the end of the day, however, the goats do not respond to the call.

Notice also that, unlike in the parable of the wheat and the tares, the sheep and the goats were separated before the judgment was pronounced (though strictly speaking, the separation was itself the act of judgment awaiting sentencing). However, those who are truly Christ's sheep need have nothing to fear. Any thoughts along the lines of: "What if I turn out to be a goat, after all?" should quickly be dispelled. Remember, his sheep hear his voice. If anyone can honestly say that they fall into that category, then they may rest assured that they will stand with others similarly inclined on the right hand side of the King of the kingdom. For those who are not so sure, it is not too late to make the transition—yet.

On the basis of this parable, it is quite conceivable that the kind person who always smiles at us in the bus queue, or the work colleague who always seems to be the only one in a good mood on a Monday morning, or the hairdresser who always asks if you have enjoyed your summer vacation, or the school's crossing patrol lady who is always the first to notice when you appear to be stressed and seems to know just what to say to make you feel better, will actually all find themselves among the goats on that day. The sheep and goats were judged on specific expressions of active service: what they had done or omitted to do. A kind word is seldom enough. Even to spiritualize it by reassuring those in difficulty that we will pray for them, when we have the resources at our disposal to physically remove the obstacle, can be considered a goatlike avoidance of the real issues at stake.

## Summary

On the whole, the kingdom parables of Jesus were designed to teach both his early disciples and successive generations of believers a number of important lessons about the kingdom of God. Among these are the nature and growth of the kingdom itself as a principle of divine rule, and the appropriate attitude and character that should be evident in its members toward God, toward other people, and toward earthly goods. The parables we have considered in this section, however, deal almost exclusively with the consummation of the age. They speak of preparedness and infidelity, of application and abuse, and of reward and retribution. Taken together, they speak essentially and necessarily of divine judgment leading to eternal destinies. May we each find assurance that ours is spent with the King of the kingdom.

## SUMMARY

We have seen that eight of the kingdom parables lend themselves to being evaluated in pairs, each couplet presenting a two-fold facet of the kingdom of God. In the first pairing, we noticed that the key principles of sowing and reaping were very much in evidence. Not only is productivity governed by preparedness, but decisions about the quality of the crop are best left for those appointed to the task at harvest time. The next couplet identified the growing and changing features of the kingdom, the key lesson being that something with such inauspicious beginnings should expand to have such global influence. The third pairing was that of buying and selling, both parables pointing to the inestimable value of the kingdom of God. Finally, we looked at separating and joining. The first parable in this section emphasized the point made earlier about the divine prerogative to judge at the appointed time, while the second one speaks of us honoring our responsibility to instruct others with all the resources placed at our disposal. We must do our task and leave God to do his.

The remaining three kingdom parables are more concerned with the Christian's eschatological hope. By applying widely-recognized hermeneutical principles, we saw that the parable of the ten virgins is essentially one that contrasts the wisdom of the alert with the folly of the ill-prepared, attitudes that each reap their own reward. Similarly, the parable of the talents addresses the need for each individual to be responsible for the appropriate dispensation of divinely given capabilities, thus maximizing their potential. Finally, the parable of the sheep and the goats leaves us in no doubt as to the criteria of the final judgment: it is insufficient to claim church membership when kingdom principles have been entirely absent in our social interaction. Eternal destiny will depend upon temporal acceptance of responsibility. What we have done—or omitted to do—for Christ's own will be reckoned as what we have done for Christ himself.

*Lessons from Jesus' Parables of the Kingdom*

    The kingdom of heaven is essentially a spiritual kingdom, and, although its principles are to be expressed practically, they are nonetheless spiritually discerned. The reason for Jesus' use of parables in unveiling such fundamentals is not subject to speculation, for he revealed that too. The parables of Jesus are far more than "earthly stories with a heavenly meaning"; they are, in fact, earthly word pictures used to convey spiritual truth. With this in mind, we must also acknowledge that the purpose of parables is essentially two-fold: revelatory and concealment. To suggest that they withhold truth from those who do not have ears to hear, however, is not to say that the parables themselves become a stumbling block to those who otherwise would believe. It would seem from the context in which they are used that they serve merely to further harden the hearts of those who are already estranged from the message of the kingdom.

# 4

# The Kingdom of God in the Present

ALTHOUGH MAN HAS BEEN faithful in filling the earth, he has generally failed to express godly dominion over it. Growth without government has resulted in chaos. The fall of Adam has rightly been blamed for humanity's inefficiency to deal adequately with the social, economic, and political needs of our day, though in Christ God's original intention remains unaltered: "fill . . . and rule" (Gen 1:28). And yet, since the fall, mankind has repeatedly sought to rule the world without first being ruled by God. Scripture continually reinforces the idea that it is only they who are themselves subject to godly authority that can rightly administer his authority. The purpose of the law given through Moses was essentially to provide a social infrastructure that might provoke the nations to seek Israel's God for themselves (see Exod 19:6). Where Israel failed in this regard, God's objective was fulfilled in Christ and continues to be so through his body, the church.

But is this a true picture? When we think of the church do we immediately identify it with a corporate organism that expresses God's rule in its actions? Can we really imagine that debates over whether or not to sanction so-called civil unions between same gender partners, to allow women roles of ecclesiastical governance, or what color of robe to wear on a particular saint's day would have been high on the apostle Paul's agenda in first-century Jerusalem?

Just as the church is not the kingdom, but an agent through which God's kingdom rule is to be expressed, so it is equally true that not everything claiming to be church is, in fact, church. I have never bought into the idea that the church in its biblical sense can be defined in terms

## The Kingdom of God in the Present

other than the corporate body of the redeemed. In chapter 2 we saw the kind of character that believers are to aspire to, while in chapter 3 we looked at certain characteristics of the kingdom of God. Both were derived from Jesus' words, not those of any subsequent entirely human agency. They are faithfully authoritative because they come from the author of our faith.

Thus, in this chapter, we will be looking at some fundamentals regarding how the kingdom of God should be—and, indeed, is being—expressed in our day. These, I believe, are hallmarks by which we may identify the genuineness of those things that claim to be expressions of God's kingdom in the present:

- is it motivated by an approach that rejoices in Christ?
- is the fruit that it produces rooted in Christ's ancestry?
- can it be identified as a legitimate response to the King's edict?

## REJOICING IN CHRIST

Kingdom rule is inextricably linked to kingdom worship. But what precisely does this mean? Depending on our particular churchmanship or denominational allegiance, the answer to that question could vary considerably. As ever in such circumstances, we can do no better than to prayerfully search the Scriptures for guidance. When we do, we may be surprised to find that true worship, according to the biblical pattern, has very little to do with liturgical expression or the singing of religious songs, however meaningful or well-intentioned they might be. Rather, it is more concerned with a lifestyle that is committed to rejoicing in Christ's person, in his work, and in our being in him. The relationship between all of these aspects and the kingdom of God is surely obvious: it is the kingship of Christ.

### Come Worship the King

We have already established that worship is more than simply words and music, though the singing of spiritual songs is one form by which we might rightfully express a worshipful heart (see Eph 5:19–20). There are a number of Greek verbs translated "worship" in our English New

Testament, the most frequent one being *proskuneo*, which means "to make obeisance, do reverence to."[1] The other words each convey a subtle change of emphasis within this general concept and, thus, allow us to formulate a more complete image of what is involved in true Christian worship. *Sebomai* relates more specifically to devotion evoked by a sense of awe, its derivative *sebazomai* is concerned with religious honor, *latreuo* identifies with the rendering of homage, and—perhaps bizarrely for those of us familiar with European football of the 1960s—*eusebio* is to behave in a pious manner.

At its very heart, worship may be perceived as a human response to divine revelation. Of course, the means by which God chooses to reveal himself are many and varied, the pinnacle of which is to be found in the person of his Son, Jesus Christ. In the types of churches that I have been accustomed to frequenting over the years, worship has often been related to Jesus as Savior, in relation to the Christmas theme, or even pertaining to the resurrected Christ. Comparatively rare, however, have been those occasions when worship has been specifically identified with his kingship.

The relationship between worship and service cannot be taken lightly. But again, we must be clear that what we describe as "service" and what Scripture identifies as such may not necessarily be one and the same. Paul's counsel to the believers at Rome leaves no room for the idea that it consists only in allowing our names to be put forward for the monthly coffee rota: "I urge you, my brothers, in view of God's mercy to offer your bodies as living sacrifices, holy and pleasing to God—this is your spiritual act of worship" (Rom 12:1).

So, if true worship consists essentially in us offering our bodies as living sacrifices, what can this mean, especially in relation to the kingdom of God and Christ Jesus as its king? Cast your minds back a couple of paragraphs where I mentioned the correlation in worship between human response and divine revelation. Well, here we have a perfect example of that relationship. The revelation is that of God's unbridled mercy, while the response is our giving of ourselves in complete surrender. Grant Osborne notes three significant features of such a sacrifice:

> It is *living*, denoting not only the dynamic nature of the sacrifice . . . but also the spiritual state of the "new life" in Christ and the Spirit.

---

1. Vine, *Expository Dictionary*, 1247.

It is *holy*, meaning that the person is wholly dedicated, "set apart" from the world and belonging to God.

It is *pleasing to God*, building on the Old Testament concept of the sacrifice as pleasing to God.[2]

All of this the apostle discusses in terms of reasonable or spiritual worship, from which William Hendriksen draws the following conclusion: "Paul is thinking [here] about . . . the wholehearted consecration of heart, mind, will, words, and deeds, in fact of all one is, has and does, to God. Nothing less!"[3]

Even a casual glance through a reputable concordance might cause us to register surprise at how often terms associated with royalty and redemption appear together, particularly in the New Testament: "God exalted [Jesus] to his own right hand as Prince and Savior" (Acts 5:31); "the eternal kingdom of our Lord and Savior" (2 Pet 1:11; see also 3:2, 18). We cannot own Jesus as Savior without also acknowledging him as Lord/King. Having delivered us, he thereby has the right to rule. Indeed, having been redeemed, no other party but Jesus has a rightful claim to reign in us thereafter, not even ourselves.

There seems to be a prevailing church culture, certainly in the UK, whereby the criterion by which the "period of worship" is deemed to be acceptable or otherwise can be almost anything but "is Jesus being lifted up?" But, just as the kingship of Christ is not restricted to a twenty minute slot on a Sunday morning, neither should our appreciation of it be confined to the words projected on a wall during that time. Wherever and whenever he is King, he is there and then worthy of our devotion. Or, as Tozer put it in his classic treatment on the subject: "If you cannot worship the Lord in the midst of your responsibilities on Monday, it is not very likely that you were worshiping on Sunday."[4] Thus, if genuine worship truly is the missing jewel in the evangelical crown, then it is also the coronet that is to be placed upon Jesus' head.

John Stott makes a strong case for worship being the primary duty of the church. At the heart of his argument is the premise that genuine worship is not related to form, ritual or ceremony, or even a quest for

---

2. Osborne, *Romans*, 319.
3. Hendriksen, *Romans*, 402.
4. Tozer, *Whatever Happened to Worship?*, 122.

the transcendent.[5] To imagine that it might be so would be to engage in the act of worship with entirely selfish motives. This is not where Scripture places the emphasis. New Testament worship does not consist in cultivating an environment wherein Christ will bless us with his presence. First of all, worship is not anthropocentric but theocentric; how it makes us feel is of secondary importance. I can get goosebumps and a tingly spine from occasions that are utterly devoid of any overtly Christian connection. No, we worship Jesus principally for who he is: "the King of Kings and the Lord of Lords" (1 Tim 6:15; Rev 19:16).

Moreover, true worship celebrates the fact that we are in God's presence. "Be still and know that I am God" might be unattractive to the caffeine-laden persona of the hyperactive. But it will unleash more of God's potency in us than the approach of those who promote the idea that the level of God's power in our midst is commensurate with the decibel level attained by our pleas for it to be generated among us as an egotistical sign of pseudo-authenticity.

### Expressing Gratitude for the Work of Christ

While it was necessary to emphasize the Lordship of Christ in the previous section, this should not discourage us from being thankful for what he has done to effect our salvation. After all, it is the Lamb of God who now sits on heaven's throne (Rev 22:3). This should come as no surprise to us at all. Whichever specific hermeneutic we opt for by which to interpret and understand Scripture, the central character is the same. Whether we focus on creation, covenant, redemption history, the church, the unfolding purpose of God, eschatology, or—as we have here—God's kingdom, Christ Jesus is—and must necessarily be—the pivotal figure.

Although in one sense the works of Christ continue, insofar that he yet intercedes on our behalf before the Father (Heb 7:25), when we speak of the work of Christ we usually have in mind those features pertaining to his atonement. This, too, is a source of great rejoicing, for should it not be with joy that we express our gratitude for being delivered from a state of direst peril into one of divine protection? Whereas we were once guilty and without hope, we now stand righteous before

---

5. Stott, *The Living Church*, 35–47.

## The Kingdom of God in the Present

God, with heaven as our inheritance. Thus, the coming day of judgment holds no fear for us, for no condemnation awaits those who have availed themselves of the opportunity to be justified by Christ's mediatorial ministry (Rom 8:1).

And there is much to be grateful for: once justified, we thereby become recipients of the promise of adoption as sons (Rom 8:23; Eph 1:5), are actively engaged in the continuing process of sanctification (1 Thess 5:23; 2 Thess 2:13), the fruit of which demonstrates the genuineness of our regeneration (John 3:7–8). This soteriological aspect of Christ's kingdom is one that is not lost on Jim Packer: "Salvation is a blessing of the kingdom of God, and like everything else in that kingdom it is both 'now' and 'not yet': *now* in beginnings and foretaste, *not yet* in completion and fulness. Hope of more grace and future glory, springing from faith that rejoices in present salvation and life in Christ, is therefore central to the Christ mind-set."[6]

We must be careful, therefore, to guard not only the truth of God's revelation through Scripture, but also to ensure that our interpretation of it remains authentic. As a younger Christian, I believed it was sufficient to teach the Bible; I am becoming increasingly aware that it is more necessary to do so biblically. A twenty-first century anachronistic perception of salvation can be detrimental to that originally conveyed. The New Testament writers are consistent with Old Testament prophecy in presenting the uniqueness of God's Messiah to deal with the human condition. Contrary to the pluralistic epithet of the age, Jesus did not announce himself to be a way, truthful, and living, but "the way and the truth and the life" (John 14:6). He alone provides reconciliation with the Father because only he can. The names of Buddha, Abraham, Mohammed, Karl Marx, Mary, Pope Benedict, Billy Graham, or any other (pseudo-) religious icons are incapable of effecting our justification, for the only "name under heaven [that] is given to men by which [they can] be saved" is that of "Jesus Christ of Nazareth" (Acts 4:10–12).

In short, any soteriology that is not at the same time Christocentric is invalid and violable. This should not be a cause for concern, but rather it is grounds for celebration. Without it, we remain in sin and without hope, for were it not for Christ's perfect sacrifice on our behalf we would still be objects of God's wrath instead of subjects of his glorious kingdom. The specifics attached to the doctrine are often

---

6. Packer, *Celebrating the Saving Work of God*, 53.

incomprehensible to finite reason. To claim that they must, therefore, be untrue is to elevate the human intellect to a status beyond its capacity to attain. Some mysteries remain veiled. "The immortal dies?" How can this possibly be? Even after many years of attempting to fathom the "whys" and the "wherefores," we are left to arrive at the same conclusion that Charles Wesley (1707–1778) reached in the very next line: "Who can explore his strange design?"

But the mystery is not primarily linked to our incapacity. It is not that these things could be known if only our capabilities were stretched further, increased to a greater degree, or our attempts to articulate them were enhanced by the pushing back of linguistic limitations. The mystery is intrinsic to the act. It is unfathomable because God has chosen not to disclose its secrets. That in itself is a mystery. Rather than seek to understand why, it would perhaps be more sagacious—not to mention judicious—of us to rest in that, rather trusting in his judgment, which can only give cause for yet further rejoicing.

Christ's work of atonement was one of penal substitution, whereby both propitiation and expiation were fully and finally addressed. Many theologians are uncomfortable to discuss it in such terms and it is beyond the remit of this work, given the immediate context, to tackle those concerns. The fact that it is so is yet another facet of the whole, for which we must express our gratitude. Suffice for now to concur with the erudite findings of James Denney: "If Christ died the death in which sin involved us—if in his death he took the responsibility of our sins on himself—no word is equal to this which falls short of what is meant by calling him our substitute."[7]

## Glad to Be a Christian

To my mind, anyone who is not glad to be a Christian must seriously contemplate whether they, in fact, are one. Now, I'm not talking about the occasional blips we feel from time to time when heaven seems like brass and other believers simply its monkeys, only to later discover that perhaps we are the biggest ape of all. I remember many years ago, Barry McGuire telling the story of his coming to Christ and the mental struggle he encountered immediately prior to his surrender. It wasn't

---

7. Denney, *Death of Christ*, 73.

## The Kingdom of God in the Present

becoming reconciled to God or having a relationship with Jesus that he had found so unpalatable, but having to get along with all the others who had made the same journey. Well, it's all part of the package, I'm afraid. Indeed, the apostle John states quite categorically that if we claim to love God but hate those with whom he has joined us in Christ, then we are liars and the truth is not in us (1 John 4:19–21). I would even go so far as to suggest that the only way to deepen our understanding of the relevance and import of the body of Christ on earth, to which we belong in principle, is to develop our commitment to the reality of expression toward that body in practice.

But what does it mean to be a Christian? When my wife and I first began attending the church of which we are now a part, there was a feature series directed toward the children called "Windows on the World." Each week, someone in the church would take a specific nation and, after a brief geographical/cultural introduction, go on to say something about the church there. Sometimes the individual(s) giving the talk might have had some personal connection to the country under review.

On one occasion, a couple who were later to become our friends, Andrew and Laura, were speaking about Holland. Being a native of that land, Laura said a few words in Dutch; it might just as well have been double Dutch as far as I was concerned. However, one word did strike me as being familiar: *Christelike* (pronounced "kris-ta-lee-ka"). It is a word that is also used in Afrikaans for our English noun "Christian." Certainly, to be a Christian is to engage in the process of sanctification by which we become more Christlike, but we are a Christian from the point of justification, even before we have had the opportunity to take such steps. According to my understanding of the biblical narrative, to be a Christian means quite simply—yet utterly profoundly—to be "in Christ" (Rom 8:1; 16:7; 1Cor 1:30; 16:24) and to have the assurance that he is "in us" (Col 1:24–29). To grow in Christ is something to be glad about, but growth can only take place from the basis of being. That must surely be the foundation for our exultation.

Kingdom expansion on a global scale is a legitimate promise of Scripture (see Isa 9:7; Hab 2:14). But its ultimate fulfillment is dependent upon the kingdom rule of God being first of all established in the individual. This, of course, should not be understood in either Unitarian or Universalist terms. The overwhelming evidence of Scripture, in my view, is one of a particular atonement. I concur with the observation of Roger Nicole that the term "limited atonement" is unhelpful in bringing clarity to what it seeks to describe.[8] But the kingdom rule of God throughout the earth is not dependent upon the whole world becoming Christian; it is—in some measure, at least—reliant upon those who are Christians expressing that kingdom rule so that the whole earth is influenced by godly standards. And that process begins with the critical establishing of that same kingdom rule in you and I as individuals. It is the fruit of our being in Christ, for which we give thanks.

Moreover, what we are is more significant than what we do, though very often the validity of the latter will be found insofar that it is a true expression of the former. This can be difficult to grasp, especially in a culture that has a tendency to define worth in terms of work. How many times have we been introduced to someone and one of the first questions they ask is concerned with what we do for a living? Sometimes, our occupation can give a clue as to what we are like as a person, but more usually this is not the case. Since leaving full-time education, I have been variously employed as an apprentice colliery mechanic, ambulance paramedic, theology college registrar, exam invigilator, and research writer. Although at the time all of these posts represented skills I had either attained or sought to aspire to, none of them could be said to have had any real bearing on who I was or am as a person.

A similar mindset can also affect the way we are as believers or, perhaps more accurately, our perception of how God sees us, which in turn governs our behavior. Other Christians can help to foster such an outlook and church leaders are not exempt, either as victims or perpetrators. What we need to re-establish in our thinking is the fact that all the conditions for our being in Christ have been fully met; this is what justification by faith means. Otherwise, it would be by works. The Lord articulated it in this way through the prophet Isaiah: "In repentance and rest is your salvation, in quietness and trust is your strength . . ." (Isa 30:15).

I trust I shall never have cause to add: ". . . but you would have none of it." Perfect peace is not to be found in striving to maintain a position in Christ, but in a steadfast mind that has learned to trust in him (Isa 26:3) and a glad heart, wherein he dwells (Ps 31:7). Thus, God's

---

8. R. R. Nicole, "Electing Love," in Boice, *Our Savior God*, 168–9.

love should not only cultivate within us a sense of gratefulness, but it should also produce from us a measure of gracefulness.

## Summary

Although the focus of both our attention and our affections in this section has been necessarily Christocentric, I am aware that such a path may be perceived to tend toward Jesusolatry, just as an overenthusiastic approach to the authority of Scripture could attract the charge of bibliolatry when, in fact, the Bible's inherent potency is derived by virtue of its source as the word of God. In the present milieu, however, it is appropriate to concentrate so exclusively on Christ, for Scripture speaks only of the Second Person of the Trinity as the King of the kingdom. We might even say that the purpose of the church is to reflect the glory of God in Jesus throughout the earth as an agent of his kingdom rule; it is not to mimic Hollywood or become a cathedral of worship to Apple.

Our joy, then, consists in three aspects in relation to the kingdom of God:

- we exult in the person of the King of the kingdom;
- we rejoice in the completed work of Christ that gives us access to that kingdom; and
- we celebrate for no other reason than that we are simply to be found in him and he in us.

## ROOTED IN CHRIST'S ANCESTRY

The title of the final piece of work for my first theology degree was *The Constant and Consistent Nature of God in both Testaments*. It was written on an old electric typewriter with every typo marked by a white blob of correcting fluid. When, some years later, I finally mustered sufficient courage to dip my toe in the waters of the computer age, one of the first undertakings I set myself was to key in all my earlier essays, monographs, and dissertations so that I would have an unblemished electronic copy of each. In order to keep an accurate record, I remember having relentlessly to resist the urge to rewrite large sections to accommodate improved understanding, better writing skills, or to develop themes that originally I had only touched upon. I managed to do so, but it was a struggle. It wasn't that I necessarily disputed my own earlier findings; I just felt more equipped to make a better fist at presenting those same arguments. The point? God doesn't change; we do.

## God's Unchanging Purpose

Matthew introduces us to his gospel account of Jesus Christ as "the son of David, the son of Abraham" (Matt 1:1). If we relate to Adam racially, then it is to Abraham that we relate redemptively. It is they who share his faith who are partakers also of his covenant promise (Gen 12:1–3), for the hallmark of the faithful is personal righteousness. Similarly, we join in the regal blessings of King David and, thereby, share his covenantal rule. The significance of David's reign is that he brought about such a change in fortunes for God's people, who once evoked only scorn and derision, to a place where they were respected by all around them. Not only did he rule in righteousness, but David also judged with justice, for one without the other is an unbalanced gospel. Grace without government is only one side of the coin. The harmony of Christ's kingdom rule is maintained by embracing both—"Seek first his kingdom *and* his righteousness" that all else may be built on such a foundation (Matt 6:33).

Our attention is drawn immediately and instinctively to "kingdom" and "righteousness." We then note that they are not our own or those of anyone else, but that they belong to God. The context may suggest a contrast with that of the Pharisees, but the evidence—such as may be conceded—is inconclusive. Finally, we congratulate ourselves that we have spotted Jesus is promoting the pursuit of them as of primary importance. But that is not the end of the matter and I am grateful to William Hendriksen for stopping me in my tracks before I moved on: "The verb *seek* implies a being absorbed in the search for, a persevering and strenuous effort to obtain . . . The form of the verb that is used allows the rendering, 'Be constantly seeking.'"[9]

Jesus' throne is founded and upheld in righteousness and justice (Isa 9:7). On this basis must all other forms of government be evaluated. Injustice and unrighteousness are twin pillars of a society that

---

9. Hendriksen, *Matthew*, 354.

has dispatched God's kingdom rule from its vocabulary. But kingdom people are those who recognize a shared ancestry in and with Christ and are prepared to embrace their God-appointed role as his agents in the earth to once more shake the foundations of those who make the decisions from Washington to Brussels. Indeed, one of the principal features of God's kingdom community is that it so embraces God's rule that it challenges the assumptions of the generation in which it finds itself. Where there is political expedience by the wealthy at the expense of the poor, we cry "Unjust!" Wherever tyrants choose to exploit the provision of the world's resources for profit, we declare "Unrighteous!" When, in a pseudo-attempt to redress centuries of racial inequality, world governments opt for positive discrimination, again we shout "Injustice!" Where the growth of food mountains is matched only by the escalation of the graves of the famine-stricken, citizens of the kingdom of God protest "Enough!" Not just "Enough! It's time somebody else did something about it," but in obedience to Jesus' command, we lead first by example and then by influence.

It is surely time for the mountain of the Lord to dispense justice and righteousness to the nations (see Isa 21:1–2; 25:6–7), to feed the hungry, clothe the naked, bring health to the sick, befriend the imprisoned, set free those who are sin's captives, and demonstrate to a watching world that true "live aid" can only be found in the gospel of the kingdom of Jesus Christ. Humanism has failed and continues to do so. Secularity promises much but delivers only futility. Base religion is but a guise aimed at proffering some semblance of God-consciousness, though denying its power. But the kingdom comes and is coming. In this respect, as the Father has sent the Son, and the Father and Son have sent the Spirit, so the Father, Son, and Spirit send the church in a perpetual re-enactment of the Christ event, that is, the incarnation (see John 20:21–22).

It is a matter of historical record that religious revival is the harbinger of social change. This should come as no surprise given that biblical Christianity is not confined to the salvation of the soul but also extends to deal with the transformation of the whole man. Indeed, it was John Wesley who commented that religious observance without fruit of repentance being evidenced in distinct behavioral change is not true Christianity. Other noted historians believe, for example, that

Kingdom

England was spared the atrocities of the French revolution by social changes brought about by the revival under George Whitefield.

The order in God's purpose is heart first, lives thereafter. The crux of man's need is to be found in the condition of his heart. To change society for the better, therefore, we must first of all deal with the root of the problem and not merely its fruit. Otherwise, we are guilty of merely treating symptoms, rather than performing the kind of invasive surgery that is required to deal effectively with the disease-ridden patient before us. Perhaps one Christian group that is particularly renowned for its social projects—certainly in my home country—is the Salvation Army, though its founder knew exactly where the priority lay. The call of the established churches has traditionally been: "Come to our buildings"; William Booth dared to "go into all the world [to] preach the good news to all creation" (Mark 16:15).

Discipled and Discipling

Anyone looking for biblical support for the notion that it is the function of the church to make converts, to train missionaries, to fill pews, or to swear papal allegiance would either have a lengthy pursuit or would be forced to abandon it as a fruitless exercise. The overwhelming weight of evidence is perfectly encapsulated in Jesus' pre-ascension mandate to his eleven remaining closest followers: "go and make disciples of all nations" (Matt 28:19a). That is the "what?" Thankfully, Jesus also provided the "how?" ". . . baptizing them in the name of the Father and of the Son and of the Holy Spirit, and teaching them to obey everything I have commanded you" (vv. 19b–20a). He had already given them the "Why?" "All authority on heaven and earth has been given to me. Therefore . . ." (v. 18).

At the outset, it is important that we understand the correct terminology here used. I have heard it said that to be a disciple requires great discipline and that the correlation of those two words should make that obvious. Etymologically, of course, the words "disciple" and "discipline" do share a common origin. Their use in Scripture, however, is vastly different. Our English "discipline" is employed to translate the Greek *sophronismos*, which means literally "to save the mind through

## The Kingdom of God in the Present

admonition," while "disciple" translates *mathetes*, denoting one who learns by applying rigorous enterprise to serious contemplation.[10]

Discipleship does not just involve learning, but also requires a teacher to convey that which is to be learned. Indeed, to view the matter from the other side for a moment, it would be accurate to say that nothing has really been taught unless something has truly been learned. The passing on of information requires that it is understood and applied before it can honestly be validated. This is why Jesus knew that he could confidently pass on the baton to those who had remained faithful to his teaching: they had been discipled themselves and were, thus, ideally suited to disciple others. It might even be said with some merit that those who were known as Jesus' disciples in the New Testament were those who responded positively to his message of the kingdom (see Matt 5:1; Luke 6:17).

This, too, was rooted in Christ's ancestry, but on this occasion it related to his eternal filial obligation. His *ways* were deliberately such as to demonstrate his obedience to the Father's will (John 5:19–30), his *words* were exclusively those given to him by the Father (12:49–50), and his *work* of atonement was fully in keeping with the Father's purpose for him (11:27). As if to further increase the sense of mystery, however, we are told that this same Jesus, who in respect of his divine nature is co-eternal with the Father, learned obedience through his painful experiences (Heb 5:7–8), and he "grew in wisdom and stature, and in favor with [both] God and men" (Luke 2:52). How could this possibly be? Well, if we knew the answer to that it would cease to be a mystery, yet we are assured that it is so.

What seems to be beyond the realm of speculation is the specific directive Jesus gave on how we are to achieve the objective of making disciples: "baptizing them . . . and teaching them . . ." I believe that it is not only these features that are important, but that the order in which they are presented is equally significant. In many of the churches that I have been acquainted with over the years, there has been a reluctance to baptize until the candidate has shown signs of adequate understanding. The reasons cited are often sincere, plausible, even logical, but on the basis of the evidence before us one could hardly say that they were authentically biblical.

---

10. See Vine, *Expository Dictionary*, 308.

Kingdom

Although it is true that the word "disciple" does not appear in the New Testament outside of the gospel accounts and Acts, the fact that it features so heavily in one of the last messages Jesus conveyed to his closest followers implies that the program suggested by it was very much in evidence in the formative years of the church. That it became decreasingly so over the centuries may also explain—at least partly—why successive generations have thus far failed to experience the same measure of growth, both in terms of numerical explosion and personal/corporate maturity.

Indeed, it might even be argued that if the sole criterion for determining the success or otherwise of the church taking its kingdom agency seriously was how many more pews it could fill from one year to another, then many local expressions might have cause to believe that they are on the right track. But making disciples and increasing the church membership roll can be poles apart. I would even go so far as to assert that one of the main contributory factors toward the fading of momentum of the effects of historic revivals has been a distinct deficiency in the area of biblical discipleship.

My understanding of Scripture is such that discipleship is not an optional extra for the elite believer who has a natural predilection for such matters, and yet that is how it seems to be presented in many, if not most, churches. Consider the words of Dietrich Bonhoeffer, someone who came to know the ultimate cost of discipleship: "Christianity without discipleship is always Christianity without Christ. It remains an abstract idea, a myth which has a place for the Fatherhood of God, but omits Christ as the living Son . . . There is trust in God, but no following of Christ."[11]

## Salt and Light

In Hebrew culture, salt had two primary uses: seasoning and preservation. Just as there is no flavor in tasteless food eaten without salt (Job 6:6), so too is humanity morally prosaic without the seasoning effect of God's people upon it. But salt also acts as a preserving agent; it postpones decay, thereby extending the usefulness of that to which it is applied. We must be clear in our understanding, however, that salt does

---

11. Bonhoeffer, *Cost of Discipleship*, 64.

not prevent ultimate deterioration, but only delays its effects. This is part of our calling into unregenerate society: temporarily suspending their destruction, that there may yet be time for them to turn to the Lord and so be saved (Rom 13:11).

Because we live in a morally corrupt age, one that is largely devoid of any sense of righteousness or justice, we are expected to have a restraining influence, one that brings God's kingdom rule to bear in an increasingly hostile environment. It may well prove costly, but commitment will always provoke reaction where compromise is the order of the day. This is especially so when such involvement is taken out of the synods and onto the streets. Committee meetings about the evils of illegal substances won't stop drug abuse; practical help, understanding of the individual background, counsel, and advice given from someone who has been touched by the love of God in Christ Jesus just might do. When we look with compassion on those at the receiving end of injustice, we simply reflect the image of our Master in similar circumstances two thousand years ago. The feeding of the five thousand was not some flashy showbiz party trick to capture the attention of the crowd before he could zap them with the message of the kingdom. It stemmed from a heart that was touched by their immediate need to be fed.

Salt affects things like fish and meat because it is so radically different. If it loses its salting qualities, however, it becomes utterly devoid of value. To conform to the pattern of the world for the sake of acceptance also robs us of our seasoning and preserving usefulness (Rom 12:2). We are called to be separate, which is the root meaning of the word "holy" (see 1 Pet 1:16). This means that, though we are to remain in the world for the time being, we are not to become part of it once more. It is perhaps noteworthy that it took a relatively short time for God to bring Israel out of Egypt but a further forty years for the influence of Egypt to be removed from Israel. It is recorded of Jesus that he was both set apart from and a friend of sinners (Matt 11:19; Heb 7:26). May the same be said of us also.

Jesus said: "I am the light of the world" (John 8:12). He also told his disciples: "You are the light of the world" (Matt 5:14). In creation, God made two light bearers: "the greater light to govern the day and the lesser light to govern the night" (Gen 1:16). The light we transmit in society is not our own, but the reflected glory of God's one and only Son, Christ Jesus (Eph 5:8, 14). We are the light of the world because we have within us God's imparted life and we are to express that light in righteous actions (Matt 5:16). Now, Scripture teaches that good works have no redemptive value; we are not saved *by* them. However, the Bible's testimony is equally clear that we are saved *for* them (Eph 2:8–10). In other words, good deeds are the tangible manifestation of God's life at work in us, a radical demonstration of a redirected lifestyle. Their purpose is that others may see and "praise [our] Father in heaven." Thus, we are to influence society for good by the good news of the gospel.

Jesus was not saying that he is able to offer or provide light, though of course that is true also. No, he is the source of all light (see 1 John 5). As artistically powerful as Holman Hunt's well-known painting is, it fails to adequately portray this truth. Again, to walk in the light is typically figurative of a progressive journey, as distinct from a once-for-all decision. We remove ourselves from the domain of darkness while ever we continue to walk in the light (John 8:12). Moreover, we become that light for others because we are to be found in him and him in us.

Light has a similar effect on darkness as does salt toward blandness and imminent decay. Its only liaison with darkness is to expose it by the fruit of the light: "all goodness, righteousness and truth" (Eph 5:9). The product of darkness cannot exist where there is light. It might even be said that darkness is the absence of light. For this reason, it has been somewhat adroitly asserted that all that is required for evil to prevail is for good men to do nothing. Thus, we are not to "be overcome by evil, but rather [to] overcome evil with good" (Rom 12:21). This is not just a nice verse to keep near the top of the promise box for when things seem tough; it, too, is part of our calling as children of light.

It is possible for salt to lose its effect by virtue of being influenced rather than being influential. It is also feasible that light might be rendered inoperable through concealment. Secret discipleship is an anomaly; it is almost a contradiction in terms. Let Jesus' own words serve as a warning: "Whoever acknowledges me before men, I will also acknowledge him before my Father in heaven. But whoever disowns me before men, I will also disown him before my Father in heaven" (Matt 10:32–33).

## Summary

Christ's kingdom must break out of the realm of religious cliché if it is to bring about an effective solution to society's needs. World governments will always fail where they seek to rule without caring values or clarity of vision. By stark contrast, godly government successfully incorporates the roles of the prophetic, the sacerdotal, and the monarchical. To the question: "Should Christians be actively involved in politics?" we could well be forgiven for responding: "Only if you believe that God is interested in the needs of humanity." Christians are potentially the best equipped it is possible to be in order to deal with the social, moral, and emotional bankruptcy of our day, but potential never bears fruit without becoming practical. What we are in essence in our closets, we must become experientially in our cosmos. This requires that we understand what God's unchanging purpose is, that we take steps to engage with his appointed training mechanism, and that we simply be salt and light in a world of decay and darkness.

## RESPONDING TO THE KING'S EDICT

As with many of the subjects touched upon in this book, a separate volume could be dedicated to how best we might respond to the King's edict. In the present context, however, it seems appropriate to consider three specific areas:

- resting in the fact that we simply are church and nothing we can do will add to or detract from that position;
- in order to express our relatedness to one another as church, we need first of all to acknowledge our mutual interdependency; and
- how the overflow of that relationship with fellow-believers extends to others currently outside its parameters.

Although the triumphalist might seek to convey all of these in a matter of fact "just let go and let God" sort of way, personal experience and the historical record suggests a more realistic approach might be required. The testimony of Scripture equally affirms that the task before us is arduous, challenging, and at times seemingly impossible. Being fraught with difficulty, however, does not in itself call into question the genuineness of the commission—far from it.

# Kingdom

## Being Church

Over the course of the past thirty-six years, I have witnessed firsthand some quite astonishing developments in the Christian church. Admittedly, these have been encountered within pretty tight parameters when compared to the experience of others over a similar period, but that serves only to heighten the amazement rather than diminish it. It seems that every so often, a feature of the whole kaleidoscope of Christian expression becomes unearthed once again, and, rather than afford it a legitimate place in the whole, for a period of time that single aspect becomes the primary object of our attention. In so doing, something on the periphery gets pushed off the edge until its turn awaits our rediscovery. Power evangelism, extensive worship, body ministry, and caring for one another beyond the limitations of a casual Sunday morning nod of the head have all at one time or another taken center stage. The more I read, the more I become aware that the pattern is oft-repeated throughout history. Indeed, the longer you are involved, it seems the more likely you are to catch more than one phase of the same feature being given prominence, just in case you didn't make the most of it the first time around.

Very often, the new "in thing" will have its own buzz-word or phrase. Some churches used to set their annual agenda on the basis of such terminology. I remember one church I belonged to in my early Christian experience thrived on this kind of red-top publicity: *He's Alive in '85*; *Preparing for Heaven in '87*; *Standing at the Gate in '88*; *Make Life Divine in '89*. I'm not sure that we came up with one in 1986; perhaps the publicist was too busy chopping sticks. The more recent phase doing the rounds seems to be alerting our attention to discover the best way to "do" church. It took a while to register with me exactly what was being asked here. Maybe it says a great deal about my background, but to "do" something to something or someone else has always carried with it the conveyance of menace—not an activity that I would immediately identify with how the church should operate ideally.

In many ways, the notion of having to "do" something to demonstrate one's Christianity smacks of an unhealthy hybrid of salvation by works and following the current Western worldview that can only identify merit with motion. The same is true of the similarly tainted ethos in many Christian circles that promotes doing the work of an evangelist, where the overriding emphasis in Scripture is simply of being witnesses. Those of my acquaintance who have been especially busy in seeking new ways of "doing" church have in reality been nothing more than seeking to present the concept of church in a way that is likely to meet with a favorable response from its target audience, the unsaved, while at the same time leaving them generally unexposed to the core elements of the gospel. Such a strategy seems to be entirely absent from the agenda of our first-century forebears.

Jesus could never have been accused of conditioning the power of his message to curry the popularity of the masses. Neither could that charge have been laid at the door of the first generation of believers. The kingdom of God functions on essentially upside-down principles when compared to the kingdoms of this world, where successful leadership is determined by a servant disposition, greatness is measured in terms of humility, true riches are attained by giving, and favor is by way of the cross. Moreover, wealth is not evaluated in terms of fiscal probity or material possessions, but by exclusively spiritual means. The abundance God has for us can only be attained through—more often than not, in the midst of—trial (see Ps 66:8–12). Despite what the proponents of the so-called "prosperity gospel" might promote, a church that is infected with affluenza is seriously inhibited in its capacity to present the gospel of Christ's kingdom.

Of course, being inevitably leads to doing, though the validity of the latter must always be determined by it being a legitimate expression of the former. Equally, believing is not merely about nodding one's head in mental assent to a system of doctrinal tenets, however scripturally balanced they might be. Indeed, for theology to be truly biblical, it must also be practically applicable or, if you prefer, prophetic. When Peter reminded Cornelius how Jesus, under the anointing of the Holy Spirit, "went around doing good" (Acts 10:38) it was simply the supernaturally natural overflow of him resting confidently in the assurance of who he was. Why? ". . . [B]ecause God was with him."

The ethos behind the "Let's find a better way to 'do' church" mentality is usually one that is motivated by the idea that is more concerned with filling pews than extending Christ's kingdom. It is frequently also linked to an empirical outlook that is chiefly provoked by wanting to fly one's own particular denominational flag in the town or city. The current predilection for wishing to plant a church where there already

Kingdom

exists a viable expression of true kingdom values, but where those responsible for that expression might have an ever so slightly different understanding of how the word "and" should be interpreted in such-and-such a verse smacks not of wanting to "do" church at all, much less "be" it. Not only would I question the motives, I would also query the source.

In his excellent book, *The McDonaldization of the Church*, John Drane asks the poignant question: "Whom are we trying to reach?"[12] In the context of this work, I would like to pose another one and trust that it will be found no less pertinent: "Whose kingdom are we aiming to build?"

## Constituent Parts of the Body

The church responds to the King's edict simply because it is the body of which he is the head. In anatomical physiology, this is but a natural outworking of the relationship that exists between the two, a point that the apostle Paul sees fit to remind his Corinthian readers:

> "Now the body is not made up of one part but of many. If the foot should say, 'Because I am not a hand, I do not belong to the body,' it would not for that reason cease to be part of the body. And if the ear should say, 'Because I am not an eye, I do not belong to the body,' it would not for that reason cease to be part of the body. If the whole body were an eye, where would the sense of hearing be? If the whole body were an ear, where would the sense of smell be? But in fact God has arranged the parts in the body, every one of them, just as he wanted them to be" (1 Cor 12:14–18).

Of course, the context of this passage is the interdependent nature of the different parts of the body to one another as a type of that which exists in the "body" of Christ. But it is not too unreasonable to take the metaphor further. Age and aching aside, when I want my feet to start walking in a certain direction, they do so almost instinctively—or so it seems. They continue in the path of my choosing until they are halted by some external influence—usually a laundry basket my wife has left for me to stumble over—or I decide to give them another instruction to obey. They never go off in a direction of their own choosing as a

---

12. Drane, *McDonaldization*, 55–84.

## The Kingdom of God in the Present

mark of their freedom from law, stand defiantly agaze until I change my mind to something less arduous, or sulk in a corner until I reassure them how much more vital to my overall well-being they are than my shoulder blades or how, if it wasn't for them, my knee joints wouldn't get any exercise.

It is to Paul's Ephesian epistle that we must turn to see the full implications of Christ's headship in relation to his body, the church, and that in the context of developmental maturity as a symbol of organic unity (see Eph 4:4–16). Arguments against the head being utilized here in the acquired sense of governance abound. No doubt, such opinions are aroused in some measure by antipathy toward present-day abuse in the political arena, commerce and industry, and so-called heavy-shepherding ecclesiastical frameworks. The idea of headship may well have overtones relating to source or origin, as William Liefeld suggests.[13] However, it is not necessary to choose one possibility over the other when both may be inferred with equal support. Moreover, to do so merely on the basis of personal preference and/or cultural comfortability are options we are not at liberty to employ.

Although, strictly speaking, the idea of the body of Christ is best understood as it relates to the church in its universal sense, each local expression is to be a microcosm of that. Remember, Paul's fondness for this particular illustration can be seen in the fact that he used it on a number of occasions in his letters to individual congregations or groups of churches in a specific location. In this milieu, we might even be forgiven for believing that the New Testament idea of church growth is primarily one of maturity. Natural bodies seldom grow exclusively—if at all—by having foreign parts appendaged to them.

Constitutionally, we can reduce the imagery even further. If I have a problem with one of my limbs, my local practitioner is often able to deduce the nature and extent of my difficulty, and how best to treat it by way of an external examination. If I have a digestive, respiratory, circulatory or similar complaint, however, she will often send me for a blood test and/or x-ray. It is amazing how much more confident she can be in her diagnosis when certain parts of me have been subject to the microscope. While on the outside it may look as if my body constitutes nothing more elaborate than a couple of arms, the same number of legs, eyes, and ears, a mouth, a nose, and a torso, closer inspection

---

13. Liefeld, *Ephesians*, 110.

# Kingdom

reveals that I am actually made up of somewhere between sixty and one hundred trillion cells. Each one has its own structure and is responsible for a different function. All the elements of a cell are held together by a membrane, consisting of a cytoplasm and a nucleus. The membrane also contains receptors, which identify that cell with others.

It should come as little surprise, therefore, that arguably the most effective growth movements in recent years—both in terms of numerical increase and advancement toward maturity—has been seen in those churches that use the cell structure of small groups, usually in a midweek home setting. Chris Brearley explains why this may be so:

> There is always a danger that the larger the Christian fellowship, the less its individual members know, care for, and are accountable to each other. It is very easy to become lost in the crowd, resulting in one's participation being either minimal or that of a spectator. Therefore, it would appear to be advantageous to divide large gatherings into lesser groups such as house meetings or cell groups. This eliminates anonymity, enables mutual accountability, and creates a close community in which everyone can play an active role by developing and fully utilizing their God-given gifts.[14]

Of course, it would be remiss of me not to acknowledge also the potential for calamity. Risks of separatist cliques developing, divisive tendencies, and individuals feeling that they are being bullied into areas unhealthily outside of their comfort zones are just a few examples of negative possibilities. Handled correctly, however, by godly leaders, who are themselves submitted to the overall church leadership, should help to minimize such problems.

## Getting the Job Done

As citizens who respond favorably to the edict of the King of the kingdom, Christians have a duty to confront unrighteousness and injustice, as we have seen. The voice of the church as a legitimate agent of that kingdom has far too long remained silent in the name of pseudo-meekness. Its complacency has merely registered an abstention of surrender against a system that imposes unfair foreign policies on less economically developed countries by the so-called super powers. It

---

14. Brearley, *Reclaiming Church*, 89.

*The Kingdom of God in the Present*

is conservatively estimated that there are approaching twenty million refugees worldwide, around half of whom are children. Although that number has remained reasonably stable for quite some time now, the provision for their needs has somewhat diminished in real terms.

And what of the homeless in the industrialized nations? Debt persists and continues to escalate, largely due to a marketing strategy that encourages people to live well beyond their resources; single parenthood, which is often symptomatic of a lifestyle that might better be described as "multiple partnerhood"; and a culture of techno-gadget addiction, which is swiftly replacing traditionally recognized dependencies such as drug and alcohol abuse, where priorities are drawn toward the latest "must have" accessory, even if that means not being able to meet more valid financial obligations. As a consequence—either directly or otherwise—many of the park benches in Glasgow, London, New York, Sydney, Paris, Rome, and Munich are no longer predominantly occupied by junkies, winos, and unshaven vagrants in tattered clothing and in desperate need of soap and water, but by those attired in the latest street-cred gear and sporting an iPod. Are they any less worthy of our compassion?

The answer to that question surely lies in the posing of another: "Are they any less needy of the kingdom of God to direct their paths?" Everyone who currently stands outside of God's redeemed community is in need of at least the opportunity to respond to the invitation to acknowledge his appointed Redeemer as their own. Irrespective of the choice they may make in that regard, they all similarly benefit from the influence of true kingdom values being brought to bear on society. That they would never admit as much is largely immaterial. The testimony of history counters any arguments they are likely to present.

The state of social deterioration is one that must surely sadden even the most optimistic of hearts. At such times, the number of reasons cited for the decadence in society is almost equal to the number of opinions sought. The rich becoming progressively more so at the expense of the poor, the promotion of "the economy" as the single most-worshiped idol of our day, and militant extremism among some religious groups can all trace their roots in some measure back to the source of all misdeeds: Adam's original sin. At the same time, however, that should hardly come as a surprise. Moreover, can we really blame the night for being dark? Injustice persists because the just have just given up. Unrighteousness thrives because the righteous have stopped speaking out for right and wrong. Darkness prevails because those responsible for bringing light to the situation have turned off the switch. And decay continues unabated because those with a mandate to bring seasoning to unsavoriness have found something less worthwhile to occupy their time.

That notwithstanding, however, a statistic that has remained almost constant throughout my adult life (and possibly before, though I was blissfully ignorant of it at the time) is that around 90 percent of the world's wealth is in the hands of 10 percent of the world's population. Increased global fiscal resources serve only to increase the measure in the hands of the wealthy; it never spreads sufficiently abroad to make a difference to the world's poorest. Each day that passes a staggering 24,000 human lives end because of hunger. We have already seen that even that word has become so devoid of meaning through misuse and abuse. This is not the kind of hunger experienced by those who cannot manage to leave their stomach muscles unused between lunchtime and teatime without the need to exercise them over a bag of cheesy Wotsits. This is the kind that cannot remember what the month was when you last ate a morsel. There is hunger and there is gluttony; they are poles apart.

Voluntary aid agencies help to alleviate the problem, and soup kitchens provide temporary sustenance for the hungry, but the real needs are spiritual and God's answer to that predicament remains constant: the gospel of Christ Jesus. His chosen channel of blessing: the church. The weapons he has placed at its disposal: the principles of his kingdom rule. It is time for the cry of the kingdom to be heard in Whitehall and Washington: "Enough of feathering the nests of the rich at the expense of the vulnerable." I am grateful to God for organizations like Help International, Tearfund, and Rainbow Africa, whose common vision it is to establish and maintain relief programs across the globe, thus demonstrating that God is present in the most apparently Godforsaken places. I thank him also for "the grace of our Lord Jesus Christ, that though he was rich, yet for [our] sakes he became poor, so that [we] through his poverty might become rich" (2 Cor 8:9). Out of the overflow of that richness, may we in turn bless the world's poor.

If kingdom justice is to extend beyond the parameters of the church walls, then so too must kingdom righteousness. Although there is a sense in which righteousness refers to the way Christian believers relate to one another as the body of Christ under his governing headship, this is but one expression of the model, however primary that expression might be. As Don Garlington observes: "Significantly, it is righteousness as the love and service of others which permits an application of the concept beyond the covenant community."[15]

## Summary

When I first became a Christian in 1976, the self-acclaimed "faith" movement was at its peak in the UK. Christian bookstores bounded with tomes on how to get faith, how to keep faith, how to grow faith, how to develop your faith, how to give it away to others as a means of increasing your own measure of faith, and—perhaps most prevalent of all—how to use faith as currency to attract God's abundant blessing. As a young and immature believer, I innocently wondered why God had given us the Bible if it required so many supplements that did not seem to have it as their foundation. The same could be said today of the kingdom of God and how we might most appropriately engage with the requirements of the King. Although much older and hopefully a little wiser, the same principle applies. Scripture must ultimately determine our belief and practice. To learn how to respond to the King's edict in terms of being church, growing in interdependency, and helping to overcome injustice and unrighteousness in society we must be guided by the owner's manual—the Bible.

## SUMMARY

What the church of Jesus Christ is in the present must be governed somewhat by the past. This is not to say that it should be dictated to by its failings or weakness as recorded in its most recent history, but to look further back than that, further even than those apparently halcyon days of the first generation of believers. As an agent of the kingdom of God on earth, it behooves the redeemed community to look to the original intention in God's heart as to how his rule might be exercised and expressed aright. Scripture is vitally important in our quest, especially

---

15. D. B. Garlington, "Righteousness," in Atkinson and Field, *Christian Ethics*, 744.

insofar as it reveals to us the basis of our being citizens of God's kingdom in the first place: reconciliation with the Father by virtue of being in his Son.

Just as worship without relationship is tantamount to idolatry, so too the genuineness of any claim to relationship with the King of the kingdom that does not extend to worship must be met with more than a little suspicion. Or, to put it another way: theology that does not end in doxology is merely a philosophical ideology in religious garb. I am not necessarily advocating that we should all seek to attain the same level of exuberant frenzy in our appreciation of who God is and what he has done for us. We are each different in temperament. Indeed, it might even be argued that many of the denominations exist not so much on the differences of doctrinal persuasion as that of liturgical preference. But our being in Christ must surely evoke some sense of gratitude even in the least naturally expressive among us.

Being ambassadors of Jesus' rule is not just about exercising dominion in our own limited sphere of operation, but also seeking to tap in to his ancestral roots and allow the goodness inherent in them to pervade every area of society with which we come into contact. The word "righteousness" is a derivation from the old English "rightwiseness." It simply means doing the right thing or bringing about a right situation where previously this was not the case. It is to concern oneself with righting wrongs. We do this in ourselves by learning to obey the intrinsic sense within us of appropriate conduct for kingdom citizens, by conveying that to others with whom we share that citizenship, and by communicating kingdom principles as salt and light in society generally.

Although we are not saved *by* good works (Eph 2:8–9), we are saved *to do* them (v. 10). In the same way, though kingdom citizenship is more about being than doing, this does not negate the fact that our passive experience must overflow into practical expression. Not only so, but what we do can only truly be meritorious inasmuch as it is a valid response to Christ's mandate and example. Although the primary beneficiaries of this will be the household of faith, it is by no means to be limited to them only (see Gal 6:10).

# 5

# The Coming Kingdom

IF THE PREMISE OF this work is a valid one, that the concept of kingdom has always lay at the heart of God's dealings with man, then there is no reason to believe that this will ever change. Even when its fullness was ushered in by King Jesus, there was a sense of living between the ages: the kingdom had come, but was yet coming. Of course, there is also a sense in which this might be applied to its progressive development through the ages and pages of history, but its coming in all of its glory will not be complete until the consummation of the age.

What we will be considering in this chapter touches upon the area of eschatology. Derived from the Greek *eschatos*, meaning "last," eschatology is simply the study of the doctrine relating to the last things. Although the word is not used exclusively in this sense in the New Testament, the immediate context in which it is employed usually suggests when this is so. In terms of kingdom revelation, it might even be argued that the period of the commencement of the last days coincided with the incarnation event. Certainly, the rendering of the opening declaration from the writer to the Hebrews lends itself to the possibility of such an interpretation (Heb 1:2). Peter's comments are perhaps even more deliberate: "[Christ] was chosen before the creation of the world, but was revealed in these last days for your sake. Through him you believe in God, who raised him from the dead and glorified him, and so your faith and hope are in God" (1 Pet 1:20–21).

Eastern mystical religions in particular conceive of history as cyclical and, in extreme cases, this has given rise to a belief in reincarnation. The Bible, however, teaches of history as being linear in the sense that creation has a specific goal toward which it is moving. In order to understand more fully what that objective is, we must first of all gain a greater appreciation of the ultimate purpose of God, not only for the redeemed, but also for the whole of the created order.

Although the church has not always been consistent in the regard with which it has held the doctrine of eschatology, seemingly fluctuating between fervent passion and dim uncertainty, the closer we come to the consummation of the age, perhaps the more needful we become of reassurance in this matter. This we will now attempt to address as we turn our attention to the fascinating subject of the coming kingdom.

## UNDERSTANDING THE TIMES

Contrary to the oft-heralded accusation that Christian believers live in the past and, therefore, have no relevance to the present, understanding the past has enormous significance for how we conduct ourselves today. This is true in terms both of being receptive to godly traditions passed down to us and of learning the lessons from the mistakes made by previous generations. But we must also apply ourselves to understanding something of what the future holds for us—and others—if we are to maximize the potential available in the here and now. This does not necessarily mean having a perfect knowledge of the precise nature of the unfolding of end-time events. The variance of opinion among even the most otherwise qualified of theologians suggests that such knowledge might be beyond finite comprehension. But it is possible to grasp some understanding of those times from Scripture and prepare ourselves in the light of revealed certainties.

### Signs of the Times

As a very young Christian, I remember many of the old-style Pentecostal preachers haranguing their audiences with the threat that Jesus could come again at any time. Their purpose was probably two-fold: to scare the unsaved into submission with the barely veiled warning that they may not have many more opportunities to repent, and to keep the faithful fearful, lest they be tempted to slacken in their witness before others. Although their objectives may have been genuine—of sorts—the validity of their premise was certainly not.

The testimony of Scripture is such that Jesus will not return at any time, but at God's appointed time (Rom 9:9). Of course, because that time is known only to the Father, it might still be considered as "at any time" from our perspective. It remains one of those secret things that still belong to God because he has chosen not to unveil its mystery to us (Deut 29:29). The point, however, is that it will not be decided randomly on a whim, but has been carefully designated to coincide with certain features that may well become known to us. Thus, what Scripture does provide are clues or waymarkers, if you will, that help us as the appointed time of Christ's return draws ever nearer. We might even call them "signs of the times."

The purpose of a sign—any sign—is to direct our attention to something greater than itself. If I have been booked to speak at a venue that is unfamiliar to me, I often ask the administrator for any unusual landmarks nearby, so that I will know when I am in the correct vicinity. Disused fuel stations, television broadcasting masts, traffic light systems that actually work, speed trap cameras that don't, and grocery stores that are not open on Sundays are just some that I have been on the look out for recently. None of them were an end in themselves but were designed to enable me to be assured that I was on the right track. Their usefulness is best served by both their uniqueness and their "up-to-dateness." If there is more than one of the particular kind of building, natural feature, or type of crossroads within close proximity, then the odds of me becoming lost are dramatically increased. Similarly, if the information conveyed is out of date, such as that disused filling station having recently been razed to the ground and a new shopping mall erected in its place, then I could be driving around for hours.

The outdated image of an elderly spinster parading up and down the local high street adorned with sandwich board declaring that "The End is Nigh" may well have provided little more than light Saturday afternoon entertainment for many of the passers-by. But nor was it the most glaringly obvious sign of the truth behind the message it sought to convey. Jesus gave us one or two clear pointers to look out for that, though they would not signal the end, would be indicative of the beginning of the end. Relaxing with his closest followers on the Mount of Olives, Jesus is recorded as having uttered these words:

# Kingdom

> "You will hear of wars and rumors of wars, but see to it that you are not alarmed . . . Nation will rise against nation and kingdom against kingdom. There will be famines and earthquakes . . . Then you will be handed over to be persecuted and put to death, and you will be hated by all nations because of me. At that time many will turn away from the faith and will betray and hate each other, and many false prophets will appear and deceive many people. Because of the increase of wickedness, the love of most will grow cold, but he who stands firm to the end will be saved. And this gospel of the kingdom will be preached in the whole world as a testimony to all nations, and then the end will come" (Matt 24:6–14).

Whichever denominationally-filtered spectacles we opt to don as we read those words, there can be little doubt that Jesus is not only discussing what to expect between the beginning of the end and the end itself, but he is also describing scenes that are very familiar to many of us today. Of course, there is a more immediate context to Jesus' words; commentators are correct to draw parallels between the predictive element of some of them and the unfolding of events surrounding the fall of Jerusalem in AD 70. But their fulfillment cannot be solely applied to the circumstances of first-century Palestine. Indeed, much cannot be ascribed at all to that time frame. The features here described have been present in almost every century of the church age in some measure. Their escalation in both frequency and intensity since the turn of the twentieth century, however, can surely mean only one thing: "our salvation is nearer now than when we first believed" (Rom 13:11).

Interestingly, neither Jesus nor Paul discussed such matters in a tone bearing any resemblance to that used by the doom and gloom merchants of our own day. Jesus referred to these as the beginning of birth pains, not an introduction to death pangs. Similarly, the apostle's context was one of night giving way to day, not *vice versa*. Thus, the New Testament emphasis concerning the climax of the age is not one in which God's people limp towards a finishing line in shame and abject failure, giving thanks to God for intervening in some divinely-appointed rescue attempt to keep us from further embarrassment. The wedding supper of the Lamb presupposes a marriage having taken place; there is no biblical warrant for suggesting that the bride will be anything other than a fitting one.

This being so, it is surely time for individual believers and the corporate body of Christ together to awake from its state of moral lethargy, to be aroused once more from its condition of social apathy, and shake off the dust of dispassion, detachment, and the predilection to plump for an easy believism. Signs of the times call not only for our observation, but also for an appropriate response to what they signify. Kingdom living is not a spectator pastime, but a participatory lifestyle.

## A Season of Opportunity

According to the writer of Ecclesiastes: "There is a time for everything, and a season for every activity under heaven" (Eccl 3:1). Thus, the era in which we now find ourselves living is not only a season of opportunity for the gospel, but—as far as the unregenerate are concerned—it is the period of their final opportunity to avail themselves of the message of the kingdom. Although many churches are aware of this, there seems to be some confusion as to how they might best equip themselves and present the gospel in these days. Advertising campaigns, marketing strategies, and prayer vigils that plead for insight on how best to "put the church in the world's shop window" appear to have conceded territory to the enemy before a proverbial shot has been fired in anger.

Much of what passes for evangelism in many of our churches today has more in common with the weekend super-saver at the local hypermarket than it does with what we read in the pages of the New Testament. The reasons for this are many and complex, and it is not within the remit of this work to identify them all or to elaborate on the causes that lay behind them. A failure to truly trust in God's Holy Spirit, peer pressure from elders/members where fruitful ministry is judged exclusively in terms of numerical increase, and a situation whereby the minister's salary is determined by the financial giving of the flock may all be cited with reasonable grounds of support. However, it is my conviction that a more common feature can be identified: a gross misunderstanding of our role in the process of growth.

This is not a new problem. The fact that the apostle Paul found it necessary to comment upon in his first epistle to the Corinthian believers should, you would think, save us from the potential for such difficulty. This is what he had to say to those who wanted to make more of his apostleship than was warranted: "I planted the seed, Apollos watered it, but God made it grow. So neither he who plants nor he who waters is anything, but only God who makes things grow" (1 Cor 3:6–7).

The fields are ripe unto harvest and will become progressively more so. My understanding of Scripture concerning the end times is that despite—or, perhaps even, because of—increasing persecution and hostility toward Christianity, there will be more added to the church in the days that remain than the historical records have accounted for thus far. When that happens, I trust that we will recognize our part in it as being but preparatory to the work of God.

Will it be a revival to top all previous such encounters? Well, I believe it will be the product of the most significant revival of the church age, but I must also qualify what I mean by "revival." It is my conviction that revival is primarily a sovereign act of the Father whereby he brings his own people to a place of genuine remorse for their hitherto lukewarmness and instills in them a fresh sense of passion for his Son and a reinvigorating for the things of God by the Holy Spirit. There will also invariably be a sense of yearning for moral rectitude with a commensurate abhorrence for behavioral turpitude, as believers begin to replicate their Lord's love for righteousness and hatred of wickedness in equal measure (see Heb 1:9). Out of this comes an awareness among the unregenerate that the Almighty is at work in his church, the product of which is many of them being drawn to the gospel. You can only *re*-vive that which has previously had the life of God in it.

In the so-called postmodern age, which prides itself on being incredulous toward metanarratives, there is more than a hint of irony that the author of the grandest master narrative known to man will ultimately triumph on the playing fields of those who most vehemently, intellectually, and psychologically deny his very existence. How can this possibly be? Well, again there are a number of possible reasons and they are not all necessarily mutually exclusive. In general terms, however, I believe that the primary factor will be that, despite confident claims to the contrary by those too afraid of the consequences on their own status, we live in an age of growing uncertainty.

Recently, one of our church elders preached on the subject of the believer's assurance. Taking his text from 1 John 3:11–24, he expounded on the basis, the evidence, and the source of our assurance: Christ's atonement, love among us, and the Holy Spirit respectively. Postmodernism promised much, and, now that the initial euphoria that accompanied those pledges has failed to materialize, many are left unfulfilled and bewildered. Technological advancements continue to offer hope in such diverse fields as medical research, world poverty, and galactic exploration, but seem more content to invest in programs that entertain for a moment than those that endure for eternity.

And what of religion? Well, so far the church seems not to have taken sufficiently seriously its role of fulfilling the needs of the genuine seekers for true spirituality. In the words of my former lecturer in systematic theology: "It's no use setting a tepid Christianity against a scorching atheism." This is particularly so in view of the fact that, in this age of uncertainty, the keys of the kingdom are at our disposal to unlock the understanding in relation to Christ's dying for fallen humanity, to remove the chains from those looking to live "good" lives and enable them to be equipped with the Spirit of God as the only one who can help them in their quest, and to unbolt the door that prevents the hitherto unloved and seemingly unlovable from finding their heart's desire.

Time, But Not As We Know It

Since the incarnation, the historical timeline has been divided into BC and AD (BCE and CE are more recent developments). The years prior to Jesus' birth we refer to as being "before Christ," while time from that point on has been designated as *Anno Domini*, "the year of our Lord." Strictly speaking, however, they are not two "ages," but distinct parts of the same age to which mankind belongs.

By contrast, the second coming (Greek *parousia*) of Christ is to signal the drawing to a close of this present age, before the commencement of the age to come (Matt 24:3; Luke 20:34–36). Where this age is gripped by sin and rebellion, the coming age is to be typified by the rule of God in Christ perfectly being expressed. As we have seen, however, the fact that Scripture teaches of believers having been delivered from "this present evil age" by Christ's giving of himself (Gal 1:4) implies that, for those who receive him, the age to come has broken in on the here and now. And so, there is an overlapping.

The key characteristic of the age to come in its fullest manifestation is to be the Father's sovereignty, for the Son will have handed over the kingdom and himself become subject "so that God may be in all" (1 Cor 15:24–28). We have not yet dined at the wedding supper of the Lamb, though it is possible to taste of "the powers of the age to come" (Heb 6:5). There is now a clashing of kingdoms because there is a conflict of ages. But it is of the increase of God's government and peace that will know no end, established and maintained by justice and righteousness from the time of Messiah's birth for ever (Isa 9:6–7). Commensurate with the growth of God's rule will be the defeat of Christ's enemies, the final conquest of the kingdom being the death of death itself.

Many of the features associated with our experience beyond the resurrection remain a mystery. This, I believe, is partly because God has not made them known to us, but also because they are—in some measure, at least—unknowable. Spiritual matters are spiritually discerned and even to the most astute of us, some things remain incomprehensible. That fact, of course, has not dissuaded some from the attempt. It seems that much so-called theological expertise has more to do with a parading of the plumage than it does the genuine sharing of wisdom. It is the product of little more than an elevation of the human intellect to such a lofty pedestal that to simply acknowledge that some things are beyond its capacity would be to see reason dethroned. To worship at the altar of academia is idolatry even if its object is cloaked in religious garb.

The concept of time in relation to eternity is one such area that we may ultimately have to concede defeat in our pursuit of understanding. Because we are currently able to conceive of time only as the product of created bodies' interaction with one another, we are incapable of imagining its existence outside of that framework. If we were to allow for the possibility that it can and maybe does, would this suggest independency outside of God and would that, in turn, imply a self-sufficiency with which God alone can truly be ascribed?

Some years ago, Chris Spicer addressed a congregation in my home county on matters of faith. He closed his message rather abruptly with the words: "Where doubts arise, hold on to certainties." We may not be privy to the minutiae of detail concerning the continuing existence of time in the eternal kingdom. Speculation aimed at only satisfying our curiosity is not the answer. We know that God alone is truly God and that everything else finds its source exclusively in him. It may be that our present understanding of time is corrupt and that time is essentially only the sequential succession of moments that we define in accordance with its current relation to our planet, which may cast a vastly different perspective in another environmental continuum. The same could be said of the occupation of space. Ultimately, we must be prepared to acknowledge that we simply do not know and not allow ourselves to be bullied beyond that just for the sake of saving face.

The consummation of this present age may well herald the cessation of time as we know it, but that does not necessarily mean that time *per se* will cease to be present. Nor must its continuing endurance in another format necessarily impinge upon the exclusive claim to eternity that resides in the Divine Being. God's eternal nature is intrinsic; the unending existence of time—or any other created feature, for that matter—is invested by virtue of it being subject to his divine will. Indeed, the existence of time is dependent upon God to uphold it; God's existence is self-dependent and self-determined because he is self-sufficient. In this sense, God is timeless and exists outside of its restrictive parameters, yet involves himself in time as the Redeemer of his creation. Thus, we may agree with Wayne Grudem's assertion that: "God has no beginning, end, or succession of moments in his own being, and he sees all time equally vividly, yet God sees events in time and acts in time."[1] Not only is this true, but it is and must remain exclusively so.

## Summary

The temptation to perceive of global issues from an entirely Western viewpoint is an all too easy one to fall prey to. This is no less hazardous when considering the state of the Christian church. When attempting to understand the times in which we find ourselves, the potential for misrepresentation seems to be further compounded. For this reason, it behooves us to evaluate world events in the light of biblical revelation rather than the other way around. Even then, it must be conceded that our interpretation may be somewhat conditioned by our environment. In an age of ambiguity, however, there are some things of which we can be assured: Jesus has earmarked certain key features that will enable us to recognize the imminence of his return; as that day draws closer, interpersonal strife and disasters will intensify and become more commonplace; and there will be—perhaps paradoxically—both an increased opposition toward and a growing openness to the gospel of the kingdom. The question we must face is essentially two-fold: "Are we ready?" and "How are we to respond?"

---

1. Grudem, *Systematic Theology*, 168.

Kingdom

## A ROYAL PRIESTHOOD

In my earlier work, *Covenant: The Basis of God's Self-Disclosure*, I remarked that Christ's consummation of the covenant with Phinehas confers upon believers the privilege of priesthood (see 1 Pet 2:5), while his fulfillment of the Davidic covenant also implies community kingship, citing Peter's description of Christ's followers as "a chosen people, a royal priesthood" (v. 9). In this section, we will discover how—or even, if—the implications of such a description translate into the coming kingdom of Christ. We have already established the validity of the royal assignation; it involves ruling with invested authority by virtue of our relationship to the King of the kingdom. But is there any legitimate biblical warrant for presuming the eternal continuance of our sacerdotal function? We shall see. Let us first take another step into the past that we may understand something of our present heritage, before we look to the future.

### A Kingdom of Priests

A helpful tool in the discipline of serious Bible study is what is simply referred to as "the law of first mention." Coined by the mid to late nineteenth-century New York preacher, Arthur Pierson, this is not strictly speaking a hermeneutical principle. It is, however, a very accommodating device, the aim of which extends far beyond merely identifying the first occasion when a word, phrase, doctrinal statement, or specific act is recorded in Scripture. The theory behind the value of this principle is that the essence of all that may be gleaned from any future use exists here in seed form. Thus, the complexity of its subsequent employment is best disentangled by a preliminary understanding of its simple first use.

The first time the phrase "kingdom of priests" (Hebrew *mamleket kohanim*) appears in Scripture is especially significant. Although it might reasonably be inferred that all the characteristics associated with royal priesthood were annexed to God's covenant with Adam, the first time it is explicitly mentioned is in connection with Moses' address to the Israelites on Mount Sinai (Exod 19:6). Again, the immediate context suggests a close link to covenant privilege and obligation (v. 5). But what lessons can we learn from the general background?

## The Coming Kingdom

No sooner had the Israelite tribes escaped the tyranny of Egypt (Exod 13–14) than they were confronted with the military might of the Amalekites (ch. 17). Apart from a whole chapter dedicated to a celebratory song of worship (ch. 15), much of the rest of the proximal narrative is concerned with the people's complaints and grumblings. Perhaps this is partly understandable. The haste with which they had left Egypt, not to mention the supernatural means by which it had been effected, had no doubt aroused their interest and evoked their confusion in similar measure. In the absence of any forthcoming explanation, except by way of further miraculous provision (16:4—17:7), Moses is summoned to appear before God to receive instruction (ch. 19).

There seems to be more than a touch of irony in the fact that God tells Moses to convey to his people that they are to be a kingdom of priests and yet they require his mediation in order to receive that message. But what lies behind these words: "you will be a kingdom of priests and a holy nation" (Exod 19:6)? The essence conveyed is one of singular peculiarity and global significance. They were chosen to represent God prophetically in the way they conducted themselves both behaviorally and relationally; and they were to rule on his behalf as those of royal descent, thus taking up the creational ordinance originally given to Adam, but subsequently neglected (see end of v. 5: "Although the whole earth is mine . . ."). But what is implied by their corporate priesthood?

A number of features may be ascribed to the role of the priesthood on the basis of the Old Testament evidence. There is the mediatorial aspect by which the incumbent represents the people before God in the same way that a prophet is God's spokesperson to the people. As part of this remit, of course, is the offering of sacrifices, the reminding one's fellows of the prescribed feast days and festival seasons, and reserved temple duties. These would all come much later and would not be carried out by all, but by those appointed for the task.

At the heart of the priests' functions, however, was one overarching theme: consecration for service (see Isa 61:6). The basis for such an appointment was holiness in its etymological sense of being set apart by God and for him. It is here that Alec Motyer correctly draws the allusion between this text and the royal priesthood of the new covenant when he affirms that: "The substantial truth . . . of the 'priesthood of all believers' in both the Old and New Testaments is access into the holy presence."² Hywel Jones makes a similar point regarding the original divine appointment of Israel as a kingdom of priests: "This is what Israelites . . . are to be in contradistinction to all others, viz. a kingdom whose citizens are all priests, each having the right of access, worship and devotion to God."³

Here, then, is the essence of priesthood. Although it is correct to say that Israel was blessed by God in order that they, in turn, might be a blessing to other nations (a responsibility they apparently took none too seriously), the advantage was in their freedom of access to the divine throne. And it is this essential component feature that we must carry through if we are fully to understand what the same promise means for us in a new covenant context of kingdom benefit.

To accept privilege without also acknowledging responsibility is both presumptuous and reckless, to say the least. The bi-lateral aspect of the Sinaitic covenant was pretty much consistent with all of the divine covenants: its blessings were dependent upon certain conditions having been met. So here too: "Now if you obey me fully and keep my covenant, then . . ." (Exod 19:5). Surely, having been saved, our status as a royal priesthood is not subject to such conditions, is it? Well, yes it is, actually. The difference is that the condition of our freedom of access has already been met by another.

### The Priesthood of All Believers

It was Martin Luther who first coined the phrase "the priesthood of all believers," though it is pretty much a cardinal doctrine of the majority of churches that emanated from the sixteenth-century Protestant Reformation. It is a principle, taken from Scripture, which holds that the effects of Christ's propitiatory sacrifice are such as to render any further mediation wholly unnecessary, thus giving free and unrestricted access to the Father by all who are beneficiaries of his Son's atonement. Although the phrase itself is a variant of that used by the apostle Peter in his first letter (1 Pet 2:5–9), the doctrine to which it relates is to be found on almost every page of the New Testament.

---

2. Motyer, *Message of Exodus*, 199.
3. H. R. Jones, "Exodus," in Guthrie and Motyer, *New Bible Commentary*, 131.

The actual phrase employed by Peter (that is, "royal priesthood") suggests priests belonging to a king, though the context does not rule out the dual role of those with both priestly duties and of royal assignation. In order to arrive at an understanding that is consistent with that of Scripture, we must rid ourselves of the concept of priestly functions as they appear to us in some current church settings. First of all, the New Testament only refers to "priest" singular in relation to Jesus Christ; all other citations are concerned with the corporate nature as it relates to believers in the plural. Secondly—as we have seen—the primary essence of priesthood in the Bible is not linked to the offering of sacrifices but of serving God and having access to him. The petitioning of God in prayer on behalf of others is a privilege we all share, not least by the one being prayed for.

That said, however, Peter does include sacrificial offering as part of this priesthood's duty, but the preceding adjective negates any notion that these are anything material in nature (see 1 Pet 2: 5). In fact, the only feature they share with those offered under the old covenant stipulations is that they are to be found acceptable by God. How can we know that this will be the case? Well, they qualify insofar and inasmuch that they are presented through the one mediator, Christ Jesus. There is no salvific merit to such offerings; they are exclusively by way of gratitude and service.

Perhaps significantly—or is it just coincidentally—those churches that are most hostile in their objection to this doctrine are also those who regard the church as the sole agent of God's kingdom on earth. Even the newer churches that lay claim to a back-to-basics approach to church structure have in many cases—though thankfully not all—merely replaced one sacerdotal system with another less obvious one. In such cases, the words "papacy" and "apostleship" have become almost synonymous in their expression, if not their meaning. There is no New Testament support for the idea that there exists a special priesthood from among the priesthood of all believers. Indeed, to admit as much would be to negate the whole purpose of the argument in favor of the common priesthood of believers; if there is a group who are to be further qualified, then all believers are not priests at all.

This is not to deny the special offices that Christ has given to the church (Eph 4:11–16). What it does mean is that—lofty though these may be in terms of attracting honor, respect, and accountability—they do not supersede the believer's personal access to the throne of grace. Although it should be obvious, let me for the sake of absolute clarity remove any potential for misunderstanding: when we say that the primary privilege of the priesthood of all believers is the right of access to God, that is to say that such admittance is direct and in no further need of an intermediary. Any requirement that may have existed for mediation has already been fully and finally met (Eph 2:18; 1 Tim 2:5; Heb 10:19). Only the enemy of our souls would seek to persuade us otherwise.

However, privilege is rarely dissociated from responsibility. We saw in the previous section that for the Israelites the attached condition was their obedience. Although the New Testament writers make no mention of our corporate priesthood being conditional upon anything other than faith, Peter does imply duty by way of expression: "offering spiritual sacrifices acceptable to God through Jesus Christ" (1 Pet 4:5).

First and foremost among such sacrifices, of course, is the giving of ourselves (Rom 12:1). As an extension of this self-sacrifice, comes prayer (Rev 8:3) and praise (Heb 13:15). The fact that both of these are referred to as sacrificial suggests that there is some inherent quality that distinguishes them from prayer and praise that is not costly. This is praying beyond "Please bless Aunt Belinda's pet canary" and giving thanks for reasons that are more legitimate than simply the news of a 15 percent annual pay increase. It is pleading for the unsaved family member for the umpteenth time, despite the fact that there are no outward signs of interest being shown in the things of God; it is being grateful to God for who he is, even during those times when heaven seems like brass. Thus, only prayer and praise that causes us to forego other pleasures may be regarded as truly priestly.

### Question: To Be a Priest or Not to Be a Priest?

Even our interpretation of the final mention of priests in the whole of Scripture is subject to a veiled understanding of eschatological events. Those blessed by taking part in the first resurrection shall, indeed, be priests of God and of Christ (Rev 20:6), but is it possible for us to know whether this will extend beyond the millennial reign, whatever that means in practical terms? And what of the coming age? Will there be scope in the coming kingdom in all its glory for the role of this royal priesthood? Many notable and respected commentators think not. If Norman Nagel's argument is consistent, irrespective of the environment, then surely he finds himself among them: "A priest is always toward some one else, toward a non-priest . . . There are only priests if there are also those who are not priests. If everybody is a priest, no one is a priest. 'Universal priesthood' (*allgemeines priestertum*), then, is self-contradictory."[4]

I must make it clear that Nagel's context is not one outside of the current time/space continuum, and so it is possible that his premise is restricted to that environ. However, the terminology he employs suggests he is positing a constant principle, which thus implies the negation of believers' priesthood in eternity. If I have misunderstood, then I apologize unreservedly. If not, however, I would like to draw attention to but two points. First of all, if the argument is to be granted warrant, then it must be consistently applicable. Are we to imagine that the fellowship of the saints, for example, is to be subject to the same measure of dismissal? This phrase also is only applied in the plural by the writers of the New Testament. Are saints only to be so designated on the basis of their contrast with those who are not saints?

But there is arguably an even more serious error to correct if, indeed, that is what it is. The basic hypothesis behind such a proposition is one that we have already dismissed, viz.: that the essence of the priestly function is principally mediatorial. Although its expression may be said to include servanthood, this is not the primary criterion by which the priesthood of believers is to be determined in any age; it is access to God. Within the parameters of fleshly limitation, we currently enjoy the highest level of entry "before the face of God" (Latin *coram Deo*). If anything, the removal of any restriction whatsoever incumbent upon us now will enable even greater access in the age to come and, therefore, the sense with which we might be called "priests" will be further enhanced rather than diminished.

The priesthood of believers is restricted by its environment, but it is the present milieu in which we find ourselves comparatively hampered in this regard. The apostle Paul spoke of it thus: "For we know in part and we prophesy in part, but when perfection comes, the imperfect disappears. When I was a child, I reasoned like a child. When I became a man, I put childish ways behind me. Now we see but a poor reflection

---

4. Nagel, "Luther and the Priesthood of All Believers," 278.

as in a mirror; then we shall see face to face. Now I know in part; then I shall know fully, even as I am fully known" (1 Cor 13:9–12).

Although Paul's context is the permanence of love, the principle he alludes to here is not without wider application. The hymnwriter put it his way:

> Face to face! O blissful moment!
> Face to face—to see and know;
> Face to face with my Redeemer;
> Jesus Christ who loves me so.
> Face to face I shall behold him,
> Far beyond the starry sky;
> Face to face in all his glory,
> I shall see him by and by.[5]

John says a similar thing that, though not lending credence to the arguments of either position, does support the idea that some things remain a mystery: "Dear friends, now we are children of God, and what we will be has not yet been made known. But we know that when [Christ] appears, we shall be like him, for we shall see him as he is" (1 John 3:2).

While I acknowledge that it would be reckless to contravene my own advice in such matters, not to mention those of my former college lecturer and such notable academians as Ludwig Wittgenstein, I will merely leave the reader to reflect on this proposition: in accordance with the cultus analogy, Scripture speaks explicitly and also implies Jesus' high priesthood in eternity (see Heb 4:14–15; 7:26; 8:1). Admittedly, this forms part of his role in eternity toward his people as priests in their temporal existence. If the priesthood of believers does not extend beyond this present age, are we therefore also to assume that his high priesthood will be terminated to coincide with that non-existence?

The writer to the Hebrews clearly thought not (Heb 7:24), unless it can be demonstrated that the permanence therein cited is one of only temporal measure. It would seem unrealistic, however, to consider Jesus' priesthood as being any different in terms of quantitative duration to the qualifying clause of that of his life. In other words, whatever applies to the "forever" of Jesus' living must equally be applicable to the "permanence" of his priesthood.

---

5. Carrie Beck (1855–1934).

## Summary

As far as the new covenant people of God are concerned, royalty and priesthood go hand in hand; we are kings and we are priests. Of course, we are only so because we honor, submit to, and come to God via his designated king and high priest, Jesus Christ. This is what Scripture reveals us to be in the present. Whether that is deemed to be continuous beyond the current age is not easy to determine from the biblical evidence. However, its fathomability becomes much less arduous as we come to understand the root meaning of the priestly ministry. It is my conviction that the correct answer lies in asking the appropriate questions. Are we to exercise God's rule in action beyond the end of the age in which we now find ourselves? If the answer is "Yes," then we will remain kings of the kingdom. Are we also to continue to benefit from the right of access we now enjoy into God's presence? If the answer to that question is also "Yes," then we shall similarly remain priests of the kingdom.

## HEAVEN BOUND OR EARTH DWELLER?

We now come to the final section before we conclude matters. The sequence of events concerning the end times has been the subject of much debate. Common agreement has proved impossible, largely because Scripture is not as explicit as we would often like it to be. Perhaps therein lies a clue. I am certainly one for stretching our intellect as far as it is possible to go in all directions in order to more fully comprehend truth. However, in some matters, maybe we should just acknowledge that it is only the things that have been revealed that belong to us; the secret things still belong to God (Deut 29:29). One such issue may well prove to be our eternal destination. Where will the glorious and glorified kingdom of God in the coming age be expressed by us? Are we destined for heaven? Or was the initial creation not a test at all, but the blueprint for the original intention in God's heart? Let us consider the evidence.

### The Presence of the Lord

The main Greek noun translated "heaven" in our English Bibles is *ouranos*. It has a number of derived connotations in the New Testament, including the skies (Acts 10:12), the abode of angels (Matt 18:10),

## Kingdom

whence the Holy Spirit came at Pentecost (1 Pet 1:12) and Christ will descend at his *parousia* (2 Thess 1:7), and where Paul was taken during his ethereal experience (2 Cor 11:2). The most common understanding to be extrapolated from these and similar verses is that heaven is the location wherein God resides. In terms of grasping something of the eternal destination of the redeemed, this has shaped much Christian thinking for centuries.

If we accept this as solely symbolic, that is, a means by which to convey the incomprehensible to finite human comprehension, then there is no difficulty. The implications that arise from a literal application, however, are inherently problematic. In view of God's essentially infinite Being, is it possible to contemplate him as resident in restricted space any more than it is conceivable for him to be governed by time? Or may they both be of a different order to those known by us in the present time/space continuum? The words of Solomon may prove helpful. Having completed the building of the temple as the earthly representation of God's presence among his people, the wise king declared: "But will God really dwell on earth? The heavens, even the highest heaven cannot contain you. How much less this temple I have built . . . Hear the supplication of your servant and of your people Israel when they pray towards this place. Hear from heaven, your dwelling-place, and when you hear, forgive" (1 Kgs 8:27, 30).

My immediate response on reading those words was: "Come on Solomon; make your mind up. Either heaven cannot contain him or it is his dwelling-place. You can't have it both ways." The fact was, however, that God had chosen to invest himself in an immanently localized way in the temple, but Solomon recognized that this did not militate against God's essential transcendence. To the boundaries of our understanding, such qualities appear to be self-contradictory, and yet to stress one at the expense of the other can only resolve in heresy. They are equally viable truths, their apparent incompatibility finding satisfaction only in the ultimate incomprehensibility of God.

Perhaps we should, after all, leave our quest there on the altar of unknowability regarding the eternal destination of the redeemed. In eschatology, there are essentially three different positions taken, each laying claim to the evidence of Scripture in support of their argument: the pre-millennialist view, the post-millennialist, and that of the a-millennialist. On the basis of the complexities of composite symbolism,

## The Coming Kingdom

I tend toward the latter, but I can see both the inconsistencies of such a position and the advantages of the others. I have also encountered a fourth view, which seems the most appealing yet; it is that of the pan-millennialist, which holds that it will all pan out in the end, anyway.

Is there a different approach that we may not yet have considered regarding the nature of heaven, which retains consistency with what we can discern from Scripture? I believe there is. In the Bible, heaven is often contrasted with hell. Although presented in parabolic form, the tale of the sheep and the goats was given in the context of Jesus allowing his disciples certain information regarding the final destiny of all. Having been judged on the basis of their treatment of the king's family, the goats are finally expelled from his presence (Matt 25:41–46). Thus, it might reasonably argued that the punishment of the unregenerate consists in being isolated from the presence of the Lord. Conversely, the blessedness of the righteous is made so by virtue of their continual abode in that presence (v. 34).

Again, is it possible to conceive of God's absence in view of what we know of his intrinsic omnipresence? They do seem at odds, and yet God himself speaks of his presence being with, going with, and being removed from certain individuals and corporate groups in Scripture. How can this be? We do not know. Perhaps when the Bible refers to God's presence in this special sense, it may be understood as our conscious enjoyment of it (or lack thereof, as the case may be). However, it does not seem unreasonable to conclude that not only are heaven and God's presence compatible, but that they may even amount to pretty much the same thing.

If ever there was a time when man experienced heaven on earth, then it was surely Adam in his pre-fallen state. No one since, with the obvious exception of Jesus, has known that level of conscious enjoyment of God's presence. If this was God's purpose for man had the fall not occurred—and being immediately aware of the need to resist any urge to remark on the infra-/supra-lapsarian debate—can we not expect the restoration of what Adam lost to at least resemble what might otherwise have been his in perpetuity? I can think of no more fitting comment to this discussion than the words of John Owen: "if our future blessedness shall consist in being where he is, and beholding of his glory, what better preparation can there be for it than in a constant previous contemplation of that glory in the revelation that is made in the Gospel, unto this very end, that by a view of it we may be gradually

## Kingdom

transformed into the same glory?"[6] Donald Guthrie seems to draw a similar conclusion: "We shall not expect, however, to find a description of a place, so much as the presence of a person . . . Paul does not think of heaven as a place, but thinks of it in terms of the presence of God."[7]

Whenever I find myself in disagreement with Wayne Grudem, I am forced to triple-check the evidence and my understanding of both it and his position before I commit myself further. That I am so rarely called upon to do so bears testament to its infrequent necessity. His counter-argument to Guthrie, however, gives warrant to just such an occasion. To say: "If a person is present, then by definition there is a place, because to be 'present' means to be 'located in this place'"[8] would be valid in a physical time/space continuum, but I am not convinced that it remains so in an essentially spiritual/eternal realm. To speak of a location as a specific placement implies that there are other locations outside of that place where the qualifying clause does not apply. Employing Grudem's logic, to say that the person(s) of God is present in this location surely suggests that he is absent outside of it.

Although it would admittedly be inappropriate to make too much of the connection, the writer to the Hebrews does present his case in a manner that lends itself to at least the possibility of such an interpretation: "For Christ did not enter a man-made sanctuary that was only a copy of the true one; he entered heaven itself, now to appear for us in God's presence" (Heb 9:24). This is the ultimate goal of being a Christian: looking forward to the presence of the Lord for eternity. Of course there is a hell to be shunned, but I thank God that the blessings associated with his kingdom, both in the present age and that to come, include far more than only escaping hell. Indeed, perhaps if the preachers of old had focused less on selling Christianity as fire insurance and more on promoting its blessed assurance, they may have met with considerably more success.

In the final analysis, any finite comprehension of God and things pertaining to him is severely hampered. He can only be known by revelation and our interpretation of that unveiling is conditioned by the only framework we have at our disposal: temporality and spatiality. God is spirit and can only truly be discerned spiritually. Thankfully, he has given us of his Holy Spirit to aid us in our quest.

6. In Ferguson, *John Owen*, 279.
7. Guthrie, *New Testament Theology*, 870, 875.
8. Grudem, *Systematic Theology*, 1159.

## A New Creation

If we are to make room for the possibility that heaven is not so much a specific location as the cognizant pleasure of God's company, wherever that may be found, then it behooves us to consider the implications a little further. In terms of God's kingdom rule, we have noted that this exists where the will of God is exercised and expressed. Jesus' prayer that God's will be done on earth as it is in heaven (Matt 6:10) suggests that its progressive attainment is commensurate with the coming of the kingdom. When that process is completed, then the entire creation will experience a radical transformation. In much the same way that our sanctification will not be perfected until the point at which we are released from this life, so too will the earth's change be one of life beyond dying.

However, we must be perfectly clear in our understanding: to speak of this life as our earthly existence in contrast to that of the renewed age suggests that the latter will be occupied elsewhere. There is absolutely no biblical warrant for such a thesis. The witness of both Testaments is of "a new heaven(s) and a new earth" (see Isa 65:17; 66:22; 2 Pet 3:13; Rev 21:1–2). This is not presented so much as restoration to a former glory as a glorious regeneration. The comparisons between the Genesis account of creation and that creation being seen in all its originally intended beauty are not lost on William Hendriksen:

> Genesis tells us that God created heaven and earth. Revelation describes the *new* heaven and earth (21:1). In Genesis, the luminaries are called into being: sun, moon and stars. In Revelation we read: "And the city has no need of the sun, nor of the moon, to shine in it; for the glory of God lightened it, and its lamp is the Lamb" (21:23). Genesis describes a paradise which is lost. Revelation pictures a paradise restored (2:7; 22:2). Genesis describes the cunning and power of the devil. The Apocalypse tells us that the devil was bound and hurled into the lake of fire and brimstone. Genesis pictures that awful scene of man fleeing away from God and hiding himself from the presence of the Almighty. Revelation shows us the most wonderful and intimate communion between God and redeemed man: "Behold the tabernacle of God is with men, and he shall tabernacle with them" (21:3).[9]

---

9. Hendriksen, *More Than Conquerors*, 197.

# Kingdom

Again, because of the symbolism employed by the New Testament writers—as much for their sakes as for ours—it is not possible to speak with any absolute conviction about many of the features belonging to "the new heaven(s) and the new earth." What we do assert must always be tempered with the disclaimer that such is based on perfect matters being pondered by an imperfect mechanism. That notwithstanding, however, we are left with no other alternative. We can only assume that affairs that have been disclosed to us are able to be understood within these confines or they may just as well have remained altogether concealed.

At the risk of sounding like Dorcas Lane, one of my many weaknesses is good quality chocolate. So much so, in fact, that I have to limit myself to special occasions when I am allowed to indulge its delights. My wife is the same, and, for this reason alone, we have effectively become each other's guardsperson. Every year, around Easter, we buy one egg each as a gift to one another, though I prefer it if my one egg consists of a single large hollow egg filled with lots of smaller "egglets." As with all presents of this nature, hiding them comes somewhat easier to me than it does to Barbara. It could be argued that if we both agreed not to look for them, then there would be no need to be so inventive in choosing our secret places. Barbara never finds her gifts from me; she can barely even remember where she has hidden her gifts to me. I always find them. I offer no excuses for doing so when challenged beyond: "Well, if you didn't want me to find them, then you shouldn't have put them where you knew I would look."

According to Louis Berkhof, such an understanding takes me out of the Calvinist camp and into that of the Lutheran position.[10] I would counter that I have arrived at my conclusions without filtering the evidence through the constitutional findings of either and have come to an understanding that presently coincides—in the matter before us, that is—with that of Luther. Those who believe otherwise, often do so, not so much on the basis of the evidence, as upon preconceived ideas about the perceived implications of giving the devil the upper hand. All I can say to that charge is that, whatever the outcome of the present earth—annihilation and subsequent replacement or miraculous renewal—how a hell-destined devil is supposed to take any pleasure from the fact is beyond my admittedly limited grasp. I take some small comfort that I appear to

---

10. Berkhof, *Systematic Theology*, 737.

be in good company: "No eye has seen, no ear has heard, no mind has conceived what God has prepared for those who love him" (1 Cor 2:9).

Hang on a minute, though; the apostle Paul carries on: "but God has revealed it to us by his Spirit" (1 Cor 2:10). Whether it will be a restored earth, a renewed earth, or a completely recreated earth, earth is to be our eternal abode. Not only so, but this "new earth" is also to be the dwelling place of men where the kingdom of God is most perfectly expressed. And yet, it will become progressively more so. This, too, stands outside of our capacity to grasp. If something is perfect in its absolute sense, how can it possibly improve? And if it can get better, then how could it conceivably have been described as perfect prior to that progression? Surely, the measure by which it advanced is also the mark of its previous imperfection. But note again what Isaiah says of the Messiah's kingdom rule: "For to us a child is born, to us a son is given, and the government will be upon his shoulders. And he will be called Wonderful Counselor, Mighty God, Everlasting Father, Prince of Peace. Of the increase of his government and peace there will be no end. He will reign on David's throne and over his kingdom, establishing and upholding it with justice and righteousness from that time on and for ever. The zeal of the Lord Almighty will accomplish this" (Isa 9:6–7).

These words were first uttered around seven hundred years before the incarnation event. That is amazing in itself. But they speak not only of Jesus' birth; they also tell of his eschatological rule—further astonishment. The key phrase to which I want to draw attention, however, concerns his government and peace. The prophet does not say merely that they will be interminable, but that their increase will know no end—absolute wonder.

It is my conviction that there are certain clues about the new creation of the earth to be found in the concept of the believer's resurrection. In each case, it appears that there is to be expected both continuity and discontinuity. Not only will our new bodies know neither sin nor the corruption evoked by such sin, but they will also be free from the potential for that ever to take hold again. The same must surely be true of the environment in which eternal life is to be lived to the full. God's pronouncement on Eden was "good" and upon his vice-regent "very good." They were not quite perfect in that they each contained the capacity to become tainted. Not so the new earth or its inhabitants.

Kingdom

Commenting on those texts that speak of "new heavens and a new earth," Leon Morris simply writes: "We should understand such passages as indicating that the final condition of things will be such as fully expresses the will of God."[11] In other words, the kingdom of God will have been revealed in all its glory.

Summary

So, how should we respond to the question set at the head of this section: *Heaven Bound or Earth Dweller?* Well, it is not a matter of either/or but both. The newly created earth will replicate that of its predecessor's former glory by being the fullest expression man has ever known of God's kingdom rule and one in which his presence is most perfectly experienced. If it sounds a little like paradise regained, then that is a fitting description. However, just as our position in Christ is far superior to that enjoyed by Adam in that he was capable of becoming estranged from God, so too this new earth can never suffer the same fate as the original creation. Not only will the kingdom rule of God's Christ and the peace that is annexed to it hold sway, but they will do so in increasing measure. Oh, mystery of mysteries!

## SUMMARY

All that now remains are my overall concluding remarks to the whole of the evidence I have set out in this work. Before we move on to those, however, it is necessary to summarize the findings of this chapter. Perhaps on no other doctrine should we be so wary of a dogmatic approach than that of eschatology. Ironically, it is doubtful whether any other subject has been as forcibly presented in recent years as the perceived unfolding of events during the "last days." That Scripture does afford some clues is without question; that these were given for our benefit is equally beyond enquiry. What seems unreasonable to presume is that they were granted for any purpose other than to warn us of the coming of the end of the age. That which was revealed was certainly not made accessible so that we might hazard a guess at the as yet still veiled.

---

11. L. L. Morris, "Heaven," in Douglas, *New Bible Dictionary*, 466.

Even the designation "a royal priesthood" is not quite as simple to fathom as might initially seem to be the case. Its identification with Christian believers who are also citizens of Christ's kingdom poses no real complication, but in what way are we also priests and how does this assignation correlate with the eschatological age? In terms of mediatorial representation, it is difficult to draw any positive conclusions. When we adopt the inherent meaning of priesthood as the right of access to God, however, any potential complexities seem to be immediately and inexorably resolved.

Precisely where this eternally-redeemed community is to exercise its priestly regality cannot be determined beyond all reasonable doubt on the basis of the evidence we have from Scripture. Although I have presented an argument in favor of "heaven" and the presence of the Lord being understood as almost synonymous terms, I am aware that there are also occasions of apparent dissimilarity that must be considered. Yes, there are certain differences of execution. But, though these may not be outnumbered, I am of the opinion that they are positively outweighed by similarities in essence.

I must confess to the difficulty I have found in presenting my understanding here, more so than in any other work I have thus far addressed. The reason for this, I believe, is largely two-fold: the relative dearth of biblical evidence in conjunction with a seemingly commensurate wealth of speculative opinion. This is why I have addressed the "Acknowledgments" section to those whose previous endeavors have proved helpful and my sincere best wishes to others whose research in the future will prove beneficial to a more scholarly understanding of this wonderful subject than I have been able to provide. That notwithstanding, however, we may only be held accountable for failing to make the best use of the tools at our disposal. I trust I shall not be found wanting in that regard, at least.

# Conclusion

THE PROPOSED AIM OF this work has been to present a biblical understanding of the concept of kingdom as the expression of God's sovereign rule over the created order generally and, more specifically, through the redeemed community. On this basis, it has been crucial to keep certain objectives in mind:

i) to determine from Scripture precisely what we mean by the kingdom of God;

ii) to identify the required character traits of those who are subjects of God's kingdom and the promised blessings associated with them;

iii) to examine Jesus' parables of the kingdom for any vital lessons that will aid us in our task;

iv) to evaluate the universal significance of the biblical presentation of the kingdom of God being manifest in the present; and

v) to analyze the specific relevance to believers of the biblical presentation of the kingdom of God at the consummation of the age.

In chapter 1, we traced the historical development of God's kingdom rule as it has been exercised on earth, both through designated individuals and through a chosen people. We saw that, though there were periods during which the expression of God's kingdom and the recognition of his kingship were very real, all too often these were undermined by a desire for self-governance, self-expression, and selfish ambition. That these were all rooted in the sin principle meant that they could only be appropriately and irreversibly dealt with by the revealing of the true King of the kingdom, Christ Jesus, and the one by whom his kingly requirements could be fully carried out, the Holy Spirit.

## Conclusion

As if to highlight the failure of God's chosen ones to appropriately and adequately demonstrate his kingdom rule throughout the Old Testament, Jesus wasted little time in spelling out the characteristics required of his people. As early as the fifth chapter of the New Testament, he embarks on a lengthy discourse that not only dispels the ethos of the age both then and now, but also annexes such character traits to divine blessing. This is perfectly consistent with the whole of the new covenant message where the standard perception of things is turned upside down. Thus, true riches are to be gained by turning away from materialistic ambition, real honor is attained in the most naturally inglorious of pursuits, genuine meekness is considered worthy of the highest reward, and purity of vision effects the purest of all to come into view.

Chapter 3 allowed us to take a more exhaustive approach to some of Jesus' parables, most notably those relating specifically to the kingdom of God. I don't fully buy into the theory that the purpose of speaking in parables was as much to conceal from the disinterested as it was to unveil to the elect. To my mind, the truths they represent are suitably concealed to those who have no interest in discovering them by saying nothing at all. However, I can see that there is a sufficient tease element attached to how much truth they reveal that their deeper secrets require more than a mere passing curiosity in order to discover them. Although they relate essentially to spiritual matters, I am of the conviction that the principles that lay at the heart of them may be beneficially applied to the natural realm also. Moreover, in this regard, they are not the exclusive right of the redeemed. The application of godly ethics by the unregenerate, though of no salvific merit, would at least make their temporal existence more satisfying.

That notwithstanding, to many of Jesus' initial hearers his parables may have seemed little more than an interesting representation of some entirely religious ideal; to those whose hearts had been touched by the Spirit of God, however, they were the very words of life. Intellectual appreciation would have proved ultimately as worthless as mere thoughtful reflection. Only when accompanied by a believing heart and an obedient will can the tenets contained within the parables really produce the fruit as originally intended.

Indeed, the true worth of the revelation of Scripture must always be evaluated in the light of its prophetic application in any given age.

## Conclusion

Thus, the fourth objective was addressed in chapter 4 when we reflected upon the kingdom of God in the present age. The emphasis here was most notably on that as experienced and expressed by the redeemed, both individually and corporately. Again, that is not to suggest that unbelievers are exempt as temporal beneficiaries. But only those who belong to Christ can truly rejoice in him, point to his ancestry as their own, and respond wholly and unreservedly to his directives as the rightful King of the kingdom.

There is an Aristotelian tendency to give prominence to the quantitative over the qualitative. Biblical scholars and teachers are not immune from such a proclivity. Arguments based on little more substantial evidence than the number of times a particular word or phrase appears in the concordance are commonplace in a number of pulpits and lecture theaters. On such a basis, it would be easy to claim that the New Testament emphasis is on the here and now, today, this day, the present age, etc. The context, however, is usually that of tomorrow being too late for the unbeliever to alter his/her final destiny. As far as believers are concerned, the significance of today pales when compared with the glory of our shared inheritance that will be realized when the kingdom of God is fully and finally revealed.

Your response to these musings, I must leave with you. But I do so with the sincere and solemn prayer that you will discard from them any untruth they may contain, glean from them any truth that is to be found there, and glorify the truth because of it.

# Bibliography

Atkinson, David J., and David H. Field, eds. *New Dictionary of Christian Ethics and Pastoral Theology*. Leicester, UK: InterVarsity, 1995.
Benson, Clarence H. *Old Testament Survey: Law and History*. Wheaton, IL: Evangelical Teacher Training Association, 1956.
Berkhof, Louis. *Systematic Theology*. Edinburgh, UK: Banner of Truth, 1973.
Boice, James M., ed. *Our Savior God: Man, Christ, and the Atonement*. Grand Rapids: Baker, 1980.
Bonhoeffer, Dietrich. *Creation and Temptation: A Theological Exposition of Genesis 1–3*. Translated by John C. Fletcher. London: SCM, 1966.
———. *The Cost of Discipleship*. Translated by R. H. Fuller. New York: Macmillan, 1963.
Boswell, James. *The Life of Samuel Johnson*. London: Penguin, 1986.
Brearley, Christopher. *Reclaiming Church: Applying 1st Century Principles to 21st Century Problems*. Lancaster, UK: Sovereign World, 2010.
Bright, John. *History of Israel*. London: SCM, 1978.
Brown, Colin, ed. *Dictionary of New Testament Theology*, vol. 2. Carlisle, UK: Paternoster, 1986.
Brunner, Emil. *Sowing and Reaping: The Parables of Jesus*. Translated by Thomas Wieser. London: Epworth, 1938.
Carson, Donald A. *Expositor's Bible Commentary: Matthew*, vol. 1. Grand Rapids: Zondervan, 1995.
Chambers, Oswald. *My Utmost for His Highest*. London: Marshall, Morgan & Scott, 1960.
Cole, Edwin L. *Maximized Manhood: A Guide to Family Survival*. New Kensington, PA: Whitaker House, 2001.
Cottrell, Jack W. *Gender Roles and the Bible: Creation, the Fall and Redemption: A Critique of Feminist Biblical Interpretation*. Joplin, MO: College Press, 1994.
Denney, James. *The Death of Christ*. London: Tyndale, 1961.
Douglas, J. D., ed. *New Bible Dictionary*. Leicester, UK: InterVarsity, 1992.
Drane, John W. *The McDonaldization of the Church: Spirituality, Creativity, and the Future of the Church*. London: Darton, Longman & Todd, 2002.
Ferguson, Sinclair, B. *John Owen on the Christian Life*. Edinburgh, UK: Banner of Truth, 1987.
France, Richard T. *New International Commentary on the New Testament: The Gospel of Matthew*. Grand Rapids: Eerdmans, 2007.
Grant, Robert M., and David N. Freedman. *The Secret Sayings of Jesus: A Modern Translation of the Gospel of Thomas with Commentary*. New York: Barnes & Noble, 1993.

## Bibliography

Grudem, Wayne A. *Systematic Theology: An Introduction to Biblical Doctrine.* Leicester, UK: InterVarsity, 1994.
Guthrie, Donald. *New Testament Theology.* Leicester, UK: InterVarsity, 1993.
Guthrie, Donald, and J. Alec Motyer, eds. *New Bible Commentary.* 3rd ed. Leicester, UK: InterVarsity, 1992.
Haenchen, Ernst. *The Acts of the Apostles: A Commentary.* Oxford: Blackwell, 1971.
Hagner, Donald A. *Word Bible Commentary: Matthew 1–13*, vol. 33a. Dallas: Word, 1995.
Hammond, Thomas C. *In Understanding Be Men: A Handbook of Christian Doctrine.* Leicester, UK: InterVarsity, 1968.
Hansen, G. Walter. *New Testament Commentary Series: Galatians.* Leicester, UK: InterVarsity, 1994.
Hendriksen, William. *More Than Conquerors: An Interpretation of the Book of Revelation.* Grand Rapids: Baker, 1998.
———. *New Testament Commentary: Galatians.* Edinburgh, UK: Banner of Truth, 1990.
———. *New Testament Commentary: Luke.* Edinburgh, UK: Banner of Truth, 1997.
———. *New Testament Commentary: Mark.* Edinburgh, UK: Banner of Truth, 1987.
———. *New Testament Commentary: Matthew.* Edinburgh, UK: Banner of Truth, 1989.
———. *New Testament Commentary: Romans.* Edinburgh, UK: Banner of Truth, 1980.
Houghton, S. M. *Sketches From Church History: An Illustrated Account of Twenty Centuries of Christ's Power.* Edinburgh, UK: Banner of Truth, 1981.
Hultgren, Arland J. *The Parables of Jesus: A Commentary.* Grand Rapids: Eerdmans, 2002.
Johnson, Paul. *A History of the Jews.* Welwyn, UK: Weidenfeld & Nicolson, 1987.
Kübler-Ross, Elisabeth. *Living with Death and Dying.* London: Simon & Schuster, 1997.
Ladd, George Eldon. *The Gospel of the Kingdom: Scriptural Studies in the Kingdom of God.* Grand Rapids: Eerdmans, 1990.
———. *A Theology of the New Testament.* London: Lutterworth, 1975.
Lewis, C. S. *Mere Christianity.* London: Fontana, 1962.
Liefeld, Walter L. *New Testament Commentary Series: Ephesians.* Leicester, UK: InterVarsity, 1997.
Lloyd-Jones, D. Martyn. *Studies in the Sermon on the Mount.* 2 vols. Leicester, UK: InterVarsity, 1976.
Matthew, David. *Church Adrift: Where in the World are We Going?* Basingstoke, UK: Marshall, Morgan & Scott, 1985.
McKechnie, Paul. *The First Christian Centuries: Perspectives on the Early Church.* Leicester, UK: Apollos, 2001.
Motyer, J. Alec. *The Bible Speaks Today: The Message of Exodus.* Leicester, UK: InterVarsity, 2005.
Nagel, Norman. "Luther and the Priesthood of All Believers." *Concordia Theological Quarterly* 61/4 (October 1997) 277–98.
Osborne, Grant R. *New Testament Commentary Series: Romans.* Leicester, UK: InterVarsity, 2004.
Packer, James I. *Celebrating the Saving Work of God.* Vol. 1 of *Collected Shorter Writings of J. I. Packer.* Carlisle, UK: Paternoster, 2000.
Parkes, Colin M. *Bereavement: Studies of Grief in Adult Life.* London: Routledge, 1996.
Pink, Arthur W. *An Exposition of the Sermon on the Mount.* Grand Rapids: Revell, 1994.
Richardson, Alan, ed. *A Theological Word Book of the Bible.* London: SCM, 1982.

## Bibliography

Shea, Nina. *In the Lion's Den: A Shocking Account of Persecution and Martyrdom of Christians Today and How We Should Respond*. Nashville: Broadman & Holman, 1997.

Stott, John R. W. *The Living Church: Convictions of a Lifelong Pastor*. Leicester, UK: InterVarsity, 2007.

Tozer, A. W. *Whatever Happened to Worship?* Eastbourne, UK: Kingsway, 1986.

Vine, William E. *An Expository Dictionary of New Testament Words*. Iowa Falls, IA: Riverside, 1975.

Wallis, Arthur. *The Radical Christian*. Eastbourne, UK: Kingsway, 1982.

Watson, Thomas. *The Beatitudes: An Exposition of Matthew 5:1-12*. Edinburgh, UK: Banner of Truth, 1971.

Woodall, Chris. *Covenant: The Basis of God's Self-Disclosure*. Eugene, OR: Wipf & Stock, 2011.

www.ingramcontent.com/pod-product-compliance
Lightning Source LLC
Chambersburg PA
CBHW051801230426
43670CB00012B/2378